My Education

D0723928

*To all who have contributed to my own education.
Many of those featured in this book had a
significant input into that awesome task.*

MY EDUCATION

Edited by John Quinn

TOWN HOUSE
DUBLIN

Published in 1997 by
Town House and Country House
Trinity House
Charleston Road
Ranelagh, Dublin 6
Ireland

British Library Cataloguing in Publication Data. A catalogue record for this book is available from the British Library.

ISBN: 1-86059-063-2; P/BK
ISBN: 1-86059-072-1; H/BK

Typesetting: Red Barn Publishing, Skibbereen
Printed in Ireland by ColourBooks

Contents

Introduction

The interviews featured in this book are edited versions of radio interviews which were broadcast under the title 'My Education' on RTE Radio between 1991 and 1996. They were much acclaimed as radio interviews, but good radio does not necessarily make good print, hence the need to re-shape the material into a narrative flow that will make for interesting reading. In doing this I have at all times remained true to the original content and have only altered the sequence of material in the interest of readability, as how we speak is most definitely not how we would write!

That said, there is much to savour here, not least from the variety of contributors. Poets and philosophers mingle with captains of industry, civil servants rub shoulders with comedians, artists jostle with politicians. Their contributions are not overtly (in many cases not at all) about schooling, which is too often confused with education. For many of the contributors, the words of George Bernard Shaw are singularly apt – 'My education was interrupted by my schooling...' For 'education' in this book read the chance encounter with a mentor, the journey undertaken, the 'failure' in one particular job, the books read, the encouragement of a parent, the sheer chance of being born in a particular time and place; examples abound. For Tony O'Reilly, rugby football was a 'template for life'; for Jean Vanier, moments of silence with disabled people 'teach us how to be at peace'; for Noam Chomsky, the most exhilarating experience was listening to the intellectual discussions which took place at his uncle's news-stand in Philadelphia...

It was my privilege to meet with these contributors over a five-year period and to hear their very individual stories. I hope this book will convey much of the warmth, thoughtfulness and honesty that marked each interview.

John Quinn

Tom Barrington

Tom Barrington was born in Dublin, just after the 1916 Rising. His father was a civil servant, who imbued the young Tom with an interest in government and in public service. Tom was educated at Belvedere College, Dublin, and at University College, Dublin.

After a brief spell in the business world, he entered the civil service, starting in the Department of Finance and working his way through the ranks to the position of principal. Tom played an important role in founding the Higher Civil Servants Discussion Group, which instituted high-level debate on crucial topics. In all, he spent nineteen years in the civil service before becoming the first director of the newly-formed Institute of Public Administration in 1960, a position he retained until 1977. He was editor of the journal, Administration, from 1953 to 1963 and is the author of several books on Irish administration. He also wrote Discovering Kerry, a Dublin man's guide to that county. Tom Barrington has argued passionately for many years for real democracy in the form of proper decentralisation and an end to what he calls 'the disease of congestion of government'.

I was born in Dublin just after the 1916 Rising and we lived in Glasnevin. My father died when I was thirteen, so I didn't really get to know him that well, but my earliest memories of him were of him laying down the law to his friends about what had to be done about this country – and to some extent I am sure my own children would have the same memories of me! He was a strange mixture of intellectual and hail-fellow-well-met – quite a combination. He was a very hardworking, committed man and he went off to a conference in Geneva when he wasn't at all well and died there of pneumonia. That gave us all a reaction against the civil service – we felt that it was no place for anybody to go – and we were all pretty miserable around that time. So, it was some time, having tried two other jobs, before I realised that the civil service was the place I wanted to be.

My mother was thirty-seven when my father died and she had a tough time of it from then on. She came from a family of eccentrics, but she was in no way eccentric herself. She was a very quiet, careful, determined sort of woman, very anxious to avoid conflict and trouble of any kind, and I think she was a big influence on me. My wife says I am a very obstinate man, but I like to think of myself as being tenacious. When I was at school in Belvedere, one of the Jesuit mottoes that stuck in my head was *Suavitur in modo, fortitur in re* – take things easy, but be firm in principles – and that has remained with me. I hate having to fight about things, but I like to get my own way, so you develop certain skills in that way. My mother was extraordinarily controlled and she was very good to us, in the sense in that she never tried to impose anything on us but we knew there was a line out all the same, so we behaved ourselves – more or less!

I went to the national school at St Patrick's in Drumcondra, which was a very good school and which I liked very much. It was a very mixed sort of school. A chap I was friendly with in class left school at fourteen to be a messenger boy on a bicycle, and it struck me that we really ought to encourage that sort of mixing in society, instead of creaming people off into special schools.

I went to Belvedere when I was twelve, in 1928, and I was there for five years. I liked Belvedere very much. I never had any interest in sport or games and I was regarded as an oddbod in that way. I would have made a fine forward for the rugby team and all sorts of pressures were put on me, but there was no way I was going to get engaged in those rough games. I was very attached to the Jesuits and when my father died they were good to me and my brother. Again, it was the mix of tenacity and smoothness that appealed to me about them. My youth wasn't a very happy one, with father dying so unexpectedly, and we were very poor. There were some very good friends of my father that stood by us at the time, but friends drift away and I led a rather lonely and detached sort of life. So I didn't really have a happy childhood, or young adulthood either, until I eventually got myself established.

I got a job after I left school as what you would now call a management trainee, in a small candle firm. I was there for three years and it was an interesting experience. The capacity to get things done impressed me very much. An order would come in from the parish priest for candles or altar oil and it was sent out that afternoon. However, they were still making the candles in the same way candles had been made from time immemorial, with the wick hanging down and the chaps with a scoop pouring the melted beeswax mixture.

I got into a kind of literary circle at that time. I became friendly with Gabriel Fallon and Leon Ó Broin and I met Father Senan of the *Capuchin Annual*. He offered me a job and I was greatly taken at that stage by the crazy literary life. I had started an evening course in UCD and I persuaded him to let me attend lectures and make up the time. I had set my mind on the civil service and I needed an honours degree to get in. It wasn't really like a university education – dashing in on my bicycle and listening to the lectures and dashing back to work. I didn't make any friends at college and it wasn't much of a life for me at all, except for the lecturers. I came up against George O'Brien in economics and he remained a friend. I can still remember the thrill I got from listening to John Marcus O'Sullivan doing the French Revolution – 'Don't mind if I have the year or the month wrong, but I'll tell you the day will be right and the hour of the day will be right!' I loved history and I got a great kick out of that. I did politics with Canon Denis O'Keefe. I don't think I ever understood the subject at all, but they were the most entertaining lectures. He was an extremely funny person.

Gabriel Fallon was very good to me. He took an interest in me and set about educating me. He had a beautiful collector's edition of the novels of Thomas Hardy and I read all of them. He taught me a lot about the theatre and how to look at plays and how they were produced. Father Senan then started a thing called the Capuchin Annual Club, which comprised a lot of his contributors. We would meet every Thursday in the Father Mathew Hall and have a meal there and Frank McManus, Roibéard Ó Faracháin, Tadhg Gahan and others would come along. Father Senan was great in attracting people like Frank Sheed, the publisher, a very entertaining customer, and a lot of people from abroad to visit our meetings.

I had begun to write a bit; not that I was any good at it, but I was learning the craft and I used to contribute the odd article. There were a lot of Catholic papers in those days, like the *Irish Monthly* for instance, and of course there were the *Capuchin Annuals*. Father Senan was very good about commissioning me to do something and encouraging me to write. He was a remarkable man.

I got my honours degree, so I got into the civil service. We were quite a little collection – Paddy Lynch, for instance, was the man who came first in the exam. I went into the Department of Finance. The civil service is a very civilised sort of organisation – an extraordinary level of courtesy and formal kindliness, backed up by a tremendous amount of absent-mindedness in terms of human relations! I was very taken by this after the rough and tumble of the business world. We were shown around and introduced to everybody and I was assigned to Maisie Kiely, who became one of my dearest friends. It was a real kind of a master and apprentice type of thing and she took a great interest in a number us who she thought were personable young men. If she didn't like you, on the other hand, then that was the end of you. She held a sort of *salon* at her flat, not in any formal sense, but she liked to give us the opportunity to meet senior civil servants and she consciously went out of her way to civilise us and acculturate us into the system of the civil service. I spent three years in Finance and that was a very interesting time.

The Department of Finance had a very orderly system – I only realised this afterwards, when I moved to the Customs House. They had a tremendous filing system. You had to read the relevant file thoroughly so you knew the background and then you had to write a minute of some sort summing up what you had read and your assessment of the letter that had come in from some unfortunate department looking for money. Then that minute was appended to the file and would be passed to various superior beings who would say 'That fellow Barrington is an awful eejit' and put snide little notes in the margin, which was very good for you because then you began to learn the game. You were supposed to use your own judgement and initiative, even if it was against the line that the department took. In those days, the department line was that any spending was a bad thing so the answer should be no, but if a good case was made then it had to be given serious consideration.

In one sense, we were at the hub of things, but, in another, we were really on the top of a mountain when all the real action was going on at the bottom. That is one of the reasons I left. The other was that there were twenty or thirty administrative officers in Finance at that time, all about the same age and all madly ambitious. A vacancy occurred in the Department of Local Government and Public Health for a private secretary to Sean McEntee. I applied and was summoned to the Custom House, where I was interviewed by a remarkable man who was secretary of the department, called James Hurson. I became personal secretary and was with McEntee for a couple of years and learned an enormous amount there. I spent time with the minister and saw all the important things that were going on in the department. Because I was reputed to have the ear of the minister, everybody was very nice and anxious to explain things, so I learned a great deal about the department, which was a very diverse one in those days. McEntee was an extremely able man. Even though he had his failings – losing his temper and that sort of thing – basically, he was an extremely intelligent man, interested in the whole business of government. Some ministers are only interested in their own department, but McEntee liked to have a finger in every pie.

I had one great success in those days. George Bernard Shaw had a little property in Carlow which he wanted to give to the town of Carlow. He wrote to Dev asking him to arrange this, but there was a lot of confusion about it and, eventually, it transpired that legislation was needed. So, a message came over from the minister on a Tuesday that the bill was to be prepared straight away and got through the two houses at once. We got our bill ready and it was approved by the government at their Friday meeting. The bill was introduced in the Dáil on Tuesday, went through the Senate on Wednesday and then, by special arrangement, the President signed it on the Thursday. Shaw was delighted and wrote to Clement Attlee, the Prime Minister of England, saying, 'You really ought to learn how to get legislation through.' I always call it the Shaw/Barrington bill!

I was eventually promoted to assistant principal and found that I had a certain gift for tidying things up and making things sensible and getting people to agree to a better way of doing things. However, the tendency is then to get arrogant and I think I must have been quite arrogant around the age of thirty or so. While I was going through that phase, I only thought of myself as exercising power and influence, but later on, when I realised that these were human machines, I began to think about the civil service as a whole. Rather against my will, I got involved in personnel work in the department and that really gave me an insight into handling people and the need to improve the organisation and the way things were run. I remember trying to get things moving when I discovered that it took a fortnight from the time a letter was dictated to the time it came back for signing! As I got a bit older and more experienced, I understood how complex such things were and became interested in how the machine worked as a whole.

There was a sort of apartheid in the Customs House. There were those of us who were in health and local government and there were the customs people and we never really mixed. Two chaps in the customs, Pat Doolin and James Waldron, went to a lot of trouble to persuade the Association of Higher Civil Servants that they ought to take a professional interest in the civil service, apart from the matter of pay. We got together and organised the Higher Civil Servants Discussion Group in the Customs House. It made quite an impact; two or three hundred people would turn up to meetings and talk about all sorts of things.

Tom Murray, who became the head of the ESB afterwards, was a very vigorous civil servant and he started the very first debate, 'In defence of bureaucracy', and that very competent piece of work set the whole thing going. Con McElligott was retiring and he opened a debate on the problems of valuation in this country and what needed to be done about that – that was quite a bombshell.

We subsequently decided to publish some papers. I took over the job as editor of the paper, *Administration*. We had a marvellous Kerry man, Michael O'Connor, who was in the publishing business and was keen to have a paper that would stir up all sorts of intellectual debate in the civil service. People seemed to think that it wouldn't be possible to have a detached and intellectual publication that was not bashing politicians or revealing state secrets!

I was a principal at that stage and getting a bit bored with the job, so I was shunted over to the town planning section, which was in real trouble at that time. They needed new legislation for town planning, but nothing had been happening, so I was given the job. I had a great assistant, Brendan Drury, who had devoted his life to planning and had in his head all the things that needed to be done. I went into the department some time in September and by Christmas we had the heads of our bill drawn up and it went on to the minister, Neil Blaney. He sat on it for some time and eventually said he wouldn't touch it. I hated town planning – it was full of artistic pretensions but had no common sense or intellectual input at all. I was beginning to become a bit of a pseudo-intellectual. I got browned off and the thought of spending years in that milieu was too much for me. By then the Institute of Public Administration had been founded on a part-time basis and a full-time director was needed, so I let it be known that I was very discontented where I was and, in the summer of 1960, I went off to become a one-man institute.

In the late '50s, I came across one book that had an extraordinary effect on me. When we were getting *Administration* on its feet, I was writing a fair bit and reading around the subject. I began to realise that I had some capacity for abstract thinking and, by an extraordinary coincidence, the librarian in Bray at that time, Mairín O'Byrne, gave my wife a book to bring home to me. It was a book called *Insight* by Bernard Lonergan, a Canadian Jesuit, and it was exactly what I needed. It gave me confidence in my writing and in arguing for the future. It had a terrible effect on my style – for a while nobody could understand what on earth

I was talking about – but, thank goodness, I eventually learned to simplify it.

Another book that influenced me was a small book that Paddy Lynch recommended to me – *Beyond the Welfare State* by Gunnar Myrdal, the great Swedish economist and social scientist. It showed how, as people became better educated and more self-conscious, central government would shed a lot of the detailed things and these would be looked after by small groups instead. The argument was that central government should be concerned about the big issues and local government should deal with everything else. As you get a more educated and informed society, people should get the opportunity to look after their own affairs. That has remained a vision for me amid all the ups and downs of the intervening years since the early '60s.

I am not too happy with the state of democracy in this country. Local government seems to be doing only about one third of what they should be doing. We are really very backward in terms of local democracy – having the smallest number of local authorities, the smallest number of councillors, the smallest number of functions being discharged by local government, the smallest amount of money spent by local government as a proportion of public money spent and so on. If you want a country to progress, you have got to mobilise the skills and talents and enthusiasms of the people as a whole, not just of a small number of people at the centre who won't even go to the trouble of learning how to organise themselves.

There is nothing so powerful as an idea whose time has come, and I am confident that, sooner or later, the time will come for these ideas, whether in my lifetime or not. I have tried to do what I can and, if people accept these ideas now, well and good, but, if they don't, it will probably happen in the future.

John Behan

John Behan was born in Dublin in 1938 and grew up in a then very vibrant part of the city, close to the dockland, where there was constant activity and bustle. An early interest in art was fostered by a neighbour, Maggie Cummins, a french polisher who allowed him to 'mess around with colours and brushes'. His formal schooling was uninspiring, apart from the influence of a couple of teachers who took an interest in John's development as an artist. At the age of fifteen, he began a seven-year apprenticeship with a major engineering firm which did both structural steelwork and art metalwork. The die was cast . . . John Behan was on his way to becoming one of the most successful metal sculptors Ireland has produced.

I was born in Sheriff Street in the heart of Dublin in 1938. I spent the first six years of my life there and I went to the local parish school, St Lawrence O'Toole's in Seville Place. That is where I first started painting and drawing, although I had done some at home. There was an old lady nearby who was a french polisher and she had all kinds of dyes and colours and paint brushes. I used to sneak into her studio when she wasn't there and mess around with the paints. That was the origin of my work as an artist.

Sheriff Street was a very vibrant part of the city then, because there were big commercial concerns there, like granaries, oil companies and coal companies. The Point Depot was a huge railway siding and assembly point for goods coming from all over Ireland to go on to the docks and be shipped away during the war. The cattle trade was enormous there – it was like Kansas City or Chicago in the 1880s. Everything was driven on the hoof in those days and one of my most vivid memories is of all these animals being shunted off on boats.

My father was a grocer in those days. He started off in the '30s just before I was born and he stayed there until the mid '40s. I was sometimes very bold – I would let the local kids in to raid the shelves and run off with the sweets. My parents weren't very happy about that!

My father was very fortunate in that we lived near the docks. He used to go into Connor's pub and meet people who had tea to sell and he would buy it from them and sell it to the local inhabitants. If you were able to get butter, tea and sugar, and all those commodities that were very scarce, you were a very popular person.

When the war was over, we had outgrown the premises – there were seven of us in the family – and we moved out to Marino. I changed schools then, from the nuns in Sheriff Street to the nuns in Griffith Avenue, and from there I went on to the Brothers in Scoil Mhuire, and that's where I ended my primary education.

I wasn't too happy with the Brothers, but Brother Coughlan from Tuam was a very nice man and he took an interest in me. I was very young when I started school, so I ended up with my primary certificate at the age of eleven. I couldn't go anywhere for another three years, so I spent that time with Brother Coughlan and he taught me quite a bit. He was keenly aware of the visual arts, but, apart from that, it was the three Rs – with a vengeance at times.

All the kids in those days did everything they could to earn a few bob. I did the milk run and then I did the paper run in the evening, and during the summer we went out to pick raspberries in Scott's, so your childhood days were over by the time you got to the age of ten. Times were very harsh; there was mass emigration in the '50s and you had to get out there and get money somehow, especially if you came from a large family.

My father came from a place called Ballybrittas in County Laois. His family had a farm where I went every summer until I was about eleven. We all had our duties – driving the cattle out in the morning and bringing them back in the evening for milking, feeding the hens and the pigs and so on. It was a terrific experience for any young child from the city.

There was a good small library there that had been inherited from a family called McLaren, so I was able to read every day – all the old classics like R M Ballantyne and Robert Louis Stevenson. It was a great escape and a good way of stimulating the imagination.

After primary school, I decided that I wasn't going any further with the academic world, so I went to the North Strand Vocational School, which had a very good art department. Bill O'Brien and Jack Pearse were both excellent teachers and Bill took a particular interest in me. We used to meet after school and discuss things. He was a marvellous man, a great influence on me.

I eventually got a job in J C McLoughlin's, a big engineering firm which did both structural steel work and art metalwork for convents and churches, all kinds of intricate metalwork. I started there when I was about fifteen and a half and I did an apprenticeship for seven years. Whilst there I had to go to night classes and I met a man called Paddy McElroy who was teaching in North Strand. He was a blacksmith and he was able to pass on all the techniques. He also showed me how to structure metal into an expressive piece of artwork.

It was tough work. You were working five and a half days a week and you had to be in on time. It was a very disciplined way of life for a young lad and the benefits were to accrue for me later. I just did it and didn't raise my head for seven years. I didn't think about anything else except trying to get into the art business eventually as a full-time practitioner.

They had a foundry there as well as an engineering shop, for welding, riveting and bolting. I learned all those techniques and by the time I was twenty I had worked with aluminium, brass, copper, bronze, steel and stainless steel. That was a terrific introduction for a sculptor into the workings of metal and, as Herbert Reade said in his *History of Twentieth Century Sculpture*, we were in the middle of the new iron age. It was a great era of technical innovation. Welding techniques and casting techniques were being taught in the technical schools and were also being practised in workshops like McLoughlin's, and I benefited from all that.

I went to exhibitions as soon as I got to know about galleries like the Richie Hendrix Gallery in Stephen's Green, for example. The Dawson Gallery later put on exhibitions of modern art – people like Arthur Armstrong, George Campbell, Cecil King, Louis Le Brocquy and Paddy Collins. Until Edward Delaney came along, I can't remember there being one-person shows of sculpture. He started all that and it gradually developed in the '60s to what it is today, where sculpture can be a feature of modern Irish art.

At the end of my apprenticeship, I spent about a year and a half in London. The intention was to study art full time. I met some people who said, 'You know enough about the techniques and, if you keep working away at life drawing and maintain your objectivity and observation and so forth, you should be able to make a go of it.' I took their advice and decided that I was not going back to work in factories or workshops, except as an artist.

The first thing I ever exhibited was in the Irish Museum of Living Art in 1960, and not alone did it get a write-up in the paper but it also sold and I have never looked back since. I have been very fortunate. I did a lot of painting in the early '60s, but then I met up with Delaney and worked with him in the mid-'60s. He was very much into serpidu loss wax casting, which was a technique that wasn't known in Ireland at that time. It was all sand-casting and piece-moulding, very complex, highly technical and time-consuming stuff, so the loss wax technique, particularly for sculpture work, was a great revelation.

Casting is very tough work. There is a lot of theory and written work done in relation to visual art, but if you want to do bronze casting you have got to get your coat off and get stuck into the work. It is hard, physical work.

The first thing I ever made was a bull. I was doing welded pieces of the Celtic mythological cycles, like Cú Chulainn, with Paddy Mc Elroy. They always held a fascination for me. As for Picasso, the bull is a symbol of all kinds of things, like power and virility and continuity.

I am also interested in flight and particularly the winged man. I suppose it is the struggle of man trying to lift himself off the ground, not being earthed like Antheus in Greek mythology. If he lifted off the ground he was vulnerable, but in my case I wanted to get off the ground. The birds in my work are a symbol of freedom and peace and of gentility.

I worked with Edward Delaney for a couple of years on and off, when he had work. One of the big commissions that comes to mind is the Wolfe Tone memorial. I helped him cast all those pieces, so I learned a lot from him and from watching him. I later went on to London and studied in a more detailed and focused way. Then I came back in 1970 and, along with Tony Stevenson, Peter O'Brien, Leo Higgins and a few more, put together the Dublin Art Foundry, which is still there today.

There was a resistance to modern art by the older academics, who thought that Picasso couldn't draw and who were stuck with the idea that William Orpen was the great master. Orpen was an exceptionally gifted draughtsman, but his imagination was limited to very set compositions of a realistic nature. My generation and the one before that, like Oisin Kelly's, had been stimulated by Picasso, Matisse, Miró and Henry Moore, so we wanted to take it a bit further, but there was a definite resistance to us.

Sculpture is not for the woolly thinker. You can't make mistakes when you are doing bronze sculpture, because it is so expensive to produce. I have a good clear idea in my head before I start and it is usually accompanied by sketches and maybe a more finished drawing.

I use welded metal an awful lot and I use welding techniques to make up models for the foundry. They are passed over and converted into bronze or aluminium. I also use a technique where I cut out polystyrene and hollow it out with hot knives. It is the quickest way of all of making sculpture in metal.

Any artist worth his salt is trying to communicate, and communication can only take place when you cross a certain barrier. It is as if there is a ring of fire and only somebody who is prepared to go through it to make the image in sculpture will be able to communicate. When I was preparing the 'Famine Ship' for my recent exhibition, I was working on a whole series of different images from the Famine, stimulated in great part by a couple of visits to Strokestown Museum in Roscommon. My images came from looking at the material, reading up history and visiting places. The Famine Ship idea came together after a visit to Portugal, where I saw the sailing ships which Columbus had used.

I read Joyce when I was about nineteen. At first I found it difficult, but then I read Ellman's book and that illuminated the whole process for me. I have always been fascinated by Joyce. I walked the same streets as his characters did for years on end. It was the same kind of city then, a mundane kind of a place in many ways. *Ulysses* is full of images that I grew up with, except that Joyce heightened them and used them in a very imaginative way. Most people lived those kind of lives and never realised it. It is only when somebody like Joyce comes along and pinpoints everything and then exaggerates it all in a comic way that they realise it. *Ulysses* is probably the funniest book ever written. To read *Don Quixote* is a very similar experience – it is so grotesquely funny that every artist worth a damn has tackled it.

Dublin was always a stimulating place and I found the people good-natured and outgoing. They had hard times of course; I don't wish to glorify the good old days, because they didn't exist. I remember going around in the 1948 election campaign and seeing the squalid tenements of the inner city. The door would open and a fetid smell would overwhelm you. I was only a young kid and I saw all that side of life as well. At the same time, it has always been a mistake to displace populations radically and unconcernedly, breaking up communities. You create a lot more problems than you solve. I knew these people in the old days and they were definitely a much tighter-knit group of people.

In the late '70s, I moved from Dublin to Galway. I was involved with so many different art groups and organisations in Dublin that my work was suffering. I am very glad that I made the move. Galway has been good to me. I get on very well with the people and I find it very stimulating. It has that distance from Dublin that a lot of artists seem to require.

I have three or four exhibitions every year. I commit myself to a date and, even if I have to get up at five in the morning, as I sometimes do, I meet that deadline. When I was on the milk run, I was up at four in the morning, so that has never been a problem to me. I work from as early as I can in the morning until about two or three and occasionally I work in the evening, if necessary, but not very often. I always carry paper for sketching, because you never know what you are going to see. It doesn't matter where I am in the world, I can use things I have seen six months or even two years later. Images remain clearly etched on my mind and if I have a reminder, in the sketch, there in front of me, I am home and dry.

Other artists stimulate me as well. I saw a marvellous exhibition in Belfast by Basil Blackshaw and when I came back I felt like rushing into the studio and getting stuck into work, because it was such an exciting show. Basil is a painter, but that doesn't matter. That kind of stimulation can keep me going for weeks and I apply it to my own work in my own particular way. I'm never stuck for ideas – what I need is stimulation like that now and again.

I try to get abroad once a year for a couple of weeks. I have been going to Italy on and off for the best part of twenty years and I have never been less than stimulated when I get back. For me, going to places like Naples and Pompeii, for example, and seeing all the artefacts and the civilisation there, is enough stimulation to keep me going for a couple of years. Until I was about thirty years of age I had not been to these places, so now when I travel I get a great deal out of it.

I have never wanted to be anything else – I am not an airline pilot who wants to be a shoe salesman, or the other way around. I am quite happy to be doing what I am doing.

Fr Harry Bohan

Harry Bohan was born in Feakle, County Clare, and educated at St Flannan's College, Ennis. He then attended Maynooth College and was ordained a priest in 1963. He studied sociology at the University of Wales and worked for some time with Irish emigrants in Birmingham. His work there and his study of the growth of British cities convinced him that 'the industrial city is wrong'.

Harry Bohan returned to his native Clare in the late 1960s, a period when the Irish economy was booming – but too much, he felt, at the expense of rural communities. He committed himself to the revitalisation of those communities, starting with his native village. His work has always been influenced by the two institutions that shaped him – family and community – and that influence inspired him to put the heart back into rural communities, building houses and encouraging families to come back from the big industrial centres. The Feakle experiment was a success and was extended to other counties through the Rural Resource Organisation.

A man of considerable dynamism, energy and optimism, Harry Bohan continues to work for rural revitalisation. His book, Roots in a Changing Society, *reflects his basic philosophy of holding onto roots, putting down new ones and nourishing them.*

I was brought up in a pub in a small village – Feakle in County Clare – in the '40s and '50s. The family and the local community were the two institutions that really formed me. The traditional family of that era was uncompromisingly dominated by 'the boss', in many ways. All major decisions, whether farming or financial or business, were taken by the father. At the same time, the mother had a huge emotional influence, certainly on me, and on most people who grew up at that time.

The family was very much a productive unit – a place of enterprise. We all had specific tasks, in a place that produced rather than consumed. Thirdly, it was very much a place of training and education. Sons grew up learning a lot of skills from their fathers; we watched and learned from what they did. Fourthly, practically every family had other adults, apart from the father and mother. There were grandparents, neighbours, aunts and uncles. I grew up in a pub, but a pub then wasn't confined to one room – people took over the house when they came into a pub in those days – so I grew up very much in an adult environment.

The entire family were very conscious of our dependence on God. Prayer was important, necessary and habitual. It was something that happened every day. Praying together was vital and the togetherness was as important as the prayer.

We knew nothing about government in those times. Feakle was a place where people worked hard; there were no handouts. People produced their own food and their own fuel and it was very much subsistence living. The wider community became a huge influence on us as well, fundamentally through three institutions – the school, the Church and the GAA. One of the things that kept us going through those years was our great tradition of hurling; the teams of the '30s and '40s won five championships. Not alone were they our heroes, they were *local* heroes. Another big influence was the Church. We came together every Sunday, from the valleys and the hills, and people had a chat after Mass. Again, the praying was important but the togetherness of the people after Mass was also important. In school, also, the togetherness of those people was as important to me as the schooling itself. Later on it was a source of great sadness to see the people with whom I went to school having to emigrate. Nine of the fourteen of us who left school together actually emigrated and all fourteen of us left the parish, and that was a symptom of the kind of place it was. It was a place of great security, of great stability, but at the same time of great sadness because of emigration.

I went as a boarder to St Flannan's College in Ennis. Leaving home was a huge wrench for me. At St Flannan's you had to be an achiever in sport and you had to be inclined towards working in the civil service, a vocation in the Church or teaching. These were the kind of things that the greatest emphasis was put on. We seemed to be educated simply to get out of where we were and go elsewhere. A lot of emphasis was put on the big job, the job with status. Looking back on that kind of education, I would seriously question the role of a secondary school that channelled people away from their own localities and into other places. Schools of that kind were *in* communities but not *of* them.

I suppose the priesthood was contemplated by almost every young fellow that went through St Flannan's. God permeated all areas of life in those times – at home, in the community and, indeed, in St Flannan's itself. I loved my local community so much that I felt that if I could become a priest and go back and serve in a place like that, it would be my ideal in life. I remember the night that I made up my mind. I was walking through a country road when I was home on holidays and I suddenly decided I was going to be a priest, and from there on, at least for the first few years, I didn't have any doubts. Mind you, I had several doubts as I went through the seminary at Maynooth later on.

I went to Maynooth in 1956. The first thing that Maynooth meant for me was that I met people from other parts of Ireland.

Feakle had been my world until I went to St Flannan's and met people from Tipperary and west Clare. Now, going to Maynooth, I met people from the North of Ireland, from Dublin and from all over Ireland. I noticed very quickly the self-confidence of the students from the North of Ireland. In many ways, I would have had a bit of an inferiority complex in the early days.

From the early 1960s onwards, the social question became a major one for the Church and *Mater et Magistra* was the great encyclical of that era from Pope John XXIII. Jeremiah Newman, the Professor of Sociology in Maynooth, encouraged us not only to study theology, but to study how that theology could be preached and lived in the context of the changing world. He asked me to present a paper on *Mater et Magistra* to the students one evening and, after I had studied it, I felt that Pope John XXIII must have known the West of Ireland. He wrote about the problems of the industrial society, the uprooting of people, the housing conditions and then he wrote about the value of agricultural society and of rural society, so that I soon got a sense that the Church was actually endorsing what I had in my soul and in my heart and head, coming from a place like Feakle.

It was a wonderful time to be in Maynooth and I will be forever grateful to have been there then. It was a most exciting time in Ireland because of all the changes that were beginning to take place. The Industrial Revolution was just starting in Ireland, but John XXIII was writing for a Western world that had experienced it a hundred years before, so in the Irish context it was a very exciting time. It was also the start of the communications age and it was the era of Vatican Two. I will be forever grateful to Jeremiah Newman for grasping the kind of teaching that was coming from the Church at that time and applying it to our lives.

The day I was ordained, Bishop Joseph Rogers told me that he was sending me off to do a postgraduate course in the University of Wales, because it was a time of change and because Shannon was beginning to emerge within our diocese as a new town and one of the centres of industrial development. He wanted someone who would have some understanding of what that change was all about.

I went in October 1963 to Cardiff and my thesis was *The Growth of Cities in Britain.* I looked at the movement of people out of Ireland, from the Famine days right up through the second half of the last century and the first half of this century, and the kind of conditions they lived in in the cities in Britain. We often hear of people emigrating from this country and dying on the way to far-off places, but what we don't always hear of are the numbers that suffered and died from diseases like typhoid in the cities of Britain. They lived in hugely overcrowded accommodation and they worked in horrific conditions in factories there. The thesis convinced me that the industrial city is wrong and that I should go back and make some contribution to the Feakles of this world.

I was asked to go and work with the emigrants in Birmingham and so I left Cardiff with a heavy heart in the late '60s. I worked for two and a half years with the emigrants in Birmingham and came to love it and to love them. I worked in a parish that had thirteen thousand Catholics and got heavily involved in their lives, in the housing and the pastoral scene there. Again, this was another step in the inevitable direction. The night before I left Birmingham, I was called down to a one-room flat where a man and his wife and six children were living. She had been beaten up by the husband and he said to me, 'I'm sorry for doing what I did to my wife, but if you or anyone else had to live in these conditions you would probably do the same thing.' They and others like them convinced me that something has to be done for families that have to uproot from rural Ireland to go and live in conditions like that. It is very definitely not a recipe for good family life.

I came back in the late 1960s to Shannon. The whole of Ireland then was flying; there was progress everywhere. Whereas people were talking about full employment in a number of 'growth centres', I felt, despite popular opinion, that we were on a disaster course in Ireland. However, to say that, which I did publicly and privately at the time, was almost considered to be a mortal sin. We were over-reliant on transnational money and transnational technology. We were putting all our eggs into one basket and we were only putting the new industries into a few centres. Effectively, that meant that families that I had grown up with would simply be suppliers of labour to those centres. We were totally neglecting our own natural resources and putting millions and millions of pounds into multinational companies. They gave a great service to this country in the '60s, but it became very clear to me that some of the companies that were coming here then would be in another part of the world – and for the most part in the Third World – ten years on. And that is exactly what happened.

I began to say publicly and privately that, if we continued on the course we had embarked on, we would soon face mass unemployment and urban breakdown. Because I was so convinced of this, I borrowed fifteen hundred pounds in 1972. I went to a bank manager and told him that, if we could get young families to come to live in small villages, then maybe we could reverse the trend. Not only did that bank manager, Johnny Mee, say that this was a good idea and give me the loan for fifteen hundred pounds, but I asked him to come onto a committee with a few other experts to see if we could build twenty houses back in Feakle. I felt that, if I couldn't do it in Feakle, I couldn't do it anywhere.

We discovered that, in 1972, in spite of all the apparent progress in Ireland, in a village population of one hundred and twenty there were only three people between the ages of twenty and forty, and that spelt disaster. In other words, the village that I had grown up in and loved had been written off. All the experts told us that people would not go back to live there. I asked the parish priest to announce from the altar that, if there were young families who would like to live in Feakle, they should come to the hall the following Friday night. We got representatives of twenty families into the hall that Friday night and, eventually, through a lot of scraping and bowing and a lot of backbreaking, we got twenty young families back into Feakle. That was an enormous input into a small village population, because not only was it an increase of about a hundred people but this was in the age group that was needed. We formed a company and we moved on from there and since then we have built 2,500 houses in a hundred and twenty communities and thirteen counties, and the spin-offs became obvious very quickly. For example, in Feakle, Con Smith built a village hotel; the school, instead of losing a teacher got an extra one; young farmers stayed on the land. People started to look at setting up little enterprises and this happened in many of the other villages as well. All of that investment by a voluntary organisation represents an investment of about two hundred million pounds in rural Ireland.

It was often said to me that I was a romantic, that it couldn't work, and obviously that was a challenge. We had to make it work on the ground and we had to make it work practically. I was convinced then and am more convinced now that the era of the industrial city is over and done with. There is too much crime, too much family breakdown. I believe that family breakdown itself has come about largely because families became consumers and not producers; they were not working together. The father and mother that I grew up with trained me in a whole lot of things. Many sons today don't see their fathers at work, so that they are seriously deprived. The togetherness, the praying together, the working together, have been taken away from family life. I am completely convinced that we are entering a new era where we'll return to the family and to the community to solve the unemployment problem and to solve a lot of the other problems we have in society.

Pope John Paul II told us in Limerick to keep in contact with our roots, with the soil of Ireland, and that is basically my philosophy. If we uproot people and if the togetherness of family and community is broken, then obviously we run the risk of building a society on a narrow form of economics which has failed to work. People no longer participate, as we did, in determining their own future. Mass unemployment results and multi-poverty systems emerge. Europe now recognises that a pull into the centre is going to do unholy damage and, if the periphery and the rural parts of Europe die, we are going to have a huge problem.

For those of us who became priests, our deep faith in God comes, for the most part, from the faith of the people. There is a huge sustenance in being very involved with people pastorally – in their marriage problems, their family problems, their work problems, their growing up problems. For people that feel beaten, defeat may serve as well as victory to shake the soul and let the glory out. All parishes are fundamentally a Eucharist community and, in spite of what we hear, so many prayer groups have emerged in the last number of years, so many individuals have gone into deep reflective prayer, so many people are restoring their faith in the Eucharist, that I think there is a whole new re-creation of parish. A lot of it is to do with the priest and the people worshipping together, working through prayer together, and, particularly in a time of noise, through reflective prayer.

I couldn't continue to be busy without a time for quiet, a time for prayer, a time for God. I have been very privileged over the last twenty years to have been given one or two diocesan retreats every year and I always say that we priests should nearly write into our diary that we have an appointment with God every day. It is from that appointment with God that we can be alive and supportive with people.

In the '60s and '70s, we set up a lot of government. We convinced ourselves that the huge number of people going into jobs then were all going into industry, whereas, in fact, there was an increase of about ninety thousand people in the public service in that fifteen-year period. When people go behind desks and phones in government bodies and agencies, the ordinary people in communities and families are made dependent. The unemployment figures and the crime figures stand witness to that kind of dependency. There has been far too much government and, linked into that, in a media age, the chat shows and the current affairs shows are dominated by politicians telling us what they are going to do for us. I would love a government minister or a Taoiseach to come on television and say, we can do nothing for you except facilitate you to do it yourself. We should go back to the talent, the energy, the creativity of people, and governments should be there to facilitate that.

There are one or two things that energise me. I'm not good with prayer and I struggle with it, but I do have a deep appreciation of praying scripture in a contemporary way, but in a very reflective way. The Lord himself coming alive in present-day Ireland and in my life at this time is of crucial importance to me. I have to say, too, that I love the Mass, and daily Mass is also extremely important. Finally, although I meet with huge obstacles in my work, I also meet with great encouragement from people, whether they are directly encouraging the work or whether they are people struggling with their own problems. I thank God that I have been so fortunate as to have been given the opportunity to do this kind of work.

Noam Chomsky

Noam Chomsky was born in Philadelphia, USA, in 1928. He grew up in an intellectually-enriching Jewish tradition, despite the severe anti-Semitism and economic depression of that era. His early education was in a Dewey school, where he relished the non-competitive atmosphere. At university he became interested in the study of linguistics and developed his own radical theory, which argued that grammar is not learned from scratch but is innate; our mental attributes, like our physiology, are determined by our genes. He became a political activist in the 1960s and '70s, leading the resistance to US involvement in South-East Asia. Since 1955, he has taught at the Massachusetts Institute of Technology.

I was born in Philadelphia, Pennsylvania. The family was essentially an immigrant family. I had one brother, five years younger, but different enough in age for us not to have grown up intellectually together. My father came from the Ukraine when he was about seventeen; my mother was actually born here, but only a year after the family had arrived from Lithuania. Both my parents were Hebrew teachers and my father was a Hebrew scholar as well and a director of the Hebrew educational system in Philadelphia. They both worked afternoons and Sunday morning and afternoon, so we had to have household help. I actually had an Irish maid take care of me for the first couple of years of my life.

My parents sent me to a nursery school by the time I was about 18 months old. It was a Deweyite progressive school run by Temple University as an experimental school. This was the heyday of John Dewey's educational influence and I stayed at the school from the age of eighteen months to about twelve years. I still have childhood memories of being wheeled to school in a baby carriage. Alongside that, from an early age I went to Hebrew school, where, as in the home environment, Hebrew education and the Jewish tradition were the fundamental values. It was primarily from the local Jewish community that my father's friends came, people who spoke Hebrew and were raising their children in similar circumstances.

The local area was not so pleasant. This was the 1930s; we were the only Jewish family in a largely Irish and German Catholic neighbourhood which was fiercely anti-Semitic, rather pro-Nazi in fact. I can even remember beer parties as late as the Fall of Paris. On the other hand, there was an extended family, which was a big influence on me. My father's family, who lived in Baltimore, were very Orthodox Jewish. In fact, according to my father, they actually regressed beyond what they had been like in their Eastern European Jewish village community. My mother's family were in New York and they were mostly Jewish working class, which at the time meant mostly unemployed.

Many of them had never been to school, but they lived in an atmosphere of quite high culture and also working-class culture, which were not dissociated at that time. They were very active intellectually in every domain.

These were immigrants, usually first-generation immigrants, maybe some early second-generation, working-class, largely unemployed. A few had gone on to school, one or two had gotten through college and become teachers. Some had not gotten past fourth grade; they had grown up in the streets. They were very deeply involved in working-class politics of the day, which meant the Communist Party for some and anti-Communist left for others, every fringe of radical opinion that you could think of. Of course, in those days that political activity didn't just mean having political opinions, it meant a life; it meant everything from the picnics to the summer vacations to concerts to everything else. A large part of their life was what we would nowadays call high culture: there would be debates about Steckel's critique of Freud, discussions about *Ulysses* and Cubist art and the latest concert of the Budapest String Quartet, as well as what was wrong with Lenin's version of Marx and what that implied for politics of the day.

Much of the excitement of this environment was focused for me around one particular uncle who hadn't gotten through elementary school. He happened to be disabled and, as a result, he was able to get a news-stand, which became a very lively intellectual centre in the late '30s; a lot of European émigrés clustered around it, many of them German PhDs or psychiatrists and so on. I remember going to work on the news-stand in the evening by the time I was say twelve or thirteen and it was a very exhilarating experience. I didn't understand much of what was going on, but it was exciting. Nobody bought many newspapers, but there was a lot of discussion.

The Dewey education was the best educational experience of my life, without any comparison. The school encouraged individual creative work, but it was completely non-competitive.

When I went to the local academic high school at twelve, I realised for the first time that I was a good student. I seemed to be getting all 'A's and other people weren't. There was a differentiation among students; people were judged by where they ranked and that was the first time that I had ever seen that happen. In the first years of my own schooling, kids had worked together and were encouraged to perform to the best of their ability and praised for what they did. It was a very healthy intellectual environment and very stimulating. I became interested in science – chemistry and the natural sciences – and I remember third-grade projects on astronomy. I was quite interested in political affairs and the first article I wrote was when I was about ten years old. It was on the Fall of Barcelona, the victory of the fascists in Spain and what that meant for the future. It was probably not a very good article, but that was the topic. There was one particular teacher who was quite stimulating and got me thinking about all sorts of things and at whose suggestion I skipped a year.

Going to the academic high school, which was theoretically the best high school in the city, was like entering a black hole – I remember nothing of the next four years except hating it. It was results-orientated, geared specifically to getting you through the college entrance exam with a high mark. It didn't matter if you understood anything at all or forgot about it the next week. I had to take a German exam to get into college and I had never studied German, so I literally sat and memorised a five-thousand word dictionary for the couple of weeks before the exam, got through the exam okay and then forgot it all a week later. That was considered quite acceptable, but it was quite different to the early part of my education.

I read a huge amount of nineteenth-century novels and history and science books. There was a science institute, the Benjamin Franklin Institute, in the city and, by the time my friends and I were old enough to travel alone on public transport, we would spend our Saturday afternoons down there learning about this and that. It was a pretty interesting, intellectual environment. It was the end of the Depression and a very lively time in political terms – I was interested in that, at least to the extent that a pre-teenager could be.

Home was completely different. On Friday night, which is the celebration of the Jewish Sabbath, my father and I would go off together and read Hebrew novels or the Talmud. I got very immersed in late-nineteenth-century Hebrew literature – the Hebrew language was revived around the middle of the nineteenth century. Yiddish literature was being translated by authors into Hebrew and there were Hebrew poets, novelists and essayists; that was the main reading fare on those Friday evenings. By the time I was fifteen or sixteen, I was going through the literature on my own. I was very much interested in, and involved in, the Zionist movement of the day, although today it would be called anti-Zionist. It was concerned with Arab–Jewish co-operation, especially working-class co-operation. That was probably my main driving interest in my youth. I later became a youth leader and a Hebrew teacher and led such activities as discussion groups and summer camps.

None of these individual activities was exceptional, but it was unusual to have them all together. In the immigrant milieu, all the kids went to Hebrew school and studied there. I was probably doing more than others, especially studying Hebrew literature on my own. My political interests were also not unusual at that time. In retrospect, it was a funny combination of interests, but none of the individual parts were that unusual, except maybe they were more intense in my case.

I went into college at sixteen, very enthusiastically, as I was delighted to get out of high school and I thought college looked exciting. The college I went to was the City College. It was academically not particularly good, but there was no question of going anywhere else. I lived at home and worked on the side – there was no money in those days. You didn't get stipends or tuition paid. I took one course after another, but I was very much turned off by them. They were taught in a very deadening, boring fashion; big classes and not very good teachers. I just didn't find it at all interesting.

After about two years I was ready to quit college. There were other things I was much more interested in, including left-wing Zionist politics. (Zionist, I would have to stress, would mean today non-Zionist, because it was in opposition to a Jewish state, though at that time within the framework of the whole movement.) I was ready to drop out and get involved in that – go and live in a kibbutz and bring the Arab–Jewish working class together; I was actually studying Arabic for that reason. Through those activities I met an older person who happened also to be the professor of linguistics at the University of Pennsylvania – a very distinguished linguist. I became friendly with him and was very impressed with his political and social ideas. I drifted back to studying, taking his graduate courses, and then, at his suggestion, began taking other graduate courses; I was still an undergraduate at the time.

Although the college wasn't a very good college, it had a scattering of quite distinguished people in different fields. Those students who were academically orientated tended to put together odd subjects, because they would cluster around points of intellectual excitement, even though they were separate in the university. I began studying mathematics and philosophy, mainly, and linguistics with this particular professor, and I got through. By the time I entered graduate school, I was nominated by a philosophy professor, Nelson Goodman, to the Harvard University Society of Fellows, which is a graduate research organisation. The Society picks up six or seven people a year from all fields and gives what, at that time, looked like an absolutely magnificent stipend, enough not to have to work on the side – I think it was about twelve hundred dollars. However, I managed to get that and spent the next couple of years at Harvard.

I had already been studying linguistics as an undergraduate, but completely on my own. In linguistics I was kind of schizophrenic. On the one hand, I took for granted that the structuralist linguistics of the day was the right approach. On the other, I could see that it really didn't work but I spent an awful lot of time trying to fix it up. I had a good background by then in logic and mathematics. I had the formal qualifications to patch up what were the obvious fallacies and gaps and errors in the system, but, on the side and quite on my own, I was working on something which later became what is now called generative grammar. It had no relationship that I could see to anything else that was going on in the field, although I later discovered that there was a long tradition behind it which had been forgotten. I continued on these dual paths until the early 1950s, when I was free to pursue my own interests. The research fellowship at Harvard was free; you could do what you liked. Somewhere along the line – I happened to be on a transatlantic passage, totally seasick, practically dying – I suddenly realised that the approach that I had been pursuing on my own made sense; it was actually getting somewhere and had results and implications elsewhere. My efforts to patch up the structuralist procedures were a failure because they were starting from the wrong basis. That was when I abandoned one and pursued the other and I have been doing so ever since.

If you think about what you and I are doing right now, we are producing linguistic expressions; I'm producing them in my system, you are producing them in your system. What you have in your head and what I have in my head are close enough for each of us to understand what the other is saying. Curiously, however, we are producing new expressions: I am saying things that I have never said before and that you have never heard before and you are saying things that I never heard before and so on. But we have no sense of unfamiliarity with them – in fact we can't tell which ones we know and which ones we don't know. The reason for that is that we have available to us an unbounded range of linguistic expressions which we interpret and understand instantaneously and effortlessly. This means that we must have in our minds some kind of computational procedure that determines the sound and meaning of an unbounded number of linguistic expressions and does it very precisely, because when I say something you interpret it instantly as meaning exactly what it does.

If we start looking in detail into how you interpret what I am saying, it becomes apparent that there is a phenomenal richness of understanding. In fact, we are only barely beginning to see how complex and rich it is. Now, the same is true of a four-year-old child, so it follows that these abilities must be part of our genetic constitution. It must be the case that virtually everything that you know and that I know is information that was somehow already available to us, that only had to be brought out by experience, when it unfolds, the way a flower grows. You pour water on it, but the water doesn't determine that it is going to be a flower rather than an insect. However, without the water it won't grow. The fact that you and I have arms and not wings and a human eye and not an insect eye doesn't result from the nutritional inputs that the embryo received but rather from internal biological endowment, genetic coding. Any complex form that arises in the natural world is determined by its internal structure. There is, of course, development that is very narrowly determined by the internal structure and is stimulated and shaped by environmental factors – so you might be taller or shorter, depending on how much food you ate, but the amount of food you ate isn't going to turn you into a bird, for example. Language growth must be exactly the same. So far, what I have said is almost just logic, but now we have to fill in the gaps and see how it actually works.

In the case of embryology, we take for granted, without information, that there is something about the biological endowment of a human embryo that turns it into a human and a chicken embryo that turns it into a chicken, but it is hard to know how that works. Linguistics is a bit like embryology. We can be quite certain that Japanese and Swahili and Hungarian and English are much the same – they can't be very different. The reason is that, in each of these communities, the child acquires extremely rich knowledge, acquires the capacity to do what you and I are now doing and does that on the basis of very scattered and limited evidence. Therefore, unless this is a miracle, it must be that the basic character of what is acquired is already fixed in advance. Since none of us is designed only to speak Hungarian or Swahili, and a child will pick up any language as easily as any other, it must be that we are all the same to start with, that the core structures are identical. What strikes us as different is just a modification of peripheral factors and the problem is to fill that in with precise detail. This has been my project for the last four years or so – to find out just what are the principles of language that determine the structures, the interpretations and the sounds and that are fixed by our nature and therefore invariable, not changing from one language to another, because they are part of our biological nature. So, that is the project and there has been quite a lot of progress made on it.

I think the 1960s had a very healthy, liberating impact on general culture, right across the board. Take the United States, which I know best, although I think it is the same worldwide. A remarkably wide range of concerns and questions that had been subdued or suppressed suddenly broke forth. Environmentalists have, in effect, recognised that future generations have rights and we have to protect those rights, we have to hand them over a world fit to live in. The feminist movement has expanded the moral sphere, saying that half the human race has rights, something very new. The civil rights movement in the United States has also expanded the moral sphere. The '60s brought about great change in colleges, universities and schools – from dress codes to patterns of obedience to not asking questions. The Central America solidarity movements of the 1980s were remarkable movements in the United States. They had no parallel in the history of imperialism. These were middle-class movements often based in relatively conservative sectors of the population, especially the churches in mainstream America. These people didn't just sign protests and give money – they uprooted and went and lived in the villages to help protect people from terrorist attacks. There has been nothing like that in other imperialist adventures.

Consider also the original sin of the United States, the destruction of the native population. That was never faced. When I was a child we were still playing cowboys and Indians and the good guys were the cowboys. Even in scholarly work it wasn't faced – there was just lying, lying. In the 1960s, it became possible for the first time for a couple hundred years to face these issues. All of these are tremendous changes and they're very liberating. As in any mass popular movement, there is a lot of craziness and there is a fringe of absurdity and violence. That fringe gets a lot of attention, because sectors of power don't like what is happening and they naturally want to denigrate it and so they point to the fringe, but the main core of what happened was healthy and had a civilising impact on society.

Shirley Conran

Shirley Conran was born in London in 1932. She was the eldest of six children whose drunken father made life miserable for them and their mother. The only bright time in her childhood was during her summer 'escape' to her grandmother's house in the country. Shirley went to art school in Portsmouth and eventually fulfilled her dream of studying art at Chelsea Polytechnic. While studying there, she met and later married the designer Terence Conran. She began work for the Daily Mail *as a design consultant and later became women's editor of the* Observer *colour magazine.*

While recovering from a serious illness, Shirley began making notes on how to do housework in a quick and easy fashion. These notes were to become the bestselling Superwoman, *whose motto was 'life is too short for stuffing mushrooms'.* Down with Superwoman *followed, to drive home the message that no woman can or should want to be Superwoman. Shirley Conran's writing career had taken off and there followed a series of novels, filled with 'adventure, excitement and passion' –* Lace, Lace 2, Savages *and* Crimson.

Shirley Conran, divorced at the age of thirty, now lives in Monaco.

I grew up in London, the eldest of a family of six. My memories of my childhood are not particularly happy. There was enough money, but my father was a violent drunk and anybody who has been in that situation doesn't want to remember any part of it. I think the reason I loved school so much was because it was calm and logical and straightforward and you didn't live in a state of anxiety and suspense all the time. Being the eldest, I felt I had to protect my mother from my father and try to distract his attention when he was violent.

Then we were evacuated during the war. My grandmother took a house in Hereford, on the Welsh border, which was as far away from the German bombs as you could get. She didn't only have to cope with us but also with our cousins. She just put a lot of iron beds in the attic and we slept there. I used to get to the library whenever I could, but my grandmother was quite Victorian and thought that reading was wasting time. Perhaps that is why I grew up to like it so much, spending every spare minute at the public library.

Grandmother was a very tiny woman. Her father had been a very poor grocer and they used to save farthings to go to the opera. He was potty about the opera and named all his children after operatic figures. We had Great-Aunt Norma, Great-Uncle Siegfried and my grandmother was Mignon – we called her Minnie. Grandmother was also deaf and sometimes very conveniently deaf. She had a huge black box of a hearing aid that she used to wear under her front and when she didn't want to hear anything she would just tap the hearing aid and say, 'Must get new batteries', and then you knew that she simply did not want to deal with what you wanted to talk about.

I know cynics say that school is an interruption of education, but it certainly prepared me for higher education, which I think is really self-education. I went to St Paul's school in London, after we came back from the evacuation. School was a very chaotic place at that time. You went down into the air-raid shelter when the siren went off and girls were constantly coming and going as their parents evacuated them and brought them back again. However, it taught us to work hard and to work by ourselves, so I suppose that was what equipped me later on for Fleet Street, because I certainly had no other training.

The best part of my childhood was when my grandmother used to take a cottage in the country, in a place called Bircher Green, for our summer holidays. We went to school there, to a Roman Catholic school, which was reached by a walk through the bluebell woods. The nuns were wonderful, but they were very stern. Our art teacher, who wasn't a nun, asked us to draw a pattern in two colours. I drew a very simple pattern in pink and orange. She made me hold up my hands and she whacked them with her metal ruler to the tune of 'pink and orange don't go', whack, whack, whack, whack. I think that was the start of my rebellious streak. I notice my favourite designs and colour combinations are still pink and orange.

The village was very primitive. There were no shops and a bus went through just once a week. We had to carry water uphill from the well, which was a quarter of a mile away. My grandfather used to catch rabbits and I did my first cooking there, because my grandmother sprained her ankle. She lay in bed and hollered down instructions. It was rather tough to start your cooking by skinning a rabbit and gouging its eyes out, and cooking rabbit stew and apple pudding! I immediately sat down and started my first book, which was called *One Hundred Ways to Cook the Common Apple*. It never got finished, but a lot of my childhood was spent writing little books.

At St Paul's, we always had our quota of people with different coloured skins, different religions and also physically handicapped people, so I never really knew what snobbery was until I left there. We had an exam called the School Certificate and I passed that with matriculation exemption, which means that I had done so well that I didn't have to take the next examination the following year. This astonished me and astonished my teachers even more. They wanted me to go to university to read English. However, there were a couple of girls from St Paul's who were going to finishing school in Switzerland and my parents said that I could go too if I wished. I jumped at the chance, because it seemed very glamorous – it was abroad, it was snow, it was skiing, it was chocolate, it was cream, it was very alluring.

However, I very quickly had enough of cream and chocolates and grew very disillusioned. I got into a lot of very bad habits. I learned to waste time, because, if you had a one-hour period and you finished your work in ten minutes, you just had to sit there with your hands on the table for the rest of the hour. So I dawdled over the work, because at that time I didn't have the inner resources to spend an hour doing nothing.

At that time my parents moved from London to Portsmouth and I felt this was the end of the world, because when you are a seventeen-year-old you want to be in London, not Portsmouth. Nevertheless, my parents were adamant. I entered an art school in Portsmouth, but I could only get a place in the fashion department, and that was full of girls called June designing ball gowns of tulle. It was extremely boring, because they didn't like me. I was wearing Balenciaga originals and Balmain and Christian Dior and you can understand there might have been a bit of hard feeling. I knew I didn't have the gift for clothes design, so as soon as I could I skipped into the carving department and there I stayed very happily.

I loved it at Portsmouth Art College, because I got a classic Victorian art education – they worked us very hard. We were made to draw, draw, draw, from plaster casts and live models, whereas all my friends studying art in London were riding bicycles through tins of paint and over the canvas. I passed the art exams and I then got engaged to a suitable banker's son. I don't think my parents ever envisaged any future for me other than getting engaged to a rich man and having four children. However, he jilted me when I was nineteen and I was quite distressed. I later found out that his father had put pressure on him because he didn't think I came from a good enough family!

My father thought it was a great failure that I had been jilted and he decided it was time I earned my own living. He gave me my fare to London and off I went, but I couldn't get a job because I wasn't trained to do anything. There was no demand for stone carvers at the time and, after about six weeks, I collapsed from malnutrition. I was taken home and when I recovered I started modelling. I sold all my Paris originals and my fur coat and I saved up enough money to go to Chelsea Art School to study painting for two years.

I had a one-man show of water-colours and oil paintings at the Architectural Association and it was about that time I met the man who was to become my husband, Terence Conran. He had just opened a restaurant at the end of the road and I used to go and waitress there in the evening for a free meal. We gradually drifted into a relationship and got engaged. Eventually, he wanted me to run his showroom, because he thought it was of more aesthetic value to the world if I sold a hundred of his chairs than one of my paintings! He is a very remarkable man who has had a great effect on the world visually, because, at that time in the early '50s, England was a visual desert. He went on, of course, to form Habitat and other design outlets. From him I had the best art education I could have had. I taught myself fabric printing and ran the showroom and handled publicity for Terence. I also handled all the Conran fabrics, but I found it very exasperating that I couldn't say what I wanted because I didn't know the technical language, so I went to night school when I was pregnant with my second son and learned to weave. I simply loved weaving and it was wonderful to be able to put my ideas into three-dimensional form.

It is never too late to educate yourself. I have just been back to school to learn to type. All my books have been written in longhand. I used to write them on a yellow legal pad and then stick it all together so that each chapter was one long wind-up scroll. I went to Queen's College in South Kensington and I sat there among a class full of girls with very long legs and black stockings and hair down to their waists. After five days, I was doing twenty-two words a minute and so was everyone else – they were going boom, boom, boom, boom, and you could hear the whole room rocking! I did two days on the word processor and then I went to the principal and suggested they ought to construct a class for women who are going back into business. So now I have planned a four-week course with them for women who are going back into the workforce and want to learn to type and be their own secretary and so on.

When I was thirty, my husband and I separated and I was without a job. I didn't know how to get a job and I was still very distressed about everything. I was design adviser with the *Daily Mail* and I eventually persuaded them to give me the job of Home Editor. I didn't have the experience, but I did have originality and considerable knowledge of the design world. I was very lucky – I had my own secretary and assistant, so I was able to get along without typing.

When I was women's editor of the *Daily Mail*, I developed viral pneumonia. I was about thirty-eight at the time and I had been having a wonderful time on Fleet Street. I was unconscious for five days and I nearly died. As a result of that I developed something called PVS, Post Viral Syndrome, although at the time it was a condition that the medical profession hadn't yet recognised. My sons were extremely supportive, though we very quickly ran into debt and had to leave the house which I had bought and paid for. We had to move about five times in eighteen months. During that time, I started making notes on housework. I had very little strength, so I worked out easy ways to minimise housework by applying lateral thinking. A publisher heard I was working on this and asked to see my notes. He said, 'Finish the notes and I'll publish it as a book' and that book was *Superwoman*. I was very lucky, because it went straight to number one in the bestseller list and stayed there for nineteen weeks. My new career was established.

The motto of *Superwoman* was that life is too short for stuffing mushrooms. The whole concept was that nobody can be superwoman and nobody should want to. You should get away with doing as little housework as possible, in order to leave you time to do something more interesting, and there is always something more interesting to do than housework. For some people that was a very unpopular idea. They felt that I was taking their job, their life, their reason for living away from them.

More recently I wrote *Down With Superwoman*. That title made my message more clear, because many people thought from the title of *Superwoman* that I was trying to encourage them to be one, whereas my aim was quite the reverse. Since I first wrote *Superwoman*, some aspects of housework have got easier, but I think home management has got more difficult. Any working mother who has ever tried to take a child to the dentist in the middle of the morning will know what I mean. You require one of the desert storm generals in order to organise such a thing.

In *Crimson*, the last novel I wrote, I was writing about my mother, my sisters and the women of that era who tended to see life through rose-coloured spectacles. We all need to wear that kind of spectacles from time to time, but, if you never take them off, you won't see your life as it really is. If there is something wrong with your life, it will never be put right. It is better to face your situation and decide either to live with it or escape. My early life with my father made me a rebel, because, until I was nineteen, I didn't dare argue. I once read about people being in a concentration camp and the way they dealt with it sounded very much like my childhood – avoid meeting somebody's eyes, try and hide if possible. It all sounded very much like my childhood.

There is always more to life than meets the eye. A situation is generally not how it appears. The truth today depends on what country you are living in and whether you are a man or a woman. The people who helped me on Fleet Street were my two male bosses. They definitely encouraged me and gave me confidence in myself. I am surrounded by men who help me. I don't actually believe in women's liberation, I believe in people's liberation. My definition of a feminist is somebody who wants the same pay as the person who is sitting next to her doing the same job, whether that person is a man or a woman. The rest is all red herrings. In America, a woman earns 70 cents to a man's dollar for the same job, and there is really no excuse for that today. Having equal pay for the same job is the only thing that is important. All the rest will then fall into place. The word 'feminist' has been degraded. The instant picture that comes to mind is of a dirty-haired, slack-breasted, foul-mouthed, baby-hating, man-hating lesbian, and who wants to be one of those?

Mike Cooley

Mike Cooley was born in Tuam, County Galway, in 1934. He attended both the Christian Brothers and vocational schools, pioneering an early form of comprehensive education. He studied engineering in Germany, specialising in computer-aided design. He worked for many years with Lucas Aerospace, where he was also a prominent trade unionist.

Winner of the $50,000 Alternative Nobel Prize in 1981, he is now a lecturer, consultant, writer and broadcaster who is especially concerned with human-centred technology systems. His book, Architect or Bee?, *sets out his thinking on the future of work and technology.*

I think that the most important influences for me were all outside of school. Schools were unstructured, they were often dangerous. Somebody once said that education is the structure on which you hang the rest of your life, but, if that were true, I would think of it as a wall in a gallery. It is flat, it is monotonous, it has a top, a bottom and two sides. Using the analogy of an art gallery, it really only becomes interesting when you begin to paint pictures which you hang on it.

Tuam in the 1940s was a typical provincial town, in a number of ways. It had the advantage that there was the sugar factory, so there was a sense of an emerging technology, as it would have been at the time. The outer parts of the town still didn't have electricity, so I was able to see at first hand the transformations which a new technology can make, both positive and negative, on the lives of people. And there were extraordinary people in the town. There was an exceptional range of skills of all kinds. Many people in the town were, in my view, unselfconscious artists. The manner in which women could metamorphose a wedding dress into a Confirmation dress for a daughter and again into a Holy Communion dress seemed to me an astonishing skill.

This influenced my subsequent thinking, because I now refer to technologies where you have a 'cascade use' of the material, using the same piece of material in different roles over a period of time. I got those deep insights in Tuam at a very early age. There were blacksmiths in the town; John Connolly was one and he used to draw the gates he was going to make in the ashes with the tip of the poker and say to the farmer, 'Would you like a twirl on it here?' referring to the metal turns on the gates. As a result of all these different skills, I was very conscious of the need to preserve them and build on them and this advised a lot of the work I did subsequently on human-centred systems. This tacit knowledge has been a great area of interest of mine.

Tacit knowledge was explained by the philosopher of science, Polanyi, who said that there are things we know but cannot tell. It is a sense we have of shape, size, form and appropriateness which we acquire through practice, through relating to materials, to working with materials. Since it cannot be written down or explicitly stated, there is a tendency for modern educational systems to ignore it or say that it doesn't exist, that the only important things are those things which we can state explicitly. I saw vivid examples of this during my childhood. There was a stonecutter in the town who made a gravestone for our family and I remember him saying to me, 'If you come back next week the head will be coming out of the stone', as though it had been born from the stone. He was really like Michelangelo; he could already see the figure in the material and all he had to do was remove all that which was not the figure.

I remember going to Galway when they still used to make the Claddagh shawls. It was an astonishing piece of textile design, in the best sense of the word. I have seen people get degrees in fine art at the Royal College of Art in London who, in my view, couldn't even begin to approach those kind of skills although they could write about them – so I became conscious very early on that our society values linguistic ability more than real intelligence and that is something I have tried to address throughout my lifetime.

The art of storytelling had an enormous influence on me. People used to gather in particular houses and they would tell stylised versions of the great old classical stories from the West of Ireland. I still have childhood images of these Rembrandt-like heads who would vividly portray a story. As children, we tried to emulate this. We used to have games where we would try to tell a story that would make somebody laugh or make them cry. I used to succeed, on occasion, in making the other kids cry with my very moving story. This convinced me that there was a real possibility of having a whole range of 'magic carpets' in one's mind. When I subsequently read about the Arabian Nights, I became aware that you could conjure up images of imaginary countries, where people cared for nature or were kind to each other, or of extraordinary machines which allowed human beings to do all kinds of things. So, through that story-telling tradition, my imagination was greatly inflamed and I still have a reservoir of magic carpets on which I can fly whenever I am moved to do so.

Playing hurling taught me more than just the game itself! Each road would play against the others and I think there were seven roads in the town. I was conscious very early on that how you defined a road often determined whether you stood a good chance of winning. If all your best players were in a road within the precincts of the town, you would try to get an agreement early on that it was only the roads up to the edge of the town that counted. We had a number of players who lived out on the Milltown Road and they were excellent players, so we wondered how we could somehow change the rules. We decided that a road would be defined as a road through which you went on your way to school, which meant that we had a much bigger catchment area. A year or two afterwards, if we found that others were using the catchment area, we might try and change the ground rules again. A lot of my capacity to negotiate in trade union work or even in complicated international contracts was established then, so, even in childhood games, one can learn an enormous amount.

I liked languages very much. I always point out that I learned German rather than studied it. As children, we used to go a lot to the cinema – the 'fourpenny rush' – on a Sunday afternoon. There were still films of the war and cuts of Hitler. I was fascinated by the resonance and dynamism of his speeches, without having the slightest idea of what they were about. I subsequently had a colleague on the Ballygaddy Road and I used to go and listen to his records, which were old 78s of Beethoven and Mozart and so on. It really did jar on me that a nation that had produced the beauty of Beethoven and Mozart could also produce the hideousness of Hitler. I felt I should try and find out something about that language and that culture. I went down to the Kaplan family – he was the chief engineer in the sugar factory – and I announced to Mrs Kaplan that I wanted to come and learn German. When she got over her shock, she agreed to this and, by the time I was eighteen, I could speak fluent German. I now present television programmes in German and I write books in German, but I have never formally studied German. That seems to me to say a lot about the educational process. One needs the excitement, the motivation and then the capacity to draw on resources around one. Even in Tuam, which was not a centre of Germanic study, if one used the imagination, it was possible to find suitable resources.

I was very very keen to learn workshop technology and have access to a lathe and that type of machine tool and also to learn technical drawing. It seemed to me to be a marvellous subject, but it was not available in the Christian Brothers school. I asked if I could have Wednesday afternoons off, because I had worked out that this was the time it was being taught in the 'tech' [Technical School]. The Christian Brothers were really horrified that anybody should want to go to the tech and they wouldn't agree to it. I then spoke to my parents about it and they agreed that I could continue Latin and German and so on at the tech full-time. I still remember the shock on his face when I told Brother Rafferty. 'If you go to that place' – he didn't even call it a school – 'if you go to that place, you will be finished,' he said. That showed me that, often, educationalists and others try to protect you from what they regard as dangerous or uncertain or unpredictable, when it is precisely through such a thing that we often gain the richest insights. So I shaped my own comprehensive education.

In the tech I met an extraordinary teacher, Sean Cleary. I am sometimes very critical of formal education but I always highlight the marvellous exceptions, the great gifted teachers I met, and he was one. He had worked in England for Vickers and elsewhere, so he could give you a vision of what engineering and metalwork could be like. He also had a deep sense of quality of workmanship and he would sometimes hold up a piece of material and say, 'Isn't that beautiful, just surface finished?' The culture that was transmitted just by doing that was very powerful. I told him I was very keen to design and build a steam engine and he was a good enough facilitator and teacher to say, 'Well, alright, let's try and do it.' The only machine tool we had was a lathe and with him I designed and built a double-acting steam engine which I have to this day. It was a very, very formative experience. We needed close-grain cast iron for the cylinders and there was simply none in Tuam. Now if I was going to be a good civil servant I would have learned at that stage that you write a report about the material you want, you then write saying there is none available and you conclude that the project can't be done. But we heard that there was an old sawmill with an abandoned fly-wheel and we knew that a fly-wheel has to stand high centrifugal forces, so it would have been made from good close-grain cast iron. So we went and cut a huge chunk of cast iron out of it, divided it up into pieces and made a marvellous steam engine.

I think the education system prepares people to analyse rather than to do. The great strength of a craft tradition articulated through a sensitive education system is that it encourages this sort of can-do mentality. I went to work in the sugar factory for about nine months before I went to Germany and Switzerland to study and there, if a great machine broke down, the whole place was geared to getting it working again. They didn't spend hours and hours talking about the things that could not be done and that for me was a tremendous reinforcement of a positive can-do mentality, rather than a can-analyse mentality. People often mistake apprenticeships for simply the transmission of manual dexterity, whereas it is actually the transmission of a great culture, of how to organise yourself, how to get materials, how to plan things. It was in the sugar factory that I also met other apprentices. There was Michael Hussey, who has done all kinds of extraordinary things in the meantime. Tom Murphy was also in the factory at that time, making up poems and plays, and Michael Brennan, who is now a trade union leader. The very first day I went into the factory, Michael came up and to me and said, 'Would you give me a bob?' because he wanted to send a telegram to Castro to congratulate him on arriving back in Cuba. This period was politically and technically formative for me.

The Kaplan family suggested that I go to the Continent and study engineering and German, which indeed I did. There were no agencies that would arrange exchanges then, so I had to write to different embassies finding out how I could go and how to get a passport and where I could stay when I got there. Eventually, I made the necessary arrangements and went abroad to Switzerland first and then to Germany and it proved to be an extraordinary educational experience in the truest sense of the word.

I worked with Lucas Aerospace in England for some eighteen years. We were working with very advanced technology – Concorde and fighter aircraft and so on. It seemed awful to us that there was all this human suffering around when technology properly applied could do so much to alleviate it. We were working on advanced guidance systems that can guide missiles to another continent with extraordinary accuracy, but the blind and the disabled were still staggering around as they had in medieval times. So, rather than accept structural unemployment, which was then being proposed in the company, our view was that all that skill and talent should be used to improve the quality of life for people. We came up with an extraordinary plan for socially useful production. About one hundred and fifty products would be made which would reduce energy consumption, would dramatically reduce pollution and would make meaningful creative jobs for people. Although we were unsuccessful, in the sense that I was sacked in a big blow-up amid worldwide protest, the ideas were broadly correct. I think the ideas are as relevant today as they were then.

In a strange way, artists and poets often prefigure the really big issues in society and we as engineers and scientists diminish ourselves if we are not exposed to those ideas. That is expressed for me most powerfully in the part of *Finnegans Wake* where Joyce describes the two opposites that make up each person: Shem and Shaun, the positive and the negative. Of those who always emphasise the negative, he says, 'Sniffer of carrion, premature gravedigger, seeker of the nest of evil in the bosom of good word. You who sleep at our vigil and fast at our feast, you with your dislocated reason, you have reared your disunited kingdom on the vacuum of your own most intensely doubtful soul.' That for me highlights a big issue in design. Do we design systems that assume all the things people can't do (where they talk about fool-proof systems, they actually mean that the people are fools), or do we look at all the greatness, talents and abilities of people and, instead of designing systems to obliterate that, to reduce human beings to abject, pathetic machine appendages, actually enhance those skills and abilities? I got that insight from *Finnegans Wake* and it is now an area of research and design methodology which is being pursued worldwide.

I was conscious very early on of what a natural treasure trove I had all around me and I really relished that, in a childlike way of course. I used to marvel when the skeins of geese would return in October; it was always the third week in October and I would wonder how they had guided themselves, whether they were using the earth's magnetic lines or the stars. That was later to excite my interest in guidance control systems. I sometimes used to spend the summers in Galway with my uncle Martin. Looking down at the salmon weir, I was fascinated by the fact that salmon could find their way back to the same river in the same part of the world, having been thousands and thousands of miles away. These astonishing features of nature really did awaken my appetite and I still enjoy nature enormously and have tremendous respect for it.

In recent years, I came across the work of Chief Seattle, which encapsulates for me many of the feelings I myself used to have about nature in the West of Ireland. I never felt separate from nature there, I always felt a part of it. I felt as much a part of it as the curlew or the beautiful cloudscapes we used to have – rain was never offensive to me. I enjoyed the whole surroundings and Chief Seattle for me expresses that feeling of closeness to nature and then presents a sort of religion and outlook which separate us from it and put us totally above it. He confronted one of the American presidents about the destruction of the buffalo and the president said, 'You're going to have our culture, our language, our literature and our religion.' Chief Seattle responded in the most extraordinary fashion, when he said, 'Every part of this country is sacred to my people. Every hillside, every valley, every plain and every grove is hallowed by the memory and experience of my tribe. Even the rocks in the sea are charged with our memories. The dust under your feet responds more lovingly to our footsteps than to yours, for the soil is rich with the life of my people. Our religion is the tradition of our ancestors and is written on the hearts of our people. Your religion was written on tablets of stone by the iron finger of an angry god.'

That seems to me to be profoundly insightful and, as we approach the twenty-first century, I think it should create a psychological stimulus to make us re-examine the strange, double-edged journey which has brought us to where we are. It's double-edged because, on the one hand, we produce the beauty of Venice and, on the other, the hideousness of Chernobyl; we produce the marvellous caring therapy of Röentgen's X-rays and at the same time use almost exactly the same technology to destroy Hiroshima. The German culture, which I love so much, produced the musical delights of Mozart and the stench of Belsen. These are very, very deep issues and it seems to me that what we have got to look at is the great creative, positive side of humanity and build on that, rather than emphasising and allowing the negative features to dominate the way in which we develop.

Dr Cahal Daly

Cahal Daly was born in Loughguile, County Antrim, in 1917, the son of a local schoolteacher. He was educated locally and at St Malachy's College, Belfast, before pursuing an MA degree at Queen's University, Belfast. He then studied at St Patrick's College, Maynooth, and was ordained a priest in 1941. He was later awarded a Doctorate of Divinity and did postgraduate studies in Paris. He taught briefly at St Malachy's and lectured in philosophy at Queen's University.

In 1967, Cahal Daly was appointed Bishop of Ardagh and Clonmacnoise and, in 1970, Bishop of Down and Connor. He was installed as Archbishop of Armagh in 1990 and created Cardinal in 1991. He retired in 1996.

A scholarly man and avid book-collector, Cahal Daly has written extensively on aspects of philosophy and theology. His episcopal career in Northern Ireland coincided with 'the Troubles' and he has spoken and written at length on the moral, social and political problems of Northern Ireland. Living amid the turmoil of that era has been for Cahal Daly a most educative experience.

My father was from County Roscommon in the diocese of Ardagh and Clonmacnoise, which was my own first diocese. He came north in the early years of the century, met and married my mother and lived in a place called Loughguile. They were a very religious family. My father died at the age of sixty and, therefore, still relatively young. I was still a student, two years from ordination. Being a boarder at college and then away from home in a seminary, I didn't have the experience of living continuously with my father, but I have very vivid memories of him and he had a deep influence on me. He taught in an outlying school in a parish to which he travelled two miles each day. I went to the nearby school which was within walking distance, but he gave special tuition to my brothers and sisters and me in preparation for scholarships because there was no way we could have afforded to have second level education without scholarships. He was a good teacher and his spiritual, religious and moral influence were very strong. He was a quiet-spoken person with a deep but unostentatious faith. We always knew, at the weekend, when he was preparing to go to Confession – there was a stillness and a sense of expectation in the house at that time. Things like that make a deep impression.

My mother lived on until I was bishop in Longford. She died in 1974, a quite aged and infirm person. She had had an amputation before she died and I learned a great deal from her serenity and her cheerfulness in that period when she was confined to a wheelchair. Long before that, she had taught me so much about my faith. She was someone who was not theologically trained and yet she had very profound insights of faith, a great reverence for God, a great love of prayer and a great love of Mass, which she hardly ever missed throughout her whole life. Even in times of illness she would force herself to go to Mass, even though afterwards she would tell me that she had had to sit by the side of the boreen on her way to Mass because she was too exhausted to complete the walk. She also taught us a great sense of compassion, of charity and of generosity towards people who very poor – and there were many people who very poor in those days in County Antrim. We often took dinner and food to homes where there was literally nothing. We were always taught to have concern for others and never to waste food ourselves, because others would be so glad to have what we left, and those lessons stayed with me. It was the first and the greatest commandment – love the Lord your God – and the second, which is inseparable from it – love your neighbour as yourself. That lesson of concern for the poor and the disadvantaged was part of one's very earliest training and these things remain.

Somebody once remarked that education is what remains after you have forgotten what you had learned. These were not formal lessons, but they were part of the whole atmosphere which one breathed growing up in that home. One lived close to nature. One grew up with a great love of nature, the fruits and the flowers of the field and the animals. We kept a cow and had its milk for churning our own butter. We were not very good at it and a very caustic neighbour used to make scathing remarks about the pretended churning that we did – 'How the dickens do they think they can get butter when they drink all the cream!'

In the latter years of primary school, I began cramming, under my father's tuition, for the scholarship examination for admission to grammar school. There was no access to Catholic second level education locally for boys in those days, so that meant being a boarder at St Malachy's College. That was quite expensive for someone on a teacher's salary with a large family, so one had to give a lot of extra time to homework and mock examinations. Fortunately, most of the members of the family acquired a scholarship and were therefore able to have a proportion of their fees paid, so it was possible, with stinting and saving, to get by.

Pocket money was very limited and from an early age I spent any pocket money I had on books in a secondhand bookstore down in Smithfield. I am afraid this became almost compulsive and I still find it hard to resist going into a bookshop. If I go in, I can't resist buying books that I hope to read some time. I have always felt that even just owning books is to some extent educative. It has been important in my life to keep reference books handy. There is a certain satisfaction in being familiar with a wider world of ideas – I have always found it stimulating.

Life in boarding school approximated closely enough to the way in which one would have been brought up at home. It was tough in many ways, but then nobody wanted to be dubbed a sissy. There is a kind of macho image which one tries one's best to live up to. It was a good experience, a broadening experience, meeting people from all parts of Antrim and Down and meeting people from the city. In no way did we country lads feel inferior to those city lads. On the contrary, we had a certain pride in being country lads. There was plenty of recreation and sport. I did a bit of hurling and a bit of football in my time. I never distinguished myself, but I think at least I excelled in stubbornness and determination and tried to make up in that way for what I lacked in skill.

Father Henley was president of the college. He was a man who had a tremendous spiritual influence on his pupils because of his integrity, his utter sincerity and conviction and his lack of all pomp. He was a man of a very compassionate heart but he was anxious not to spoil his students, anxious that nobody would have ideas beyond their station and that we would genuinely give thanks to God for the gifts we had and not pride ourselves upon them. I had done the equivalent to the junior certificate examination and I think I probably had the leading results in Latin and Greek, which were my favourite subjects then and afterwards. I came back rather proud of my results and not unwelcoming to any compliments that might be directed towards me. I met the president on the stairs on the first night and he looked rather sternly at me and said, 'Daly, you didn't do very well in your mathematics. You'll have to pull up your socks in mathematics.' I discovered afterwards that he was in fact quite proud, because he had taught me Latin and also mathematics, but he just wanted to make the point that I mustn't get ideas above myself, and I think that was good for me.

The study of these languages was a great help to me then and afterwards, particularly when I went on to specialise in the ancient classics in my university course. I did honours in Latin and Greek with subsidiary subjects in modern history and philosophy, which was part of the requirement for admission to a major seminary. I liked philosophy and was to specialise in it afterwards, but at that time my horizons were within the world of Greece and Rome. I still remember the classes in translation and in Latin prose conducted by the professor, R M Henry, who was a venerable figure, just as old as I am now but I thought he was as old as the hills then. When he had a good student, he took a great personal interest and was very encouraging. He gave compliments sparingly but when he did they were worth receiving.

The appeal of the classics for me was the insight they gave into the structure of a language, into how language works and how you construct a sentence that will concisely and grammatically express your meaning. Thinking yourself *into* a language with a different structure from a modern language, and yet which is at the root of modern linguistic development, was a tremendously mind-stretching experience. There are very few experiences in life that have ever stretched me intellectually to the same extent as Latin prose translation. The philosophy of translation which R M Henry taught was that you take an English paragraph and ask yourself, 'What did this writer mean to say?' and then you say it in the language that Cicero might have used in his time. It is not a question of word for word literal translation, but a thinking *into* the meaning of the English sentence and then thinking yourself *into* the mentality and thought patterns of a Ciceronian. In an examination, for example, when presented with a Latin prose text, one would have been expected by R M Henry to spend at least half the time just thinking into the meaning of the passage and then saying it as a contemporary of Cicero might have said it. You didn't take your pen in hand until at least half the time had elapsed and the rest of the time you spent in sheer hard thinking, thinking *into* the mindset of the person who wrote the passage.

Only one other teacher had the same effect on me as R M Henry and that was Dr William Moran, the priest who was professor of dogmatic theology in Maynooth. Again, when a written examination was required, his questions were so penetrating that he would ideally have wanted every student to spend more than half the time thinking about the meaning of the question and preparing a clear and succinct answer to it. The sheer thinking involved was quite an exhilarating experience, exhausting but exciting.

Plato, Aristotle and Aquinas were the three people who had most influence on my teaching and my thinking. They are not thinkers of the past. They are thinkers of the present, participants in today's philosophical debates. It is quite remarkable and exciting that some of the leading philosophers of today derive much of their inspiration from Aquinas. So far from being an outmoded and outdated philosophy of the past, so far from our being caught in a time-warp, Thomistic philosophy is a genuine participant in contemporary debate and continually illuminates contemporary questions.

I can't remember a time when I did not wish to be a priest. What I understood by priesthood would have developed of course. At the beginning it would have been somewhat romantic, somewhat superficial, but there was always a desire to be a priest and it was part of a desire to give one's life to God and to serve God and serve others.

Just as going to St Malachy's College from a fairly sheltered life in Loughguile was a broadening experience, even more so was going from St Malachy's College to Maynooth and meeting people from every county and diocese in Ireland. A large number of us had come from the diocese of Down and Connor, but there were obviously opportunities in class and in recreation to mix with other groups of students. Mixing with lads from Kerry, Cork and Mayo was quite an experience for me. I thoroughly enjoyed my time in Maynooth and my years of postgraduate study in a special section there called the Dunboyne establishment.

I was bookish in those days and I spent my first summer almost exclusively in study instead of in vocation, because, together with my theological studies, I was preparing for a master's in Queen's University. That was on the topic of the Christian Church in North Africa at the time of Tertullian, which I found quite exciting. It was directed by R M Henry, but I couldn't do very much work on it during Maynooth term time. I had to devote all my summer holidays to it, so I was quite a recluse that summer. It gave me bad habits, in that I spent a very large part of what should have been free time and recreation in reading. However, I survived.

I spent a sabbatical year in Paris in 1952 to 1953. That was a tremendously exciting and very formative year. I hadn't a very good knowledge of French before I went. I had a reading knowledge, but my pronunciation was something else – it was a language that the Parisians never knew! I gradually got into it and I have a reasonably good knowledge of French now. It is a language which I love. It was a very exciting time in France. Existentialism was in full spate. Sartre was becoming very well known and people like Gabriel Marcel, Merleau-Ponty and others. I had access not only to the Catholic Institute where I was enrolled as a student but also to the Sorbonne and the Collège de France. Many distinguished philosophers of the time lectured in all of these institutions and, in addition, there were many other centres for philosophical debate where one could meet visiting lecturers from other European countries. There was endless variety and richness of intellectual experience.

Apart from the philosophical ferment of ideas in Paris, it was a time of great theological, pastoral and liturgical renewal. In a certain sense, the Second Vatican Council was already being prepared in France and, especially in Paris, there were many great theologians, all of them tremendously stimulating people. A great deal of what later emerged in the documents of the Second Vatican Council was already being adumbrated in their writing at the time. Then there was what was then called liturgical experimentation, which was later officially adopted by the Church, with a great emphasis on the participation of the congregation in the celebration of the liturgy. This was tremendously novel and exciting. I revelled in it and each weekend I would visit a different parish – particularly the parishes which were noted for their liturgical celebration. All of this gave one ideas for renewal in Ireland itself and influenced one's preparation for the Second Vatican Council when it came along.

I had a second sabbatical leave of six months in 1960 and in between I had visited Paris during the long summer vacation, mostly in connection with research and reading. This gave me an opportunity to visit other parts of France. I liked visiting Romanesque cathedrals and these were tremendously educative experiences. I reflected on what a sense of mastery of the cosmos must have come to all those who worked together as planners, designers, architects, craftsmen, stained-glass workers and so on in a cathedral like Chartres. I have often thought that they must have had a sense of triumph, not unlike that of the first space travellers. The sheer scope and size and grandeur of these buildings was breathtaking and no books or pictures can give one the same experience as just entering and drinking it all in, in all its grandeur and majesty and glory. The care with which the acoustics and the gradations of light and shade were planned is just astonishing.

Eventually, in the late '60s, I was raised to the episcopate in Ardagh and Clonmacnoise. It was a totally new and uncharted life. There had been nothing in my previous training which had prepared me for this. I knew very little about the extent of the diocese or about its individual parishes, its priests or its people, so it was all a new journey and a journey without maps to a very large extent. I was the first bishop to be ordained in Ireland after the Second Vatican Council, so I had the whole spirit of renewal to guide me. It was a marvellous challenge, trying to implement the conclusions and spread the spirit of the Council, so I found these to be tremendously exciting and rewarding times. Of course, I was blessed with a remarkable body of priests and religious and people.

Initially as Bishop of Down and Connor and latterly as Cardinal I have witnessed some very violent times in the North of Ireland. It has been a learning experience from many points of view. The dark side of it is that one has learned something of the power of evil to corrupt people, people who perhaps originally entered a paramilitary organisation with a certain idealism and a sense of a noble cause who now find themselves accepting and doing things which they would never have thought possible. This is something quite frightening, and the capacity of the human being for evil, the evil that there is potentially and sometimes actually in each one of us, has been one of the lessons learned.

Against that, there has been the tremendous example of people who have been deeply, deeply wounded and hurt through the murder of their loved ones, or people who have themselves been maimed or had their businesses destroyed by all this senseless violence. Again and again one has prayed by the coffins of young men, almost always young men, brutally murdered by the IRA or by loyalists and simply wept with the bereaved. It is not just a question of trying to comfort them, sharing in their grief and their tears, but of being all the time inspired, uplifted, edified and humbled by their spirit of forgiveness.

It is easy to talk about forgiveness, easy to preach about forgiveness, but to see people living it in a way that maybe I would never be capable of is a tremendous lesson in faith. I have greatly benefited from that and felt it a privilege to be allowed to share such grief.

James Deeny

1906–1994

James Deeny was born in Lurgan, County Armagh, in 1906, the son of a local GP. He was educated by the Jesuits in Clongowes College, County Kildare, and qualified as a doctor at Queen's University, Belfast, at the age of twenty-one. The fact that he was a Catholic debarred him from hospital experience in Belfast. He joined his father's practice and continued postgraduate studies, acquiring further academic honours within a short time.

James Deeny's work with the poor country people in County Armagh influenced much of his later innovative work, particularly the Mother and Child Scheme and research on tuberculosis. In 1944, he was appointed chief medical officer to the then Department of Local Government and Public Health in Dublin. With a handful of other devoted public servants, he was the architect of much of Ireland's health legislation. He conducted a national tuberculosis survey from 1950 to 1953. Subsequently, he had a distinguished career with the World Health Organisation and as scientific adviser to the Holy See. In retirement, further 'careers' involved farming and community development. He published his memoirs, To Cure and to Care, in 1989.

James Deeny died in 1994. In 1995 his family published The End of an Epidemic, his collected essays on public health.

I go back an awful long way. I grew up in what you would call an extended family. My father and mother and my sister and brother and I lived next door to my grandfather, my grandmother, two aunts and an uncle. We were a bit like a commune. In addition to that, we were reared with a governess, a remarkable woman, Miss Finnegan, and then my mother had a housekeeper who came to her as a girl of fifteen and stayed with her for thirty-five years. My father also had a driver, known in those days as a chauffeur, and next door there were a couple of girls to help. We had a big farmyard and paddocks right in the middle of town and there were a couple of men working in the yard. They all took care of us and minded us.

Life went at a very even, slow kind of pace and there was a feeling of security. Every Sunday afternoon, my two aunts took my sister and me out to Derrymacash, which was a hamlet about two or three miles outside the town. We went there for benediction, so it was a solemn walk, and that happened every Sunday unless it was raining. My uncle would take us to the pictures. He had a motorcycle with a sidecar and, if he was going to a fair, I would be put in the sidecar with the collie dog in the back and we would go up to Stewartstown, where we would visit another house and get a great big 'tuck-in'.

My other grandfather lived up at Dungiven and I had about five or six aunts and uncles there who were still unmarried. My grandfather was a contractor and he had land and a mill and various other things. One of my uncles ran the contracting business and he was also head of the Vincent de Paul Society. As he went from one wee job to another, like building a bridge up in the mountains for the county council, some old lady in a little pony and trap might stop at the side of the road and he would have a wee chat with her about help from the Vincent de Paul, maybe. In this way I learned from him. That grandfather took me for a walk every Sunday and we would sometimes go to Banagher Old Priory. Because he was a builder, he could tell me about all the ruins at Dungiven, or he would take me up to Poll na Péiste, the dragon's pool, which is now flooded for the waterworks for Derry. People took time to teach you, so you got a wonderful education.

When we were walking along the street with Miss Finnegan and stopped to look at a shop window, we would walk another twenty yards and Miss Finnegan would say, 'And what did you see in the shop window?' We would tell her as many things as we could remember and then she would take us back again to see how many things we had missed. So I learned a touch of RIC observation – and I still miss nothing!

I used to run wild through the countryside. I had friends like the lock-keeper on the canal. He built me a wee boat for two quid like the ones that the farmers used to get from one side of the canal to the other. I used to sail it and, in fact, nearly drowned myself. Then there was Herbie Andrews. He was head of the waterworks and he had three or four daughters and no sons. He was fed up with women, so he loved having me around. He showed me how to run the waterworks – which valves to turn, what to do when the filter-beds got clogged. Further along the shore there was Hughie McAlinden. He was a fisherman and he used to take me out on his boat.

I used to be sent to get shoes soled at Lavery's the shoemaker's down in Edward Street. I would sit there half the morning talking about shoemaking and the difference between putting in the woodpegs or the tacks. Then Mr Lavery would go to feed his pigs and I would go down and help him and I'd forget to come home and they would have to send for me. I really was a dreadful child and I never stopped talking! I had a wonderful childhood, running wild one minute and the next strapped down and taught to play the piano.

My mother was a very fine musician – she was a great harpist. My father was a doctor, and a very good doctor – he was a tremendous worker. He had a huge practice, which he gradually brought me into. I got my driving licence at fifteen and I used to drive him on his calls and I would even be brought in to help at times. General practitioners then had many more skills than they have now, some even setting all their own fractures. Maternity cases were attended to in people's houses – my father once did five maternity cases in one night and I drove him from house to house. My mother ran the practice to a very high standard. When my father was needed on a case, Miss Finnegan would be hauled out from giving lessons, handed the maternity bag and sent out to the golf links on the bicycle to find him. In those days, if you were a doctor and you got a call, there were no answering machines or restricted hours. If you got a call, you went. Answering the door was a major thing in our house. If somebody came drunk to the door on a Saturday night, you had to know how to handle them. If somebody came along spurting blood from a cut, you had to know what to do. So, we gradually became involved in the whole process.

John Dillon, who was a great friend of my grandfather, was recruiting for the Benedictines, so I was taken and dumped in Mount St Benedict's School in Gorey. It wasn't a success, because I broke my arm and was always in trouble and I learned nothing. I loved running wild through the country, snedding turnips and such like. However, they then sent me to Clongowes College. I had a very good time there, even though I got the hell beaten out of me by the Jesuits. We had wonderful teachers, people like Father Fergal McGrath, Father John Ryan, Father Aubrey Gwynn, Father O'Dea and Father John Joy. Cyril Power taught me mathematics. He had been in the Cavendish laboratory when they split the atom and then he joined the Jesuits. Charlie O'Connor sat beside me at school. He was a descendant of the last High King of Ireland. He has given up a huge estate in Castlerea to go off and join the Jesuits and live like a poor man. These were all remarkable people and they were devoted to teaching you.

As you came out of Clongowes chapel, there was a statue of the Blessed Virgin and a prie-dieu. A lot of the boys, as they came out of the chapel in the evening, would kneel down and say a prayer before they went to study. There was a card there with a prayer on it for success with study. This was the prayer of St Stanislaus Kostka, which had come from Thomas Aquinas before that, and I learned it off by heart. I was then about thirteen years of age and I have been saying it ever since. It is not that I was particularly pious nor was it to get first place in an exam or win a prize, but it was just a prayer to enjoy studying. I have always enjoyed learning and I am still learning. Study was never a chore. I loved it because it was so interesting and so I was always learning.

During my time in Clongowes, there was a social studies club. This would have been in about 1924, at the very beginning of the State. We boys used to sit around and worry about how the turf could be developed in Ireland and about the forestry. At fourteen years of age, the Jesuits were teaching us to start thinking this way and many important Jesuits with interesting ideas would come and talk to us. This gave me a notion of social responsibility and social care and it altered my whole life. There was also a meteorological station in Clongowes and I learned an awful lot about meteorology there. I was always looking for wee jobs and nobody ever knew where I was or what I was doing. I could even have a smoke if I wanted to!

My preparation for medicine was very funny. I said to my father one day, 'I'm fed up with school. If I can pass my 'matric', can I start medicine?' So I sat the matric at Queen's when I was sixteen. I was actually in medical school in my sixteenth year and I qualified at twenty-one. You could do that in those days. Really, my father had taught me my medicine, although I was very well taught at Queen's. Queen's was a very bigoted place, but naturally you became the best of friends with the others in the class. There were only two Catholics on the staff of Queen's, right down to the cleaners, and yet I got a first-class training; there was never any difference made. You could still win a prize, but, on the other hand, you never had a hope of getting on the staff!

I started hanging around the laboratories in Queen's and there were two or three remarkable men there. Dickie Hunter, who was the secretary of the university and a lecturer in anatomy, became a great friend of mine. He taught me all sorts of little things about research and anatomy. Eventually, I got my nose into bacteriology and I gradually worked my way in there. This gave me an interest in laboratory work and research.

I went into my father's practice in Lurgan. Again, my father taught me many skills, like how to pull teeth. In those days, there was no free dental service and old people didn't have the money. An old man would come in and say, 'Dr Jim, could you pull that tooth?' I would get my father's forceps and jack it out, but I would freeze it first so he wouldn't feel it. During the hungry '30s, people got a bit of dole and there was a bit of outdoor relief, but eventually they would be cut off and people were literally faced with starvation. The Vincent de Paul Society did their best and there was also an organisation called the Ladies of Charity, but it was all pretty ineffectual.

I was taught by the people of Lurgan. I had my eyes opened, coming from a posh school down the south and then coming home and living and working with these people. If you delivered a mother's first baby, you were her friend for life. You became part of the family. We always earned money, but for weeks during the really bad times I never saw a fee. They hadn't got it and you didn't ask them for it. When the war came and people got work and there was money floating around, every one of those people came and paid me. When I left Lurgan, there was very little bad debt – they all came and paid you when they had it and, when they hadn't it, you minded them and there was no nonsense about it. You had a responsibility.

Every year I wrote a research paper. It was very simple research, but I was on the ball with it. I discovered the 'blue men' [a diet deficiency] and, within three days, I turned a man pink who had been 'blue' for thirty years. I became world-famous for about a week! Eventually, I came to Dublin as chief medical adviser to the

Department of Health. One of the extraordinary things about Ireland has been the integrity and quality of the senior civil servants in this country. I have seen the inside of fourteen governments all over the world and I have seen crookery and knavery, but the senior civil servants that I worked with – and not only the medical fellows – like J D McCormack, McWeeney and Hourihane, were all outstanding people.

This country is blessed in the people it has in the civil service. Look at the Hospitals' Sweepstake money. They spent hundreds of millions of pounds building hospitals and not one penny of that money went astray. There is no other country that could do that. I was very young relative to these people and one of the things I came to respect was their judgement, their wisdom in the old-fashioned sense of the word. These men had all worked their way up in the civil service in different ways. Some of them had been in prison or had been condemned to death because they had fought for their country. Others had simply worked their way through the county councils and so on. They taught me to stop and look, stop and think, be careful what you say and then stand up and say something unpopular if you know it to be right. Old Berry, son of a bishop of Killaloe, a colonel in the RAMC and a wonderful old man, taught me my job – how to handle the files, how to deal with people and all that sort of thing. I was a mere general practitioner when I was brought in there. Later on, I went off to work with the World Health Organisation, which was a wonderful experience. I was chief of the mission in Indonesia and did national TB surveys in Sri Lanka and Somaliland.

I love art. I have seen all the great art exhibitions in Europe, because, when I was sent to a conference, I would get up early in the morning in order to visit them. I always made sure that I saw anything worth visiting. When I was a medical student, I used to travel up and down from Lurgan to Queen's every day.

There was a bookshop beside the station and, if I had half an hour to wait for my train, I would poke through the books. One day, I bought a wee book called, *Simplicity*, by Pastor Valmer. His belief was that you should make your life simple and not complicate it with possessions – don't complicate life by riding one hundred horses at once! He was echoing a medieval scholastic, William of Occam, a Franciscan from England whose philosophy came to be known as 'Occam's Razor' – one cuts away all the extraneous things in any philosophical hypothesis to bring it down to one central thought. I followed this idea in my research. If I had a job to do, I did just that and cut out all other distractions. It is like those people who want to write a novel but never do because they have too many other irons in the fire. If you want to write a novel, you get on and write it. There were many other suggestions in this book. For instance, if something is very, very important, you do it immediately. Another theme was prevention, which became central to me throughout my medical career – so much disease is preventable. A final theme was simplicity.

I developed a great interest in the old Irish monks, way back in the Golden Age of Ireland, and, wherever I went in Europe, I used to look for their history. It was a very emotional experience, to visit somewhere like the library of St Gall in Switzerland and see all the old Irish manuscripts, beautifully illuminated. I would imagine some poor character starting off in Clonmacnoise or Durrow or Bangor with that same book in a leather satchel on his back and carrying a staff and wearing an old wool habit, crossing seas and marshes, being attacked, starving and sick and, eventually, reaching one of the great monasteries that had been founded by the Irish, like St Gall. Imagining all that, it is then incredible to see the actual book, eight or nine hundred years later. Three years ago, when I was eighty, I went out to Skellig Mhichil and climbed the Skellig. It frightened the wits out of me! But such places have inspired me. In one way, it is their austerity, but, in another way, the Irishness in me makes me glory in what these men achieved.

Eventually, I came down here to Wexford and got very much involved in the whole idea of community development. The ordinary people of an area like Tagoat or Rosslare have educated me greatly. I meet more brains in the course of a day than you would in a university and an awful lot of them never had a chance in life. Some of them have a contentment, they are perfectly happy at what they are doing. I went to Moone recently and a lovely Cistercian monk heard my Confession. After the Confession, I sat back and said, 'Now, father. Most men of my age must begin to think about their end. Is there anything in particular that you would want to advise me?' He looked at me and said, 'Ach no, son. Just go on as you are.' There are a lot of people in a place like Tagoat who are content and wise and this is a very good thing. Everywhere, even right under your feet, there is something to be learned, something to be done, and this is the important thing about community development. I have been educated by wonderful men like Pat Stafford and Lar Doyle, and ladies like Jenny O'Brien and Mary Murphy. They have taught me goodness – there is an awful lot of good in people. Once you start community development, it brings out the creativity in people. Our education system smothers creativity, but we need to bring it out in people.

I have two regrets about my education. One is that I really should have had my last year in school. Character-wise, I would have been better rounded if I had. The other is that I never really learned Irish properly. I have a few words, but I really regret not learning to speak it properly. My grandchildren speak it and I sent all my own children to Ring, to make sure that they learned it. I think it is a very important thing to have – you may not use it, but it needs to be there. It is like belief in God; it is like music; it is like an interest in study and learning.

I am still learning. I read philosophy and I read about the quantum theory, systems analysis and that kind of thing, even if I do not understand it all. I have had a marvellous life. I have a wonderful wife, who has given me a postgraduate course in humility. I am not very good at it yet. In fact, she says it's not working...

Denis Donoghue

Denis Donoghue was born in Tullow, County Carlow, in 1928 but was reared from a very early age in Warrenpoint, County Down, where his father (an ex-RIC man) was a sergeant in the RUC, an unusual position for a Catholic to hold at the time.

The young Denis developed an early passion for music and literature, thanks to the influence of a teacher and neighbour, Sean Crawford. He was educated at Abbey CBS, Newry and later at University College, Dublin, where he studied arts, although his first love was law. He later taught English at UCD and became one of the most distinguished critics of English literature. He has written many works of literary criticism, in particular studies of W B Yeats, Jonathan Swift and Emily Dickinson.

In his student days, Denis Donoghue developed an affinity for American literature and scholarship. He currently holds the Henry James Chair of English and American Letters at New York University. His memoir, Warrenpoint – an intimate, unsentimental portrait of his coming of age – was published in 1990.

I grew up in Warrenpoint, County Down. My very earliest memory is of the death of my brother John, who died of pneumonia at the age of fourteen months. There is one photograph of him in his pram a few weeks before he died, looking out with a big smile over his face. I was much too young to attend the funeral, but I do remember my father carrying the small coffin single-handedly down the stairs.

My father was a sergeant in the RUC there, in charge of about nine or ten constables and a number of what at the time were called B-specials. It was an unusual position at the time. He was a Catholic and there weren't very many of his kind. The RUC then was predominantly a Protestant institution and this made for a degree of awkwardness. I didn't feel any allegiance at all to the source of my father's rather meagre salary, in so far as he was paid by the British government, ultimately. My sense of self as a private individual growing up in Ireland was based upon Dublin and the whole of Ireland. I was certainly an anti-partitionist, which indeed I still am, so that Dublin to me was the centre of the universe. All of my mother's family, and indeed my father's family, were living in the south, so we had no attachment to the North of Ireland as a place. When I went back to Warrenpoint recently, I came to appreciate that it is really remarkably beautiful, so my memories of it are perhaps unfair, because when I was living there I had a sense of alienation from the place and certainly from the structures in Northern Ireland.

My father grew up in the Black Valley, a very mountainy district in Kerry, and his father, a boat-man and a small farmer, was drowned in a notorious accident. My father was the eldest of a large family, so he had very little in the way of formal education. Writing a letter was a serious business for my father, even though he was a highly intelligent and gifted person. He would sit very formally at the table and he would push up the sleeves of his jacket and take his pen, almost as if he were a draughtsman or an artist, and he would compose his letters with extreme precision. But, certainly, in the way of formal education he was pretty well bereft.

My mother had no discernible, or at least no audible, politics. I never recall her emitting a single political judgement. She made no comments whatsoever on the conditions of our lives, nor indeed did my father. He had a remarkable ability to keep his thoughts to himself and usually concentrated on local details, such as how we were getting on at school and was my brother playing in a football match. He was not a man for the grand gesture in conversation. Certainly, he never made any comment about the conditions of his service or about the fact that he would never be promoted, that lesser people would pass him on the inside track because they were Protestant and members of the Orange Order. He never showed any resentment about that, even though he was immensely more gifted and intelligent than many of them.

In a curious way, a great deal of my father's personality was reflected in his bearing and how he wore his uniform and the way he walked along the street. When he walked down Charlotte Street or up Church Street, you would discern extraordinary character and power and personality, far more than in anything he might say if you stopped him to have a conversation. His carriage was unusually erect. There is a wonderful passage in one of Emerson's essays where he talks about the way in which a word will bury its meaning. He mentions the word 'erect' – which in the dictionary means straight, upright – but Emerson was saying that it is also the term for moral uprightness; you appear, or indeed you *are*, morally upright by being erect.

He was extremely suspicious of all relationships. For example, I was approached at one stage, with entirely innocent intent, by a priest with nothing more on his mind than urbane conversation, but my father was suspicious of all friendships. I remember him telling me in a phrase that has its own finesse that one's relations with other people should be civil but strange. That, of course, betokens a certain circle of reference and a certain constraint. He was not open to the world. His behaviour was always impeccable, so he too was civil but strange. I doubt if he had many close friendships in the vicinity, whereas my mother was quite different. Everybody loved my mother, but she was available for friendship in a way he was not.

Warrenpoint is a seaside town and the square was the centre of its activity. Even if you didn't have the money or have any access to things like boats or yachts, at least you could see those things. In the summer the square was filled with chair-o-planes, dodgems, all kinds of activities. It was a very lively place to grow up, but one lived there with a certain circumspection. I was never unaware of the religious factor – we were split pretty well fifty-fifty, Catholics and Protestants, and if you were a Catholic you did not talk much to Protestants. My mother never bought as much as a pound of butter in a Protestant shop, even though she never expressed any political views at all. We did not cross the tracks in any respect. Once I was having a debate with Captain Terence O'Neill about the North of Ireland and he was giving his own rather decorous, urbane and civilised impression of what it was like and I said that, as far as I was aware, the divisions were so deep they were virtually second nature and that I grew up with the ability to spot a Protestant at a hundred yards by their bearing and carriage. It was simply the case that, when I was growing up, Protestants walked differently. They walked differently because they were triumphant, they had won. It may be a gross retrospective delusion now, but it seemed to me that they walked, they moved, they conversed with an air of authority and victory. I may be quite wrong about that, but I don't think I am.

I went to the local Catholic school, St Peter's, a small three-teacher school. One of the teachers, Sean Crawford, a rather remarkable and genial character, lived a few doors from us, just in the square. We had the run of the Crawfords' house. I formed with him and his daughter a little trio and we used to play music. Even more to the point, he was a literary person who made available to me his small but fairly select library. In my family we had no books at all of the slightest significance. Apart from school books, I recall only one book in the house and that was a book my father had, called *A Guide to Careers*, which indeed was a very useful book. When I wanted something to read, I would go through Sean Crawford's collection of books, so the beginnings of my readings were done with the aid of his library. It had the standard works of English fiction – Jane Austen, George Eliot and so on. There was a magazine at the time called *John O' London's Weekly* and he had a very large bound volume, an entire year's issue. I think what first started my interest in literary criticism was this bound volume, because, in addition to stories, it had several critical essays by people like Robert Lynd and Frank Swinnerton, who were men of letters at the time. I got my first introduction to what it was to write a formal essay and perhaps even to have it published through *John O' London's Weekly*, because these were civilised English essays that had a beginning, a middle and an end, in that order.

Sean Crawford used to write little essays and little squibs for the *Irish Press*. He was a strange, angular and rather daft individual, but extraordinarily humane. I remember him vividly as a teacher, not in terms of anything very tangible he taught me, but in the sense that he really made it clear to me that there was a larger world out there that was full of all kinds of magical things: novels and poems and music.

I was largely self-taught at that stage. No one told me what the difference was between good writing and bad writing. I kept lists and I would write down words which struck me as interesting or words that I came across in my reading which were unfamiliar to me. It was in some ways a forerunner of my situation when I came to Dublin and I would steal the book dockets from the National Library so that I wouldn't have to buy jotters. I would come across a sentence that struck me as memorable and write it down and commit it to memory. I began in Warrenpoint by simply writing down single words, words which struck me as either having some resonance or some interesting meaning. When I tried to write an essay, I used some of these words, morally disreputable and pretentious of course. In the same way, when I became a university student, I would try to work these flashy quotations into my formal essays to dazzle my teachers.

Eventually, I moved from St Peter's into the secondary school, which was the Christian Brothers' school, the Abbey CBS in Newry. That wasn't a place of very happy memories. One of my great difficulties there was that I was preceded by my elder brother, Tim. He certainly was not a hard-working student, but he was something far more important in the school at the time – a great footballer. He played Gaelic football for the inter-provincial team and I have to say that he was by far the most intelligent Gaelic footballer I've ever seen. Tim played Gaelic football in the way in which the young Georgie Best played soccer. His career came to a very sudden end, because he did a very foolish thing. Instead of preserving his body for the purposes of college football, which was relatively civilised, he played in the local Warrenpoint team against Mayo Bridge and various other Gaelic football teams and, eventually and predictably, had the cartilage smashed in his right knee and never played again. Brother Newell, who was besotted with Gaelic football, regarded Tim as a hero and I was of no account at all, because of my absolute indifference to all sport, and most particularly to Gaelic football. So my days in the CBS were very much darkened by my complete contempt for all sport and, in that sense, my years there weren't very happy.

It was very much a Christian Brothers' education. Irish history was taught essentially in republican terms – seven hundred years of Irish slavery; in each generation a small band of heroic figures would raise a revolution which would subsequently fail; the degree of success tended to increase over the centuries; from the Fenians up to 1916 it was really one story, and 1916 was nearly a success. I shouldn't give the impression that the Christian Brothers were recruiting for the IRA, or even for a republican movement, but they did imply that the history of Ireland was one story – the story of repeated attempts over a period of centuries to remove the British presence. We were left to conjure with the possibility that at some stage this might be successful, but I would emphasise again that there was no overt campaigning for violence.

I was taught English very badly. It was merely a matter of memorising ostensibly critical observations: if we were talking about romantic poetry, we should bring in the following seven points and so on – a fairly deadening exercise. It was never explained what literature was about or why it existed or what the imagination was or what was the difference between transcribing an event and imagining one. There was no indication that literature was anything but material you learned by heart – a poem was just something that didn't hit the margins of the page. There was no sense of literature itself, as distinct from history or geography.

My favourite subject was Latin. I admired its composure, the way in which the words were placed, the movement of the sentence. I was taught very well by a remarkable teacher, Pádraic Crinion. His way of teaching us Latin was not to simply go through Latin grammar but to start with Cicero's letters, thereby learning the grammar by reading Cicero – a very daring thing in certain respects but quite wonderful as a method. We weren't just chanting phrases and rules of grammar; we saw what Cicero was doing in the speeches and we saw that there was a relation between the grammar, the syntax and the rhetoric of the speech and how it was persuasive. I learned an immense amount of Latin from that and also a sense of a different culture.

When my father retired from the police in September 1946, we all drifted in different directions. I went to Dublin and my father and mother went down to Tullow, where there was a house available. My first inclination was to study law. I saw myself as a barrister and it took me about a week to discover that there was no question of that. My father couldn't possibly have afforded all the King's Inns nonsense – the dinners and the fees and so on. Very reluctantly, I switched to a degree in arts. At that time we did five subjects in UCD in the first year and my five were Latin, English, Irish, history and mathematics. Latin and English were the major subjects I wanted to concentrate on, but it was still a sadness to me that I was unable to do law. I have a strange reverence for law and for the verbal precision, the majesty of it. I always read law reports with great interest and I like their finesse and delicacy. I like talking to lawyers. I like having a conversation with someone who is a trained lawyer, someone who is trained in the niceties of the law, not just in the sprawl of human life. I like that sense of there being order and precision, even though living may be a much more chaotic business.

I didn't really enjoy college life. Even by Irish standards at the time, I was very impoverished. I resented the fact that, for instance, medical students who were my immediate colleagues were far better dressed and lived in fancy houses in Foxrock or Stillorgan, while I was living in miserable digs on the South Circular Road. So, at a very early stage, I shifted my centre of gravity from UCD in Earlsfort Terrace to the Royal Irish Academy of Music in Westland Row. I was very lucky to be able to lead a kind of double life in Dublin. I was far happier in the Royal Irish Academy of Music than I was in Earlsfort Terrace. It wasn't that I despised the teachers or the lecturers – I recognised, for instance, that the late Jerry Hogan was an immensely learned and civilised person – but I did most of my reading and studying in the National Library. They were the good old days when the National Library was open from ten o'clock in the morning until ten o'clock at night. I read omnivorously and took copious notes and also acquired a kind of low cunning in manipulating other people's ideas.

The great writer during my time growing up was T S Eliot. I managed to arrange a couple of meetings with him in London and he was my hero. He was for me a great writer, a great poet, a great critic. At a very early age, I started getting in touch with American writers and critics, major figures like Kenneth Burke, John Crowe Ransom, R P Blackmur. These were the people I revered and, indeed, still do, so that I was oriented much more towards America than Cambridge, where I was living and teaching. I was becoming very Americanised. I was reading a lot of American literature and American poets, so that American criticism and scholarship meant more to me then than English criticism and scholarship.

At that time, in Fleet Street in Dublin, there was a small building called the United States Information Agency, which has long ceased to exist, and which had a quite considerable library of American literature, music and film. I had the run of this library and was very well in with the librarian. I was trying to write a few things and dealt briefly with Francis McManus at Radio Éireann in Henry Street. He pointed out to me that if I did something a bit unusual I'd have a better chance of getting a few programmes on Radio Éireann. So I prepared six radio programmes on modern American music. I made full use of the resources of the United States Information Agency and the librarian got me works by Copland, Bernstein, Samuel Barber and so on. In this way, my ideas gradually moved a little aslant from what might have been called 'official literary culture'.

Lelia Doolan

Lelia Doolan was born in Cork and spent most of her childhood and schooling in Dublin. But much of her 'real education' took place in her parents' native County Clare, where she spent successive summer holidays. Lelia studied languages at University College, Dublin, and it was here that she developed her great interest in drama, an interest she later pursued in a year's study in Germany and, ultimately, as artistic director with the Abbey Theatre. She joined Telefís Éireann in its infancy in the 1960s and worked as producer-director in a wide range of programme areas, from politics to light entertainment. As the station developed, Lelia, with others, notably Jack Dowling and Bob Quinn, began to question the role, the methodology and the very model that the television service might adopt. Together, the trio set out their views in the book, Sit Down and Be Counted.

Lelia later worked in journalism and drama before moving to Belfast, where she studied anthropology in Queen's University. More recently, she has been chairperson of the Irish Film Board.

She now lives in County Galway, where she lectures in communications and maintains her interest in film and drama, as well as studying homeopathy.

Most of my childhood memories outside of Dublin would be of Clare – both my father's part, which was a place called Kilshanny, and my mother's part, which was near Ennis. Those early memories of Clare are very strong in me. We children always used to say to each other that we had penitential holidays in Clare, saving the hay and out in the bog, picking the blackcurrants and gooseberries and doing all the various things that people do around a middle-sized farm. We regarded ourselves as very important slave labour from Dublin and I remember well the experiences that we used to find hard, like pumping water, because you had to pump the water up from a stream into a great tank that was on the roof in order to have running water inside the house. We used to make hay in large meadows that seemed to be unending and my brother Matt, the youngest, was the greatest one for telling the stories of films that we had been to and this used to keep us going for days. He could tell a story better than anybody I have heard since. They are great memories, not just of the daily grind as we would have thought of it then, but the whole sense of community, the Catholicism, the rosary in the evening, the devotions on a Sunday which I suppose we had fairly mixed feelings about, even though you were full of the sense of devotion with the incense and the music. (My aunt used to play the harmonium in the church.)

Clare for me was the fields, all of which had names – 'the cows' field'; 'the hens' field'; 'the well field'; 'the calves' field'; a place called 'the garden' which wasn't really a garden but the wood from where the cows would come running on a hot day to go to the stream and to which they would have to be driven back again; the bog. When the parents didn't want us to be sitting around listening to them talking, they would send us out to find horseshoes in the horses' field. I remember smells from then, emotions, all those things that you begin to know for the first time; the extraordinary vista from the top of a hill looking down across to Doolin and the Aran Islands. Equally, the small fields, the rushy fields, the look of a frog that's been cut in two by a mowing machine, the feel of hay sticking up by your bare legs when you're sitting down in the meadow having the tea. I think that your earliest memories are probably etched most deeply which is why, perhaps, older people remember most clearly what their earliest experiences were. I remember driving my mother out from Ennis to her own place, which is about six miles, and she named every householder in every single house going along and had stories of all of them.

My parents were very steady, very steadfast people. My father died when he was 62 in circumstances that were most tragic and unfortunate; perhaps one could call it a medical accident. That was a very great and awful anguish for my mother, and for all of us, but I think it was something that she never got over. She would have been in her early fifties when he died. What I remember most about him was a kind of quietness and a reflectiveness. I remember also once when I was ill he read aloud to me two books which were the most extraordinary things to read to a child. One was *Flush*, about Elizabeth Barrett Browning's dog, and the other was *Memoirs of a Fox-Hunting Man*, by Siegfried Sassoon. I remember him also as being a bit of a free thinker, a man who thought things out for himself. He wrote diaries as a young man. These were injunctions to himself about how to do things better and reflections on books he had read when he was in England, where he had gone as a boy clerk in the British civil service and where he grew up.

He and my mother were a very happily married couple. My mother was an unforgettable character. She was never a woman to mince words if she felt that something was wrong or had been done in the wrong way, and she was never a woman to shirk a job or several jobs. She was a tremendous worker, faithful, steadfast, strong and loyal. They were a most remarkable couple and gave us a tremendous feeling of security. They had a certain strictness, which was part of the culture at the time. These were people from the country who had come to Dublin to live, to make a life, to bring up children, to see that they got an education. All of this came from a kind of background where learning was regarded as important and where the pursuit of intellectual matters was in itself a good thing, and that slightly puritanical thing was part of the menu as well.

I went to a most unusual primary school in Rathgar, which was run by four sisters, the Miss MacDonalds – small Miss MacDonald and tall Miss MacDonald, Miss Cassie and Miss Frances. They were a foursome of amazing qualities, particularly small Miss MacDonald, who was in fact the boss. They were very strict, they were very precise and they were very good on grammar and arithmetic and headline writing. They even taught French, so, by the time we left, at the age of ten or eleven, we were probably a bit more advanced than others of our age. In fact, I didn't go to school until I was nearly seven. I think I was regarded as delicate and my brothers used to teach me, sitting in front of the fire, various things that appeared to them to be quite important, the catechism mostly. The journey to school is the thing I remember most when I was small. My brother Matt and I used to walk to Rathgar, where the school was. It was about a mile and was always a wonderful walk. You could dawdle for hours along the way, picking things out of walls, finding little insects and, of course, if you were lucky you could hitch a ride on the milkman's cart when the milkman wasn't looking.

I then went on to Beaufort, a Loreto convent school, a school I remember as being fairly liberal and probably a bit snobbish at times too. There were certain dos and don'ts that do not appear to me to have a lot of relevance now. Most of the nuns had nicknames. 'The Bee' was a marvellous small nun who looked a bit like a bee because she wore dark round-rimmed glasses. She taught me German and we went through Schiller and Goethe and all of the verbs and declensions and several other unpalatable matters which stuck in a curious way. I went on and did French and German for my degree in UCD after that.

I became interested in the theatre and maybe just enjoyed being a bit of a show-off. I joined the dramatic society and the musical society in UCD. John F Larchet and his marvellous wife ran the musical society and used to put on Gilbert and Sullivan operas. I took part in those and I was also in the dramatic society with all sorts of luminaries. I directed Paddy McEntee in a most presumptuous and impertinent production of Goethe's *Faust.* I played Brian Farrell's mother in *The Lady's Not For Burning.* In one of those years in UCD, we played host to the Universities Drama Festival. Michael Garvey came from UCG with a production of Arthur Miller's play, *The Crucible.* They had discovered the play and did a marvellous production of it. Then a number of them from UCG and some of us from UCD decided to make our fortunes by taking a theatre in Kilkee for the summer and putting on a season of plays. It was the best summer that Ireland had seen for years and years, so nobody wanted to go to the theatre, but we put on a dozen plays in two months.

Our professor of German was Doctor Kathleen Cunningham. She was known to all of us as Katie and through her we had the opportunity to spend a semester, first of all in Tübingen University in Germany, and then, when we had finished our BA, I spent a year in Berlin. I had a German academic exchange scholarship for a year to Berlin and I wanted to do an MA on Brecht. Unfortunately, it wasn't particularly popular for somebody to go to a university in West Berlin and study somebody from East Berlin, so I wasn't able to do it. I took theatre lectures and appeared in a few plays in German. I spent a very enlightening, enlivening and interesting year in Berlin and I went to quite a number of rehearsals in the Berliner Ensemble at the time when Helena Weigel was playing *Mother Courage* and Brecht was directing *Galileo Galilei.* They also did a most unusual pre-Gary Hynes production of *The Playboy of the Western World* which was shocking to me at that time because I was a truly conventional type. It was something that affected me in the sense that doing the thing has always appealed to me as much as the theory of doing it. To be able to see the work in progress was very, very important and I think perhaps it gave me the notion of trying to work in that way afterwards.

I eventually found my way into the then bright new world of television. I just simply worked at whatever came along. I had been working in the theatre and so I did bits of drama there in television plays that were directed by people like Shelah Richards, Chloe Gibson and Jim Fitzgerald. I did some interviewing on programmes like *Broadsheet* and little bits of scriptwriting and then I trained as a producer-director in America of all places. I don't know if you could call it training, but I went there for three months and sat in on television studios: NBC and CBS, and CBC in Canada. I came back and started directing the news, which was the most scary thing. In those days you had to actually remember what came in what sequence and call it up and make sure it actually happened at the right time, but people like vision mixers and production assistants saved the bacon of many a producer-director many a time and I'm sure they saved mine too. Later, I directed *The Riordans* and I produced *Seven Days* and did some drama as well. Then I became head of light entertainment, looking after programmes like the *Late Late Show*.

I got involved in debates about the meaning of television and the kinds of things we could be doing. The influences at that time, apart from Gunnar Rugheimer, who was a very feisty, very argumentative, lively and humorous controller of programmes, were people like Jack Dowling, who was a titanic figure in the intellectual sphere within the station, and two directors who were working with me, Dick Hill and Eoghan Harris. Together with quite a few others, we began to question and raise issues to do with what were perhaps not the safe things, not the expected things. We felt in some instances that it would be possible to push things to the limit and then found that it wasn't quite possible to push them right to the very edge. Bob Quinn, who at that stage had been away for a year, came back and found that the station had turned into something of a factory for the production of Anglo-American products. He left and we began a debate, based upon his letter of farewell, which more or less escalated into a large series of talk-ins in the canteen. Jack Dowling and I resigned and subsequently wrote a book about what we thought our experiences had been, what we felt television could be in a small country like Ireland which had different cultural traditions, a language of its own, values of its own, and a way of life that in fact the television had been set up to protect and enrich and which we felt had been somewhat diluted and emaciated instead. We suggested that, if we looked at the model of television that we had and if we examined it more closely and interrogated more or less what we were doing, we could do it better. In any event, that didn't happen. The book was called *Sit Down and Be Counted.*

To be around the people who were in television at that time was to be around people who were your teachers. I was learning from everybody there. The unfortunate division of labour which dictated that the intellectual was a higher animal than the manual was something that I had never really been able to assent to. I felt television was a place where the intelligence of the engineer or of the camera-person was of equal quality to the intelligence of the director, but in our hierarchical system the director inevitably managed to get the kudos. I think a large number of producer-directors would be in skid row had it not been for a tremendous bunch of women production assistants and other technical grades who kept the boat afloat. Frankly, I would have perished many a time. The quality of a man like Jack Dowling was endlessly stimulating and indeed he wasn't the only one. Jim Plunkett Kelly, Muiris Mac Conghail, Donal Farmer, Michael Garvey, Deirdre Friel – all of these were people who were thinking on the job and presenting questions about politics: what was the government at, what were we supposed to be doing. What should be the stance of a semi-state organisation charged with the good of the commonality but set up under legislation and also unfortunately set up in order to make a profit? Nobody for a moment was saying that you could run programmes for nothing. Never. But the question was whether we should try and think of another means, another method, another model for television than the one we had. We felt that the local area was important as the focus and the locus from which the work should come, rather than that it should all come from one centre and then be diffused throughout the countryside. Why does television have to be show business? Could it not also be a two-way event in part?

After I left RTÉ, Mary Kenny invited me to write a weekly column for the *Irish Press* which, to my surprise, I started and continued to do for about six years. I think it taught me the terror of a blank page, which I don't think has ever left me. After that I went to the Abbey and worked there for two years as artistic director. That was a time of mixed emotions and mixed fortunes. I thought of studying anthropology, because I had always felt that we had had a very literary education in school. Girls from my era were offered science, but it wasn't really very much of an option and I certainly hadn't ever taken it up.

I was a person who really had a very sketchy view of the social system. I wanted to know more, so I went and lived in Belfast in '74 and I was there between then and '79. It was a most instructive and enlightening period, not least through listening to and knowing John Blacking, who was the professor of social anthropology at Queen's in Belfast, a young man, vigorous, lively, stimulating, endlessly provocative on a number of areas to do with the nature of society and the nature of nature, so to speak. I had a chance to reflect for a while on what made up the curious thing that humankind is, what kinship systems operate in other societies, what then could be thought about kinship systems in Belfast, for instance.

I was studying and researching ritual in an industrial setting, and that meant street rituals. Do people have to have an experience of religion in their lives in order to give life meaning, in order to give themselves a sense of identity? And if you are not an adherent of a formal religion, do you nevertheless partake in ceremonies and rites and rituals that have a transcendent meaning or give some kind of overarching meaning to your life? Certainly, if you look at the Orange parades, at the Republican marches to Milltown Cemetery, at the various ceremonies relating to adherents of military or paramilitary organisations, you could see that people were conferring meaning on their lives through these activities. As somebody coming out of RTÉ, a large organisation, then the Abbey Theatre, another large organisation, I found this interesting, especially as a Catholic from the south with very little understanding or knowledge of Protestantism, and the different elements of Protestantism, together with the complacency that you bring with you from living in the south in relative security.

I didn't have a lot of money and I didn't have a lot of security, but I did have the experience of John Blacking as an intellectual, provocative, middle-class middle-aged man, and of Desmond Wilson as a very stimulating, demanding radical thinker. Father Wilson was trying to provide a house and an education centre for people who were otherwise very severely deprived in terms of both physical and intellectual activities or experience. He provided theatre, photography lessons and video. I began to teach myself how to work with video and I joined the people's theatre. Instead of doing plays that others had written, local people wrote their own material and we did a good deal of political and rather funny cabaret, pretty close to the bone on political matters up there.

You become what you are. Your family makes you. The town makes you. The countryside makes you and your friends make you. School has a little bit to do with it, but not much, I think. Books make you, too. The books that remain with me are the novels of Dostoevsky and the works of Sophocles. These are works that came out of a country society that is quite small and at the same time has huge ambitions and huge questions to ask. All of these things have come to me from my past in Clare and hopefully they will remain.

Gerry Fitt

Gerry Fitt was born in Belfast in 1926 and grew up during the 'hungry '30s' amid severe unemployment and poverty. When he was nine, his father died of TB. This placed an extreme burden on his mother and, to help alleviate the situation, Gerry went to work on leaving school. He later went to sea and spent the war years working on ships.

In the 1950s, he was drawn into politics and was initially elected as a city councillor, before finally making the breakthrough as an MP in 1965. At all levels of politics, he has been a non-sectarian representative. In 1968, he was prominently involved in the emerging civil rights movement and, when people like John Hume, Ivan Cooper and Paddy Devlin were subsequently elected to parliament, Gerry Fitt joined with them, reluctantly, to form the Social Democratic and Labour Party.

In the ill-fated Sunningdale Executive, Gerry Fitt was appointed deputy chief executive. He was always an outspoken critic of the IRA and was often attacked for his stance. In 1979, he left the SDLP and, in 1983, he narrowly lost his West Belfast seat. Shortly afterwards, his house was burned out and he moved to London. He was created Lord Fitt in 1983, but, as far as Northern Ireland is concerned, he will 'always be there'.

I was born on 9 April 1926 and Paisley was born on 6 April, so the two of us were born in the one week. My mother used to say that the devil was busy that week! One of my very earliest political memories was, when I was about seven, coming home from chapel and a fellow giving me a leaflet. I couldn't read it very well at that age, but I kept it for years and years. It was a quotation from James Connolly and it has played a great part in my political thinking. 'Ireland apart from her people means nothing to me. The man who is full of love and enthusiasm for Ireland and can yet walk through her streets unmoved and witness all the wrong and suffering, shame and degradation that is wrought upon the people of Ireland by Irish men and Irish women without burning in his heart to end this wrong is, in my opinion a sham, a liar and a cheat, no matter how much he may profess to love that combination of chemical elements which he is pleased to call Ireland.' It was the people of Ireland that Connolly was concerned with and it is the people of Ireland that I have been concerned with.

My father, who was very ill at the time, had been involved in the labour movement in Ireland. He worked in Gallagher's tobacco factory, but he died in 1935 when I was very young. I lived in a Catholic ghetto beside the New Lodge Road, where we felt very hemmed in. We never thought about it, but we began to develop a big boulder on our shoulders: we were second-class citizens. There was massive unemployment in the area; lots of people were living on what they then called 'outdoor relief'. When my father died, there were six of us left, three boys and three girls. My mother had to go out every day to work as a domestic. I think she was paid two shillings a day. I used to meet her coming home. I remember vividly how tired she used to be.

I was thirteen when the war began. When I turned fourteen, I got a job in a barber shop and earned five shillings a week. In 1941, I went away to sea, down in the bowels of the ship shovelling coal. My brother-in-law and my brother were the other two firemen, so they did the heavy bits.

When we were living in a place called Dock, we didn't like the Protestants because we knew they didn't like us. And we didn't like the English because we felt that they backed the Protestants and didn't back us. So we were against the Protestants and against the English. When I went away to sea during the war, I met my first Englishman, my first Scotsman and Welshman, and my first Norwegian and Greek. I met lots of people. And I began to think, well these people are not the baddies that I had envisaged. Every nationality has good and bad, but, being at sea with them and being under attack by German aeroplanes and submarines, we were all in it together. All the ghetto bitterness I had about being a Catholic, about being a second-class citizen, evaporated.

I read whenever I could at sea. On a ship, there was a class system – the cowboy books were all down with the crew and the biographies were all up with the officers. I used to argue with the officers that I wanted to read biography, so I got to read everything they had up there. There was nothing else to do at sea.

I met my wife at Hyde Park Corner, in 1947, a wee girl from Castlederg. We were married in November of the same year. I didn't want to go to sea after I met Ann, so I came home. In 1949, a very nasty election took place in Northern Ireland. The whole partition issue came very much to the fore. The anti-partition league decided that they would fight every seat in Northern Ireland. They had collections outside churches after Mass all over the Republic, so the Unionists sneeringly referred to it as the 'Chapel Gate Election'.

I came home just before the end of the election and I got involved in a minor way. A by-election was called for October 1951 and Jack Beatty was a Labour candidate. That was when the political bug bit me, and it's been with me ever since. I went out campaigning for Jack Beatty. I starved myself, I didn't want anything at all, I just wanted to see him elected. We fought the election tooth and nail and, after five recounts, Jack Beatty won by twenty-five votes. It was a very emotional time for me and as soon as he was declared elected I started to cry. Little did I know that the next time that seat would be won would be fifteen years later, and it would be won by me.

It was quite an induction into politics and I've never been out of it since. In May 1958, the council elections were coming up again. We didn't seem to have much of a chance because the Unionists had a majority on the register. I borrowed fifty quid and I managed to split the vote. I won by twenty-seven votes and that was me a councillor!

My formal education was with the Christian Brothers until I was fourteen. I could have gone on to secondary school, but I didn't want to. I wanted to leave and get a job and help my mother, because my father was dead, and then I wanted to go away to sea. I wasn't particularly concerned about getting a university degree. Any degrees I have are from the University of Life.

After I came home from sea, I used to go to classes at the Workers' Education Association, run by the trade union movement. I went there and learned a wee bit about economics. And then there was the International Correspondence School. They sent a book and the work was all done by correspondence – you did the work and then you sent it back to them for marking. It cost seven quid at the time. I think I did three different papers and I passed them all, but by this time I was rearing a family and I couldn't afford to give up another seven quid. Also, I belonged to the library in Belfast and I read whatever I could get my hands on. I became very interested in economics, but I never had any great urge to go to university. I was too busy doing other things.

Those three years, between 1958 and 1961, were the most important years in my political life. I didn't get paid for being a councillor. I had no money and I was rearing a small family. But I was absolutely obsessed with being in politics and being able to help people. I read all the National Insurance Acts and

I used to go down to the local tribunals representing people. I became known as the Perry Mason of the local tribunals!

When I was elected, I deliberately set out to prove that I wasn't a Catholic representative but that I was a non-sectarian representative. I remember Protestants coming to my door in 1958 and they would say 'Councillor Fitt, I'm a Protestant,' and I would say, 'Look, I don't care whether you're a Protestant or not.' Those people were living in exactly the same conditions as the Catholics and they were having the same problems. There was massive unemployment at the time and a whole lot of them were on the dole or on sickness benefit. I began to represent them and news of this travelled like wildfire all over the place. The more I helped them, the more they sent their relations to see me. It took a lot out of me. I had to neglect my own home and family, going to local tribunals and then going to meetings of the city council. I made a lot of friends in those three years.

In 1961, I defended the seat and I won it with a big, big majority. And then in 1962 the parliamentary seat came up for re-election. I went out and fought the seat and won. That gave me some sort of economic wherewithal to stay in politics. I had seven hundred quid a year and I thought I was a millionaire, but at least I was able to look after my wife and kids. In 1965, Terence O'Neill had taken over from Lord Brookeborough as Prime Minister and he called an election for November. I was very, very apprehensive about this election, because the history of Dock up until then had been that no political party had held the seat at successive elections. Here I was, the second time around, fighting against history, but I fought like hell and I won with an even bigger majority. So I beat the record in 1965.

In 1968, the civil rights movement began and I played a reasonably prominent part in that. I was interested in bringing in legislation which would help the underdog living in the Catholic ghettos in Northern Ireland. I went to Derry in October for the famous civil rights march. I had taken the precaution of bringing Labour MPs over, because I knew what was going to happen. I knew they were going to beat the hell out of us, and so I got some photographers over as well. I was grabbed by the police and they beat me over the head with a baton. The blood ran down my face and the cameras were there to see. It caused a great big furore. When I returned to Westminster, I made speech after speech, saying 'I got this for asking for the same rights for my constituents as you have for yours.'

The civil rights movement was totally justified, but it scared the life out of the Protestants, because they saw it as an attack on their privileges, which it actually wasn't. And that began the trouble. The Unionist underdog began to rebel against what he saw as concessions being given. There was awful fear in West Belfast. The Catholics thought that they were going to get slaughtered in their beds. I telephoned Jim Callaghan who was the then Home Secretary and pleaded with him to send the army in, because there was a real fear that a pogrom could have broken out in Northern Ireland. I remember what Jim Callaghan said to me. 'Gerry,' he said, 'I can get the army in, but it's going to be a devil of a job getting it out.' And how right he was proved to be.

I had a very nasty election in West Belfast, because the IRA were coming to the fore and they were beginning to attack me as being pro-Brit and so on. I won that election again in 1970. Then, in 1971, the IRA started shooting. When this happened it changed my whole political life, because I could never understand how the IRA could be guilty of some of the terrible atrocities that they committed. Internment came in in August 1971 and that just tore the whole community asunder; the Catholic population were totally opposed to it.

In 1969, John Hume, Ivan Cooper, Paddy O'Hanlon and Paddy Devlin had been elected because of the civil rights agitation that was then taking place. There was great pressure on them to form a new political party. I had reservations about it, because I was from Belfast. I knew Belfast, I knew Protestants, but the others who were elected didn't have that same sort of political experience. They were Catholic representatives, as such. I formed with the rest of them the SDLP, the Social Democratic and Labour Party.

Bloody Sunday, in 1972, was a big watershed in politics in Northern Ireland. Because of that and our agitation, Stormont was abolished and then we came under direct rule. In 1973, we went to Sunningdale and we had the Sunningdale Conference.

I thought then and I think now, and I will continue to think, that Sunningdale was by far the most hopeful development that we ever had politically in Northern Ireland since its creation. There were two tangents to it. One was the setting up of a Northern Ireland executive, composed of both Catholics and Protestants. I thought that was a tremendous advance. In that executive, I was the deputy Prime Minister, the deputy chief executive. John Hume was the Minister for Commerce, Austin Currie was the Minister for Development, Paddy Devlin was the Minister for Health and Social Services, Ivan Cooper was the Minister for Community Relations. They were four of the most important offices in any government. The second part of the Sunningdale Agreement was the part which actually killed Sunningdale. A provision was made for a Council of Ireland which would involve the ministers in the Republic sitting with us. And that scared the living daylights out of the Unionists. When the executive fell in May of 1974, it caused great bitterness. People then realised that we should have done more to hold on to it.

Paddy Devlin was a socialist like myself, with a trade union background, and the Belfast wing of the SDLP were the Labour men. We were the socialists; the ones outside were the Catholics and the Nationalists. So there was always this conflict within the party. And then Paddy Devlin left in 1977, which left me isolated with a few others from Belfast, and I was becoming increasingly despairing of anything ever happening.

The IRA were trying to kill me and they broke into my house in 1976. I will never forget the job I had getting them out. I had a licensed weapon at the time and, had I not had that, they would have beaten the hell out of me with iron bars. I felt particularly incensed, because I was a Catholic and these people were doing things allegedly in my name and in the name of Ireland. Whenever I appeared on television, I would make my position clear – that I detested them and everything that they stood for. I charged them with dragging the name of Ireland through the gutter and said they were not speaking on behalf of the Irish people.

But there were some of my colleagues in the SDLP who, when the IRA committed some terrible atrocity, would keep their heads down. It got to such a stage in 1979 that I left the party, because I felt I was on my own. In 1981, the hunger strike took place and that was a really big disaster for Northern Ireland. It tore the heart and soul out of the Catholic community and the Unionist community. The Unionists saw those hunger strikers as people who had murdered their friends, the Catholics saw them as patriots or just some misguided young Irishmen, and it just tore them all apart.

I had an awful time during that period around my home on the Antrim Road. They used to gather around my home every night and throw stones and petrol bombs. They would stand outside the door and shout 'Gerry Fitt is a Brit'. It was the worst word they could have thrown. I was no more a Brit then than I had ever been. I didn't go into politics as a Catholic or a Protestant or a Republican or Unionist. I went in as a working-class candidate to try to help people, but the whole thing was going awry.

In 1983, I had to defend my West Belfast seat. The SDLP was under the leadership of John Hume. Gerry Adams, the Sinn Fein candidate, came into the field and the SDLP deliberately put up a candidate. Again it was a nasty election. I couldn't send out my election addresses, because the IRA wouldn't let the postman deliver them. Gerry Adams got 16,000 votes, Joe Hendron, who was the SDLP candidate, got 10,900 votes and

I got 10,400. The SDLP got that result with a pretty good election machine. I had no election machine at all. I only fought that election to prove to myself that I had done no wrong. Nobody ever said that I was a bad MP or a bad candidate or that I didn't represent them. Even in defeat, half of my votes had still come from across the political and religious divide.

All through this campaign, my wife had asthma and she suffered very very badly. How, in the name of God, she stood by me through all the terrible times with this asthma I do not know. We went over to England, where I had just got a wee flat. Three weeks after the election, the police telephoned me to tell me my house was on fire. I flew back to Belfast but I wouldn't let my wife come with me, because she was very houseproud and I didn't want her to see the house in ruins. I went in and I saw how the house had been gutted and the windows broken and all the furniture had been taken out and burned in a bonfire. Just before I left the house, I looked down and saw on the ground what looked like confetti. I picked it up and I can feel that sickening feeling now. I don't think it will ever go away. It was my wedding photographs.

Although I am no longer physically living in Northern Ireland, I am never very far away from it. The *Irish News*, a local newspaper in Belfast, published a list of all the people who were killed, year by year, in all the years of violence. I have it up on my wall and, every morning, when I walk into my office, I look at it. Out of those 3,000 people who have been killed, I went to 167 of the funerals, both Protestant and Catholic. Some people might think that I am long enough away from it now not to be so closely identified with it or to feel so strongly about it. If I live to be a hundred, I will still be concerned about all that is happening in Northern Ireland.

Dr Garret FitzGerald

Garret FitzGerald was born in Dublin in 1926, the son of Desmond FitzGerald, who was Minister for External Affairs and Minister for Defence in the Free State government. He was educated in Bray, Ring and Belvedere College, Dublin, before going on to University College, Dublin. He was called to the Bar in 1947 but joined Aer Lingus to pursue a career in air transport, thus developing an interest in airline timetables which he had acquired as a youth. At the age of twenty-five, he was in charge of the economic planning of the airline and 'discovered' economics in the process. He returned to university as a lecturer in economics in 1959.

Garret's parents had imprinted the notion of public service on him from an early age and, on entering the Senate in 1965, he began a long and distinguished career in Irish politics. He entered Dáil Éireann in 1969, became Minister for Foreign Affairs in 1973, leader of Fine Gael in 1977 and Taoiseach twice (1981–2 and 1982–7).

A man of great energy and intellectual capacity (although, on his own admission, 'not an imaginative person'), Garret FitzGerald, in retirement from politics, remains active, writing and contributing regularly to the media. He relishes debate, having come from 'a very argumentative family'. His autobiography, All in a Life, was published in 1991.

M y parents were both people of strong character and
they influenced me greatly. School perhaps played a
lesser role in my education, proportionately, than is
normally the case.

My mother came from a northern unionist Presbyterian
family, but she was republican in her views. After graduating
from Queens University, Belfast, she went to London and did
a post-graduate course at London University and did some
teaching there, but she also acted for periods as secretary to
George Bernard Shaw and George Moore. She and my father
met in the Gaelic League in London, my father being the son
of Irish immigrants who had come there in the 1860s from
Cork and Kerry. My father's interests in Ireland were
particularly literary; his great hero was Yeats. My mother was
the political one in the family and it was obvious from their
early correspondence that she was the one who wanted to go to
the Gaelic League meetings, while he was saying 'Can we not
go to the theatre instead?' In the Civil War, she favoured the
republican side – as many women did – though not actively.
When my father was a Minister in the first government, she
remained for years strongly republican. However, in the late
'20s she came round to my father's political position. She was a
very strong character and influence, and she was a very good
teacher. That was a practical help to me, even as late as my
entrance scholarship to UCD. I would never have got that
scholarship but for her tuition, particularly in English, but in
other subjects also.

We were an affectionate family, beyond what is perhaps
considered normal. I can remember on one occasion my parents
coming to school in Belvedere and I rushed over to embrace
them. They were slightly embarrassed lest, in showing so much
affection for them, I create problems for myself with my school
companions. However, it was instinctive – we were an unusually
demonstrative family.

My mother remained a Presbyterian until very late in her

married life, but she took her obligations to bring us up as Catholics very seriously and we were taught our religion by her rather than by my father. He had a more intellectual approach and wouldn't have felt as capable of tackling the practical problems of teaching as she did. Much later in life, when she became a Catholic, she had difficulty with the emotional elements of Catholicism as it was then often expressed. In the last conversation I had with her before she had a stroke, I had to reassure her that she could be Catholic without having to use the kind of extravagant language which some of the prayer books used in those days.

I was in some ways an only child, in the sense that my next brother, Fergus, was six years older, so that some of the time I was a lot on my own. At the same time, when Fergus was around he was a very imaginative child who stimulated me considerably. He was full of ideas which he shared with me when he wasn't away at school. He was enthused by the ancient civilisations of Egypt, Peru and Mexico. He copied out the grammar and syntax of the Inca language and we taught each other to speak it to some small degree. He was interested in astronomy. I became a founder member of the Dublin Astronomical Society at the age of twelve, under his influence. We played all kinds of games that stimulated my imagination, which I badly needed because I am not an imaginative person. I don't think he succeeded in making me one, but he certainly did things for me which I wouldn't have done for myself.

I went to a private school in Bray, St Brigid's, run by a Miss Brayden. She was an excellent teacher. I had four years there, which gave me a real head start in life. After the first year or so, after First Communion, I was the only boy in the class and I came to several early conclusions about girls. Individually, you can get on well with them, but, *en masse*, they can be rather intimidating. This brought me to the conclusion that I should concentrate on just one and, at the age of eight, I decided that I should get married young and, indeed, had some idea as to

whom I would marry! It didn't work out like that; these things
never do. I also remember an occasion, in 1934, when it
transpired that some of the girls knew about the murder of the
King of Yugoslavia and the French Foreign Minister. The fact
that I didn't know must have been evident and I felt humiliated
by my lack of political information, *vis-à-vis* the girls. This
encouraged me to read the newspaper every day from then on,
so as not to meet that fate again. My interest in international
affairs was stimulated indirectly by that experience.

My mother was concerned that we read widely. She probably
detected in me an imagination which required stimulation, so
she pushed me hard to read literature. When I was about
fifteen, she pushed me through the whole of Thomas Hardy. I
needed imaginative literature. I needed education through
fiction and it has always struck me in life that if you don't read
fiction you may lack a whole dimension. You may not have the
capacity to empathise with and understand other people. I
know people who don't read any fiction and who seem unable
to cope with many aspects of life. Without my mother's
influence, I probably wouldn't have coped either. My father had
read the *Boy's Own Paper* when he was growing up in London.
It certainly didn't convert him to British imperialism, but he
enjoyed the stories. I still have the whole lot of them. There
were stories by Jules Verne and Talbot Reid and articles on
subjects like – 'How to win at noughts and crosses' and 'Can
man fly?' They were fascinating reading, so I had a good
grounding in late Victorian literature, as well as in our own
national literature.

All my brothers had gone to Ring College for at least a year,
so I went in 1935 for a year, which I enjoyed greatly. As a result,
I never had to work at Irish in school though my vocabulary
didn't extend to the political and economical spheres. I went
back there for three Easters afterwards in order to maintain the
Irish I had acquired at that period. I enjoyed those Easter stays
there, especially sharing the dormitories with the other boys. I

wouldn't have learned Irish well other than in a boarding-school situation, but if I had gone to boarding school for the rest of my schooling I would have lost out a lot, because the fact that I was at home with my parents meant that I learned an enormous amount from them, which I have valued greatly since. My father died when I was twenty-one. If I had been at boarding school, I really wouldn't have known him very well, I suppose, so the day school at Belvedere suited me much better.

It was a very liberal education, in the sense that you were not forced to do things; for instance, there were no compulsory games. It was a healthy, open atmosphere and relations were good. Physical punishment was a feature of the system at that time which one had to put up with, but I enjoyed Belvedere.

I went there when I was ten and Father Rupert Coyle interviewed me and decided to put me into first year, which was two years ahead of my age. He judged it right, because it meant that I was under pressure all the time. I was in a class where I could never imagine being first or even second, so that I had to work to keep up, and that was good. It had some disadvantages, however. I am very poor at mathematics, as opposed to arithmetic – two opposite disciplines, I think. Arithmetic is concrete and mathematics is abstract. Being younger than the rest of the class and bad at mathematics anyway, I was always the last to understand anything. If the master saw a glimmer of understanding in my eyes, he would move on to the next proposition, which meant I never really grasped anything properly and I have suffered from that ever since.

Politics featured quite largely in the school. The war was on and most of the lay teachers were anti-British and, therefore, to some degree, pro-German, which I found difficult, not to say offensive. The priests, with one exception, were all pro-Allied, so it was an interesting division. I had very strong views on the subject. These were matters for argument the whole way through school – domestic politics, going back to the Civil War and the time of the Treaty, and the War itself. I can remember in the school yard in 1939 trying to persuade some of my school fellows against the Nazis – using Pope Pius XI's encyclical condemning the treatment by the Nazis of the Christians and Jews – and having difficulty in persuading them that the Germans could possibly be bad when they were fighting against the British.

The seeds of a political career were sown early on and, in fifth year, Father Ronnie Burke-Savage, who ran the debating society, encouraged me not only to think of taking up politics later on in life but even to think of being Taoiseach. I noted that as a possibility at the time, but not one that I would be very upset about if I didn't achieve it.

Transport was another interest of mine which developed around that time, because the 1930s were the period of Zeppelins and autogyros and pioneering flights, and to a small boy that was exciting. I remember missing my lunch one day in Ring to watch the air circus over Dungarvan and then, in 1937, I remember having an argument in the post office in Crewe with the postmaster on the relative merits of British and American flying boats. In 1938, *en route* to France for my first exchange with a French family – a very important influence on me thereafter – when my mother was buying my ticket in the tourist office, I picked up all the airline timetables and I still have them. They kept me going during the war, mulling over them, so that air transport became the initial focus of my interest, with politics as a later one. In any event, my father disapproved of any of us going into politics on the strength of his name or in his lifetime. It was twenty-two years after leaving school before I entered politics – a long enough gap to fulfil his wishes.

My father was a Francophile. I think he spent time in France before he was married and my parents lived in Brittany for almost two years after their marriage in London. He spoke French well and was passionately interested in French literature. He was a friend of French philosophers like Maritain and

Gilson – he went to see them occasionally in Paris in the '30s. We were all sent on exchanges at one time or another. I went to France on exchange in 1938 and I went back in 1939 for another seven weeks in the summer. I was young enough not to be too self-conscious and therefore willing to tackle the proper pronunciation of French. I learned to speak it very quickly and the family I stayed with then are still close friends.

When I started in first year in UCD, I took ten subjects. I dropped economics immediately, because it seemed to me so dull. I intended to do English and French to degree level. My mother had taught me so well that, on entrance into college, I got first place in English and that deluded me into thinking that I could perhaps do well in English. I took it in First Arts, but I only got a Second, and I then realised that your mother may get you a First in the entrance scholarship and a Second in First Arts but she can't get you a good degree at BA level. So I switched and took history instead, with French and Spanish.

It was a wonderful period in my life. The college was smaller then. The war years were a very sheltered period for us. The appalling tragedy happening outside was something we were terribly aware of, and following the events of the war, absorbed an enormous amount of my time, but nonetheless we were sheltered from it. It was a very relaxed existence. There was no question of working in the summer holidays; there was no work to be done anyway. We learned to do nothing for three months on end, which I think is a marvellous thing to have experienced for some period of your life. I have never regretted my total idleness for those summers.

College was a marvellous place and I met Joan there quite early on. I proposed to her about the time the War ended and we got married two years later. All the happiness of the rest of my life goes back to that period, meeting and falling in love at that time. Ours has been a very interactive marriage in which everything we have done we have done together. I have been constantly under challenge from her in the positions I have taken up, everything has had to be argued out, or if I take a wrong turning in some way I am told so very quickly! So education goes on through life, especially in marriage.

My father wanted me to be a barrister – I think he had a feeling that it would be a respectable career. It would have been years before I could have got married if I had gone to the Bar, but also I was interested in air transport. However, he couldn't accept that. When I took the job in Aer Lingus he was very upset and didn't speak to me for several months. Then he saw that I was genuinely interested, and he relaxed, and our relationship was restored – happily, because he died only a month later.

In Aer Lingus, my interest lay in the economic operation of the airline – in routes, services, timetables, choice of aircraft, how to make the thing pay, how to make it efficient – and by the time I was twenty-six I was in charge of the economic planning of the airline, which was a great opportunity for me. In order to take the decisions as to when to operate a flight or when not to, when it would pay or when it wouldn't, on what basis to open a new route, whether an aircraft would be economical or not, what was the optimum fare that would yield the maximum return. You had to have some criteria. I had to work out for myself the theoretical basis for answering these questions. I developed both a marginal costing structure and price economics theory in order to provide myself with the basis for making such decisions, and I didn't even know that this was economics.

Thus I came to economics in a curious way, having to invent it for myself in order to do my job and also by writing articles. I was journalistically inclined, as was my father. I eventually wrote for the *Irish Times* and they pushed me into writing about national economic matters, so I became an economist by popular acclaim, like saints in the old days before canonisation was introduced! I went back to UCD as a full-time lecturer in 1959, which was just thirteen years after I had left the college.

I had been a part-time lecturer there for the previous three years.

On leaving Aer Lingus, I had gone into academic life and had become a consultant. I had in mind that the work I would be doing – particularly in relation to Irish industry preparing for free trade – would be a very good learning process to prepare myself for politics. Politics wasn't a firm decision, but it was certainly a possible path and then, in 1964, I finally took the decision to go into politics.

Politics has been a great educator for me, both in terms of domestic politics and experience in international affairs, and, indeed, in dealing with Northern Ireland, to which I suppose I brought a great deal of my background. The basic issues of principle that I learned early on have remained with me and the concept of service – and of politics as one of the highest vocations of service – is something I learned very early on indeed in my life. On domestic affairs, my views have changed over time; I was very conservative when I was young, as my father had been in his views, but later in life I moved to being more of a social democrat and liberal.

A large part of my change of view was due to the influence of my own children – who are great educators of their parents, reinforced by the fact that I was teaching in UCD, where the students also challenged whatever implicit views I had during the many debates we had over coffee and in other places apart from the classroom. I found that my instinctive and inherited conservatism on many issues did not stand up to the challenge posed by the younger generation in the 1960s. I was forced to re-evaluate my position throughout that period, eventually establishing a different social and political stance to what I had had at the beginning. That is education in reverse – while you educate people, they are educating you.

For the last ten years, I have become interested in an aspect of knowledge that I have no capacity to cope with – the origins of the universe and the way the universe has developed, and also quantum physics. I have read a lot on these subjects but I can only grasp little bits here and there. These are two very important areas and it is a great pity that the educational system does not deal with them.

I think it is a mistake to divide education into the humanities and the sciences. I think these basic scientific issues are part of the humanities and children should not grow up without being exposed to the issues that are raised by the development of the universe from a certain point in time, say fifteen billion years ago, and about the nature of reality, which, when we look at it at the level of particles is quite different from what we conceive it to be. I worry now that education is too narrow as it deprives people of any knowledge of these issues. I particularly regret that I didn't apply myself more to mathematics at school. I don't think I could ever have really grasped it, but I would have liked to have been able to understand more than I can now of these crucial matters.

My parents were largely the shapers of my life. They were remarkable people, very different, but deeply attached to each other. It was a very close marriage and both had very high standards. In fact, Joan once remarked that I am really half Presbyterian and half Jansenist! For me the idea of public service was instinctive, coming from that background. It seemed to me from early on that one's task in life was to find ways of serving the community through whatever talents one had. My parents had sacrificed themselves so much in the period of the National Movement. My father had been in gaol four times, which he had accepted quite readily, so that whole background of work in the National Movement was obviously a profound influence.

Fionnula Flanagan

Born in Dublin in 1941, Fionnula Flanagan joined the Abbey Theatre School in 1964 and survived expulsion from there to become one of Ireland's most distinguished actresses on stage, screen and television. Having starred in the New York production of Brian Friel's Lovers, *she remained in the United States and developed a highly successful career there, particularly with the works of James Joyce. She played Molly Bloom in* Ulysses in Nighttown *on Broadway and in Joseph Strick's film of* Ulysses.

Fionnula developed her own very successful one-woman show, James Joyce's Women, *on stage and screen. Her work on film and television has extended well beyond Joyce and she has recently won acclaim for her role in the film,* Some Mother's Son.

I went to school first of all in Scoil Mhuire in Marlborough Street, Dublin. My primary schooling was all *as Gaeilge*. I spent a year living with my grandmother and I went to a little school in Loughlinstown, out on the Bray Road. I then went to Sandymount High School for about three years, venturing out to the other side of the Liffey, the south side. I was a scholarship girl and I picked Sandymount High School because it was 'co-ed', and that seemed to me to be extremely desirable. This was, of course, very adventurous, because, to my knowledge, it was the first Catholic co-ed school in Dublin, possibly in the whole of Ireland. The people who ran it were quite visionary. After that I completed my secondary schooling at Scoil Chaitríona, which is the Gaelic-speaking part of the Dominican College, then in Eccles Street, Dublin.

I am immensely grateful today that I had a bilingual education. I think that having a second language at a very early age, and specifically having my own mother language, was terrifically important. If you have an early introduction to Irish, you are actually being given access to a whole world of literature and culture in its native tongue that you would never otherwise get successfully. Later on, when I wanted access to the literature of French, Italian and Spanish, it was easier for me to learn a third and a fourth language, having learned two as a child. When I was going to school, Irish was compulsory and, although stories are legion about teachers who were cruel and used the compulsory aspect of learning Irish to tyrannise children, by and large I think that probably the only way to learn a language is if it is compulsory from an early age.

I was very lucky. I had a great facility for language and I am enormously grateful for that because it introduced me into the nuances of *Gaeilge* and it gave me insights into the Irish character. Since I chose the path of being a creative artist, being Irish has been very important for me because it is the wellspring of where I come from. My source will always be Ireland and all things Irish, be they good, bad or indifferent, and I would hope

I can draw from modern Ireland every bit as much I can from the Ireland of my youth.

I am grateful, too, for the amount of reading I got to do. If I were born today, I would be a child of the television age and of the technological age. I would probably be more inclined to reach for a CD or a disk than I would for a book. I was brought up on radio and on books. Radio was a wonderful, wonderful gift. It forced you to listen, it forced you to imagine the pictures and it gave one a breadth of access. I regard all of that as part of my education.

I was dreadful at sewing. At school they tried to teach me how to sew and I cried bitter tears. They tried to teach me how to make buttonholes. I ask you, have you ever met anybody who made a buttonhole? It seemed to me to be a totally absurd pursuit, to force young girls to make buttonholes when they were never going to go out into the world and make them. It was medieval. It reminded me of ladies sitting in turrets darning or doing embroidery, or making these wretched buttonholes.

Mr and Mrs Cannon ran Sandymount High School. Mrs Cannon introduced me to Italian, which is such a beautiful language and I'll always be grateful for that, though I'm sure I gave her a very hard time. Mr Cannon put me into the Greek class and I was grateful for that, too. In Scoil Chaitríona I liked the nuns very much. An tSiúir Aquinas was one of the world's greatest teachers, a fine, fine teacher who could inspire people and a woman of immense intellect.

Then there was Sister Columbus, who was my French teacher. She was instrumental in getting me to go to Switzerland, where she helped to get me a job in a hostel for American students in Freiburg. When I was a child growing up here, if you met someone who had been to the landmass of Europe, they had probably been on a pilgrimage to Rome or Lourdes. At that time, the package holidays of the Costa del Sol had not yet begun for Irish people. Suddenly I had this opportunity to spend time in a place where they spoke French and this opened up Europe for me. I worked in Italy as an interpreter for a couple of years, which gave me access to the sheer beauty of those places and the people I met there.

Politically, my parents influenced me very much. They were socialists in the '30s and '40s and my father's politics in particular were very left-wing. That gave me a view of the world that was very different from the kind of repressive Ireland of the '50s that I was growing up in. Many of my school friends who came from quite conservative families were somewhat shocked by my father's political views. My parents moved among a bohemian or intellectual set in Dublin and, among the political people that my father associated with, it was indeed fashionable to be socialist or communist. Nowadays it is a dirty word, but I was influenced very much by the way they looked at things. They weren't into making money for the sake of making money and they never held that out as a goal for any of us. Nor did I suffer when I wanted to go into the theatre, as many of my friends did. For many of them it was frowned upon, the next best thing to being a fallen woman or some kind of showgirl who worked in the theatre instead of Las Vegas, but my parents didn't take that view. They really thought that artists had something to say and were important contributors to the mainstream of life and of value to the society in which they lived.

I lived for a year with my grandmother when I was quite young. She lived in Shanganagh in south Dublin. At that time the cliffs around the beach were not built up as they are today. I used to wander around those cliffs and woods and daydream a lot and pick cowslips and primroses in the late spring. I have great memories of the whole pastoral landscape, which was so lovely. My grandmother, who was a very devout woman, thought I was rather a wild child, but she used to do something that gave me enormous pleasure. She used to build May altars – she had a great devotion to the Virgin Mary – and, following in her footsteps, I would just put May altars all over the place. I could never understand why it wasn't done after May had passed. It was an unhappy time, because I was a very young child and I didn't understand why I was being sent away from my parents. They loved me and came to see me and their reasons were complex and largely had to do with having a large family and needing some assistance to cope with so many children in a small house. I did have the feeling of having been sent away, and I thought it must have been something I had done or something that was lacking in me. It was to be many years before I was able to look at that at all, or even to say it. It wasn't that I didn't have loving aunts and a grandmother and loving parents; it was just a very difficult thing to deal with as a small child.

There were always books at home. I was a member of the library from a very young age, because my parents, my brothers and sisters and my aunts were members; that was just the way we were brought up. We went to the library and used the library. I think if you learn that when you are young, it is a terrific facility to be able to make use of. One of my favourite things when I go to Galway is to sit on the floor in Kenny's Bookshop and just read the books. It is such a pleasure to do that and to talk with people who know about books.

The radio was wonderful in those days. I remember hearing *The War of the Worlds* and being terrified by it and refusing to put my legs under the table at teatime. We used to listen to all of the radio dramas. I listened to virtually everything the Radio Éireann Players broadcast. I also used to listen to the Irish Hospital Sweepstakes programme, which was on very late at night. I had to ask to be allowed to stay up and I remember I fell in love with Bart Bastable's [the presenter] voice. Later, my mother pointed him out to me in the city one day and I was horrified, because to me he seemed horrendously old. Of course I had pictured this young prince with the lovely voice.

One of the things I did as a child was to write little plays or shows and have my sisters and brothers act in them, just to amuse ourselves and my mother, who was a captive audience, and anybody else who happened to be there. I bossed everybody hideously and they would say, 'I don't want to play anymore, I don't want to be in this game.' I would scream and throw a tantrum and stamp my foot and say, 'It isn't a game, it isn't a game! It's my show!' Nothing much has changed. I'm sure I am still behaving that way!

I went straight to Europe from secondary school. At the time I could not afford to go to college here – university was far beyond my family's means – so I took a job as a maid in a hostel in Switzerland and went to classes there to study French and later Italian. I did my French certificate as a translator and interpreter at the university of Freiburg.

When I came back I worked at various things. I worked for a wine merchant, I worked for a travel agent and then I got a job teaching in the technical school in Naas. At the same time, I auditioned and got into the Abbey school, which had reopened under Frank Dermody. Among the people who were accepted as students with me were Donal McCann, Des Cave and Clive Geraghty. It was a vintage year. Eighteen months later, Frank Dermody threw me out of the Abbey school and I was desperately disappointed. I felt awfully rejected. He was a man who was extremely volatile and his mood swings were notorious. He had had a fight with another student and had expelled him and I thought that was very unfair. I went and said so and challenged him on it, so he threw me out too.

I licked my wounds as best I could for a few months and then, magically, I met Tomás Mac Anna, who had seen me in a play years before in an amateur theatre festival. He was doing a play at the Damer Hall for the Dublin Theatre Festival, a play called *An Triail* by Máire Nic Gráda and he offered me a role in it. I then took over the leading role and that launched my career. I did it in Irish on stage and then I went on to do it in English when Phyllis Ryan directed it. Then I did it in Irish for RTÉ and they gave me a Jacob's Award at the end of the year. It really did launch my career.

Tomás Mac Anna had a great influence on my life. The man is a consummate artist and a visionary. He was also a man of generosity, which counted very much with me and does still. I'll always be grateful to him for reaching out and picking me out of my despair, putting me in that play in which I just thrived and blossomed. Of course, Frank Dermody was an influence, too. Heaven knows, if you could survive Frank Dermody's onslaughts of insults you could survive pretty much anything if you wanted to be in the entertainment industry.

It is very hard to say when James Joyce entered my life. In my childhood my parents would say things like, 'Well, Joyce knew that' and 'Joyce said' and I always assumed they knew him. It was no longer surprising to me when I, too, read his books. Also, coming from the north side of Dublin, many of the shops and small businesses, the streets and the pubs that are named in his books were still there when I was a child. Vestiges of the Edwardian Dublin that Joyce knew were still in existence. My grandmother, who had lived in Portland Row and later in Marino, would hold musical evenings in her house on Sundays and these pale young Irish tenors would bring their sheet music and sing their party pieces, a lot of which were the kind of songs that I was later to encounter in Joyce's work. So the world of Joyce was all around me. When I came to read it, I was just reading about the people I knew. I was reading about a Dublin that still had shadows and echoes in the Dublin of my childhood.

Ultimately, that writing got to me. I had been living in the States and my career was going along quite well. I was doing a lot of television work, but I really wanted to do something that made more of a statement about me and how I think and who I am as a woman. I had been putting together some material for a long time, from the political writings of Rosa Luxembourg to the poetry of Edna St Vincent Millay, with the Joyce fictional women and lots of other things thrown in. I couldn't really find a hook to hang them on in the planning of a one-woman show, other than the fact that they were my favourites. Then I hit upon the idea of looking at who were the real women in Joyce's life. I had actually met Sylvia Beach when she came to Dublin. My father had been instrumental in helping with that first 'Bloomsday' event when she came to open the Joyce tower. I began to read about her and discovered what a sustaining influence, a great friend and a courageous person she had been, and that is how the show, *James Joyce's Women*, came about. Burgess Meredith had cast me to play Molly Bloom on Broadway with Zero Mostel in the revival of *Ulysses in Nighttown* in 1973. Forces conspired to make the two things happen: my one-woman show and to work with Zero and Burgess on the Joyce material.

Joyce has obviously been an influence on my career, but I think it is probably perceived as a greater influence than it really is on a day-to-day basis. Two of the people who greatly influenced me in my early career were Micheál Mac Liammóir and Hilton Edwards. It was Hilton who gave me the role of Maggie in Brian Friel's play, *Lovers*, in its first production at the Gate, and that's what took me to the United States. It was Hilton who fought to have me in the Broadway cast, even though the Broadway producer wanted an American actress for the role. Mac Liammóir was a great influence on me because he was so completely theatrical and such an artist; so very gifted. He was a *Gaeilgeoir* and I was a Gaelic speaker, although I was an Abbey product. Very few people in those years made the cross-over to the Gate – you either worked at the Abbey or you worked at the Gate – and the Gate was perceived as being a sort of Anglo-Irish set up. I think I was one of the first to move from an Abbey training to working at the Gate with Micheál. We always spoke Irish when we met and he was always favourably disposed towards me. I was very young and frightened and very eager and ambitious and confused – all of those things – and to have someone of his stature give me encouragement and someone like Hilton believe in me and encourage me, give me a job and take me to America in his production was a wonderful gift.

Someone who is very precious to me and has indeed influenced me is the man I am married to, Garret O'Connor. He is a physician and psychiatrist and someone whom I think of as a very fine Irishman. He taught me a different way of thinking and brought me into the world that he was privy to, by virtue of his training, and he introduced me to a whole other literature and a whole other set of thinkers that have greatly enriched me.

I think a sense of humour is extremely valuable. I have a good friend in the United States who is in his eighties. He had once been the dean of the medical school at Yale and I asked him, 'Why did you leave? Everybody was crazy about you and you were so popular. You could have stayed there forever. Why did you leave?' And he said, 'There were no more jokes,' and he really meant it. I think that, when there aren't any more jokes in life, then something is terribly wrong, but I am very happy to report that there are a lot of jokes left in my life . . .

Marilyn French

Marilyn French's birth in New York coincided with the arrival of the Great Depression, resulting in the impoverishment of her family during her childhood. In the home, it was her mother who did the worrying, made the decisions and generally pulled the family through. And yet, as Marilyn observed from an early age, in the world outside, women did not seem to matter. 'Only men mattered . . .'

The seeds of feminism were sown early in the young girl who wanted to be 'a book writer'. When she eventually found the language of feminism in the writings of Simone de Beauvoir and Kate Millett, she was liberated. Her first novel, The Women's Room, *was written 'out of direct experience' and became a controversial bestseller. Marilyn French has also written two books of literary criticism and two hard-hitting polemics on patriarchy and the suppression and abuse of women,* Beyond Power: On Women, Men and Morals *and* The War Against Women. *'After millenia of male war against them, women are fighting back on every front . . .'*

I was born in New York, about a month after the Depression hit. The Depression was probably the most formative context of my childhood. It ruined my father's business and meant that my parents had to live with my mother's mother, and they didn't really pull out of that until World War Two.

My father had an automobile business, but it went bust with the Depression. It took him a while to find a job with the electric light company as a troubleshooter. It gave him thirteen dollars a week and somehow we lived on that. We lived in a small neighbourhood in Queens, almost entirely Catholic, mainly Italian and Irish. It was a poor neighbourhood in a poor time and I was a very bright kid, so they didn't know what to do with me. They put me at the back of the room at school. I would be asked to teach other children. I would write the school plays. After about the sixth grade, they sent me to the library during the day to catalogue the books or to work in the vice-principal's office, because there was no point in my attending the classes. I felt very cheated because I felt I could be learning something. I had read all the books they had available, but I didn't really have any guidance with them. I think the only real sadness I have about that time is that I didn't learn to speak foreign languages. In some ways, it wasn't a bad way to learn, because it made me very independent. All my thinking went on by myself. No one ever knew the answers to my questions. They always sent me off to look them up for myself. In a funny way, it led to a lot of confidence in my own intellect.

There were no good books for children then. What I read was very sexist and very conventional. I remember in my early teens just going into puberty longing, longing, being hungry for books that dealt with a young girl who had all kinds of ambition. I was a pianist of some talent and I had thoughts of being a composer. I wanted to be a writer. I wanted to be and to do. And the only things I could find were *Sue Barton, Student Nurse*. Being a nurse is a good thing and it is certainly demanding, but it certainly isn't the most challenging work imaginable for a girl. And, of course, the other thing was that Sue Barton was destined to find Prince Charming, and certainly not before losing her virginity. Those books were useless; they did not help a girl grow up.

My mother went to work when I was twelve, because she knew I had to go to college and she knew she had to earn some money to get me there. But she mainly stayed at home; she stretched this tiny, tiny pay cheque so that we ate really beautifully and were dressed beautifully. We didn't even know we were poor. The only way you would know we were poor was that we sometimes had a car and we sometimes didn't, depending on how cold the winter was and how much coal we needed. Someone gave us a record player and three records. I remember that one was Tchaikovsky's *Piano Concerto Number One*, one was Gounod's *Faust* and one was Bizet's *Carmen*, and I listened to these endlessly. My mother made all the decisions, my mother did all the doing. My father was very happy with that arrangement. He came home and handed her the pay cheque – whatever was decided was her idea. I remember listening to them talk long into the night with her urging him, now that things were gearing up in the war industry, to look elsewhere for a better job. In fact, he did get a better job and things eased up for them in their middle years.

In all of the families I knew, the women made the decisions, the women worried about the children, the women worried. And the men sat there and were affable and were all very nice, but they didn't have a whole lot of interest in anything. And then I would go out in the world and it was as though women didn't matter. Men were the only ones that mattered and this seemed very strange.

I didn't go for Communion instruction until I was nine. I was very bright at nine and most of the kids in the class were six and seven, so there was a huge difference between us. The nuns liked me, because I always learned my catechism. I loved one nun, Sister John the Baptist, and she was a very smart woman. One day, the priest came into the classroom and the sister kneeled down, with her head on the floor. I can't tell you how shocked I was. I never got over it. I never felt the same way about anything afterwards.

I was the elder of two sisters; my sister is four years younger. We eventually moved from that poor neighbourhood to a middle-class neighbourhood, where I was very unhappy. I hated middle-class kids; I hated their values. I went through the teenage years when I had giggling girlfriends, and the Frank Sinatra craze and all the apparent surface similarities to others, but I was very much at odds with the world I lived in.

We moved while I was in high school and it was too hard for my mother to get anywhere from where we lived. She didn't drive, so she couldn't go out to work. Instead, she sat up in the bedroom making nurses' caps at home; she was paid ten cents a piece. She would make hundreds of them a week. Hours of isolation and daydreaming. She would save and save and save and then my father would lose his job (never his fault) and she would have to help out and the money would go. There was never money for me to go to college, despite all her efforts.

I loved going to school in New York city. In those days, they would take us, for instance, I think it was for fifty cents, to see Paul Robeson in *Othello*, Maurice Evans in *Hamlet*, Katharine Cornell in *Antony and Cleopatra*. We heard and watched the New York Philharmonic Orchestra rehearsing. I had classes in music theory. The teachers were excellent. And then we moved to this wealthy suburb, where the kids were all so convinced that they were superior and that their schools were the best, yet there was not even an art class and they had never heard of music theory. But they were so sure of themselves, so superior, so complacent. It was really disturbing. Of course, you find little friends and you find people to hang out with, you find people you can talk to or play with or go to the movies with. But you don't find kin and I never really found kin until I went to graduate school when I was thirty-eight years old.

I wanted to be a writer. In first grade we had to write a composition on what we wanted to be when we grew up. I wrote that I wanted to be a book writer. My mother saved it and showed it to me many years later.

I was an independent reader. We had inherited some books that were in our bookcase. I don't know where we got them from. Nobody in my family ever read them. But I read them – Nietzsche and Schopenhauer and Thomas Paine and people like that. The way they wrote about women! I would sit there and read and think how could they say that? I would look at my mother, who was so good to us, and at the one strong man in our family, who was an uncle who was horrible. He used to beat his children with his belt and he dominated everybody in his household. It all confused me terribly.

I didn't begin to speak about these things until I was married, which was in the 1950s, and then everyone around me thought I was completely neurotic and crazy. So, when feminism arrived, it was just a huge relief. It gave us a language, as Adrienne Rich suggested in her wonderful book of poetry, *Dream of a Common Language*. It gave us a terminology, a set of concepts that we could use to base theory on and with which we could talk about these things, and it was a tremendous help. I don't know what would have happened to me without it. I had already written two novels, but they were oblique. They didn't get published. They were very feminist but not in an overt way, because there wasn't any language for that.

I was very confused at college, too. I was always getting flak from guys that I shouldn't be doing this, I shouldn't be doing that. I wasn't supposed to speak up in class, I wasn't supposed to be smart, I was supposed to be deferential. They didn't use that word. I remember one guy, puffing on his pipe, who stopped me one day. I was smoking and he said, 'You know girls aren't allowed to smoke on campus.' Girls had rules. They had to be in at certain hours; boys didn't. I left that college. I couldn't stand it. I had a lot of friends and there were a lot of people who weren't like that, so that wasn't all there was to it, but it was a constant source of irritation.

I started out majoring in philosophy at the next college I attended, but the entire philosophy department consisted of three retired Protestant ministers. I very soon shifted to English literature. I now think of English literature as the rag-bag of studies, because, for instance, when I went to Harvard many many years later to study English literature, we were, every one of us, a failed something else. One was a failed concert pianist, I was a failed novelist, several friends were failed writers or jazz pianists. We were interested in other things but we either couldn't make it in those things or those things hadn't satisfied us, so we brought those interests to English literature, which is why I think it's such a rich field. People come to it with all kinds of other interests.

My era was the '50s. The war was ending. The government and large corporations wanted to repopulate the country and fostered this 'back to the home' idea – every woman in an apron and every family with two and a quarter children and a station wagon. It was a time of tremendous domesticity, everybody buying houses and all of that. I certainly got caught up in it myself. It wasn't very satisfying. That generation of women raised daughters, maybe a generation a little bit older than I, who saw the emptiness of their mothers' lives.

When the Vietnamese War began and the anti-war movement really got off the ground, there were a lot of women in it. By this time, there were a lot of women in college and these were intelligent, educated women who were being treated like servants – she makes the coffee, she does the typing and then she shares your bed. That's the way the guys were treating them. They went into these organisations as equals, but, just like the women who married their male equals in college – as I did – they translated you into servants. These women rebelled, they pulled out of the anti-war movement and started the feminist movement. They did it in an outrageous way, to call attention to themselves. They were splendid. There was the great Women's Strike for Peace march, the women taking on the House unAmerican Activities Committee. Those women weren't especially feminist, they were just women against war. All of these things happened probably largely because of that war.

I was extremely unhappy in my marriage and I realised I could not get out of it. There were no jobs I could have gotten that would have paid me enough to support my children, and I was not about to abandon my children. I wanted more than anything in the world to get those children away from him. I couldn't get out, and even when I did get out with help I was pursued and harassed. I was not physically battered, I was emotionally battered. I thought he was going to kill us. He came and drove up in front of the house with a rifle one night, but I guess he thought better of it and drove away. Marriage seemed an irrevocable act then. There wasn't any way out of it in those days. I was married for seventeen years. I felt I was never going to be able to get out of it. I did, eventually, but it took a terrible toll on me. I loved this man. It wasn't an easy thing – he was in some ways lovable. But I understood helplessness, just as if I had been a baby. It was complete paralysis.

My daughter was born first and then my son a year later. I think that that was truly educational, because I had had a male education. I had been raised on Plato and Aristotle and all the Western thinkers, and I believed all this garbage about mind and body being separate and mind being superior to body and body being base and emotion being shameful, and all that whole bag. When you're giving birth, you can't go on buying it. You are bodily tied to these babies. I was just a neuter until I had children and then it became clear I was a woman and there wasn't any way out of that. I really loved my kids. They were so adorable and so wonderful and so interesting, because you didn't know what was going on inside them. Here was this new little intelligence, looking at you with wide eyes, and you never knew what they were going to say next. It's just a fantastic thing.

It's a kind of education I can't talk about, because it has been too sentimentalised and idealised. It's not ideal and it's not fun raising children, especially if you're in a bad marriage or you don't have money, but it is a glorious experience.

I certainly had feminist notions when I wrote my first book, the book on Joyce, although it is not considered a feminist book. My feminism has just grown over the years. The novels came out of life, out of direct experience. After the first two, I was doing a lot of thinking and I was giving a lot of talks. Everywhere I went, women would ask me, 'How did the world get this way?' I felt that I knew and I thought I could write. At that time I had planned to write a thirty-five-page essay on how the world had gotten this way, and I would include a number of my speeches and have it all published. My publisher was very happy with this idea and so I sat down to write the essay and it ended up being eighty-five pages long. He handed it back to me and said, 'I don't understand what you're talking about', so I had to do it the hard way. I wrote *Beyond Power*, which took five years of my life, during which I did almost nothing else. It was just constant research and constant thought. The whole notion of patriarchy became more palpable to me, and what it does to all of us, not just to women, but to men. The Book of John says, 'In the beginning was the Word'. In the beginning was *not* the word; in the beginning was the mother. The word began patriarchy, where the word becomes the truth. You say the father is the main parent and you say we will name the children after their father. But the mother is the main parent, the mother is the only parent you are sure of, and children should be named for their mothers. The most basic, vital, essential task we perform on this earth is giving birth. The whole world should be arranged so that having, raising and educating children should be safe, felicitous – a joyful experience. It is the least valued thing that you can do on this earth. It is unpaid, it has no status. This is a perverse world.

Look at what's going on across the world. Greater and greater areas are being brought under the hegemony of one power. They are going to be controlled by global economy, the international monetary fund and television, most of which are emanating out of my country. The rich are getting richer and smaller in number and the poor are getting poorer and larger in number and I see us headed for a really awful stratified world.

The thing about feminism that is so wonderful is that it frees your mind. When I wrote *The Women's Room*, I was really setting out to describe the process of liberating the mind from a whole lot of superstitions and fake images. Feminism frees the mind beautifully and it empowers you as a result, so that it's more pleasant to be alive. I always say that it is the first revolution that asks people not to die for it but to live for it. You don't have to win. You don't have to reach the end, the feminine utopia, the egalitarian world, to be enriched and empowered by it. This is lucky, because we can't figure out how to accomplish the egalitarian world. If you have a lot of feminists in your world, that world is quite a nice place to be. What I am really concerned about, and wish someone else would do, is to come up with a design, a blueprint, for a different way of organising the world, so that it is not arranged into hierarchies as a means of domination; a different kind of political and economic structure that would be more egalitarian, more mutual, that would permit true participatory democracy, which we don't have. I am so grateful to feminism, feminist thinkers and other thinkers, for allowing me to feel this tremendous joy of thinking, of being. The intellectual ferment and what I feel to be the fertility of the last ten or fifteen years of my life has been tremendous. It's just wonderful.

Bernadette Greevy

Bernadette Greevy was born in Dublin in 1940. A mezzo-soprano, she has won international acclaim through her concert appearances with many of the great orchestras and her numerous recitals in all the major capitals of the world. She has specialised in Mahler's lieder *and has featured regularly on radio and television, as well as recording works by Mahler, Handel, Bach, Brahms and Berlioz.*

I was sixth in a family of seven. My father used to read a lot – we were always falling over books because he would buy up little libraries. In the end, it was a case of who was more important, us or the books? My mother was a very bright, go-ahead person. I wouldn't describe her as a *feis* mother, but she always made sure that we were involved in as much as possible.

The older family members were already established in their own lives and their interests filtered down to me and my sister. My earliest memories are of my father teaching us songs like 'The Mountains of Mourne'. Every time I hear that it really takes me right back. We learned all sorts of funny little songs from him. He also used to take us for walks around Clontarf, where I was born and raised and educated.

I attended the Holy Faith School in Clontarf. It was certainly a very good education. We were fortunate that there were some marvellous nuns in our school. They didn't just stick rigidly to the curriculum but would branch out and make it interesting for us.

My earliest memories of school are of myself and my sister Pauline dressed up as two very large ducks who were going to be killed by the farmer's wife. It was a little kids' presentation; we must have been very small when that was put on. We used to have huge projects in school, where we would have not only to put on a show or a play, but we would also have to make all the costumes and the scenery. I remember when we did the story of Catherine Labouré and the miraculous medal. A few of us had the brilliant idea of getting four huge pieces of white cardboard and making a medal, with me as Our Lady as the middle bit. And then the Goddards used to teach us drill and George Leonard, a marvellous Irish dancer, used to teach us Irish dancing, so it was a non-stop carry-on from morning to night, as far as I can remember.

The school term from September to Christmas was spent preparing the school opera – terrific work went into that. From Christmas to Easter we had all the *feiseanna*, like verse-speaking, choir, school choir, solo singing. And then we only had a little term from Easter to summer to do the work, but we all survived and seemed to get through our exams.

When I was quite young, I became fed up with *feiseanna* and the whole business of dressing me up as Pitti Sing or some other character. I remember one time going out and singing so quickly that the adjudicator stopped the whole thing. 'Make that girl come back,' he said. 'This girl has the best voice but she is not going to get the prize because she doesn't want to be in the competition.' How right he was, but it taught me that you just can't do what you like all the time.

I started to win things at about fifteen. I was actually a joint winner with another girl in the Father Mathew *feis*, and the adjudicator made very glowing remarks about what might be possible for me. I then went in for the solo in the *feis ceoil*, which in those days was a huge event, and which to any young performer is the first major platform, and a very valuable one too if you intend to go on.

Gradually, I won more and more and then came the *Deep in My Heart* competition. I was still at school when I went in for that, but, although I didn't win (I got into the final by default because one of the four who were picked dropped out), it was a great experience for me. This suddenly took it out of the small arena and into the national. I enjoyed the experience and then I did one or two things in England and actually won a few competitions there.

I'm always fascinated by my colleagues whose ambition knows no bounds. My ambition is always to do my very best. I wouldn't waste an opportunity. You may have ten minutes or half an hour and are you going to make the best use of that? Have you done your work? I go through a whole litany of questions to myself beforehand. I still do it to this very day. I do my very best and, each time I perform work that I might have had some difficulty with before, I find I have learned enough to improve on it.

I got a huge amount of encouragement from home. Jean Nolan, my teacher, said I should have two lessons a week. She charged something like five guineas a lesson, so that meant we had to find ten guineas a week, and that was a lot of money back in the late '50s, early '60s. My father agreed to pay one of the lessons and I applied to the Arts Council to pay the other. Their response was that, unless I was going abroad for lessons, they wouldn't pay for anything at home. I believe that persists to this day and it is absolutely ridiculous. Anyway, I didn't get the grant, so the older ones in the family coughed up the rest.

Jean Nolan was my principal teacher here in Dublin. She was tough. She had a lot of experience and had been trained herself in Paris. I came to her towards the end of her life. I just feel that she was old when I got to her and she was also, like a lot of teachers, very possessive of her pupils. Now that suits some people, but it didn't suit me. I'm always ready to take advice and to be told and so on, but you have to leave some decisions to the person; make mistakes if you have to and then you learn by them. However, she really wanted to guide me body and soul. I remember when my late husband, Peter, came on the scene. He got a rough time from Jean, because she thought that I might think of getting married – having another life was just taboo. I said to her at the end of her life, 'Do you not regret that you didn't marry?' She half said she did, but she wouldn't actually admit it. She had a good sense of humour, though.

I remember all the gobbledegook when I first went to Jean – what you do, what you don't do, what you might do – and I said, 'Well, Miss Nolan, with the greatest respect' (I was thinking of the struggle to find this vast sum of ten guineas every week) 'if you don't sing and show me what you're doing, I really can't follow this at all.' And she said, 'Oh, I haven't sung for years.' So I said, 'You're going to have to sing for me. Whatever sound you produce doesn't matter, but I have to see how it's sung.' She started to sing and her whole demeanour changed. She came to life, I felt, when she started to sing herself.

You had to sing everything in front of a mirror. You had to sing it and look at yourself. To a young one, certain technical things – like a loose jaw, a stretched palate and so on – sound crazy, but as time goes on you find that, when you encounter problems, you actually do what you were taught to do. Singing well is not much of a big deal at all. If you have the voice, the actual technical business of singing well, focusing and projecting the sound, is quite a reasonable regime.

Because I went from secondary school to professional training, I never finished my schooling. There was just no way I was ever going to be allowed to be anything other than a singer. I would love to have tried to be an artist. My son does animation, so he is doing the sort of thing I would like to have done. I probably wouldn't have been as good at that as I was at singing, though. I would also have liked to have gone to college and studied English and history – which I still might do as a very mature mature student! However, I got into a groove and that was that.

When I look back on my life, it has been very interesting. I have been fascinated with the voice, and particularly my own voice and the way it has served me, but it has been a very pressured life, a very dedicated life. Not only for me but for the people closest to me, who had to understand how difficult the life is. My late husband did this very well. He always said that the job I had was hard enough without having to do an awful lot in the house. When he died, I was completely at sea in that whole area, because he had always taken all that worry from me. Even though our life together was short, in a sense, I made absolutely the right choice. Occasionally in your life you make the right choices and that was certainly one.

After my time spent with Jean Nolan, I went to England. I always wanted to see what the big world was like. I didn't want to be a big fish in a small pool and I could have been. I wanted to be out there with the best and I wanted to prove that, if you are good enough, living in Dublin on the edge of Europe shouldn't make any difference. Where you live is your own business and Dublin is only fifty minutes from London. I wasn't going to leave, like so many others. Looking back now, this certainly worked artistically, but in many other ways it was not a good idea. It was not a good idea at all. I suppose familiarity breeds a certain amount of contempt. Albert Rosen, our conductor here, said to me, 'You cannot confuse the general public and that is what you are doing. They know you are singing abroad and then they see you walking around with your trolley in the supermarket. You are destroying the whole image and they won't accept it.' To a certain degree he was right. I ruined the myth of the artist in Covent Garden or the Festival Hall or whatever. That was his view as a foreigner who lived and worked in Ireland and knew Ireland well. I feel that we still have this terrific cap-in-hand attitude towards foreigners which I just don't understand at all.

My first major breakthrough in the international scene came about when I was working here with Tibor Paul, learning all the Mahler that has served me so well throughout my life. I was also making records, although I had no reputation at all; I recorded the Handel arias for Decca. At that time I auditioned for Sir John Barbarolli and he took a shine to me. I always come in at the end of people's lives, sadly, but in two years I did an enormous amount of work with him. When he came here in 1970, I was his last Angel in *The Dream of Gerontius.* It was my first Angel, but it was his last one. He taught me the Verdi *Requiem.* I did several Halle Messiahs with him and I did my first Mahler Three with him, so he was a huge influence in my life at that stage.

I did an audition for the BBC and they failed me the first time and I never got over that! They said I was to come back in six months, but I said I'd never sing for them again. Six months and a day later, I was back and got accepted the second time and I have worked for them ever since. In the recent past I have recorded most of the Herbert Hughes material and all the

Anglo-Irish songs – Stanford, Hamilton Harty, Moeran – for their archives, which is very nice.

If Barbarolli was a big influence as a conductor, then I suppose as a composer Mahler was my great musical mentor throughout my entire life. For about eight years, I sang with the Royal Ballet at Covent Garden whenever they did the *Song of the Earth*, which was fantastically choreographed by MacMillan. I had learned Mahler earlier on in my life and then suddenly he became very fashionable. Now everybody is an expert on Mahler. If Mahler is performed, you get a full house; they absolutely adore him.

Dietrich Fischer-Dieskau was a great influence as a singer. He was a wonderful singer in his great days. I always listened to him for the German language, because his diction is so magnificent, and he was a very elegant performer. It wasn't a huge voice. I heard him live lots of times, but he was a wonderful recording artist. Of the others, I loved Victoria de los Angeles, because she was like a breath of fresh air, even on a record – a wonderful performer. There was also nobody like the young John McCormack. At his best he really was the best, just heaven.

I was always attracted to the German school of singing. It's a very disciplined school, a school that really cares for the voice. It's very thorough – nothing slipshod at all. The sound is clean, there are no huge vibrato things, which are terrible. It treats the voice with great respect.

I was also a great fan of Karen Carpenter. She had a real alto voice; if you sing along with her, it is pitched very low. She had a lovely easy way of putting a song over.

The great influence in my life was my late husband, Peter. Sadly, we were separated a lot throughout our marriage because of my work. The separations were never too long and I feel that it enhanced our life together. There was always great rapport between the two of us. We used to be fascinated when we went out to dinner and saw people sitting silently staring at each other, whereas we never shut up talking. When Peter died, our son Hugh said he didn't know what I was going to do on my own – his memory of his dad and me was that we sat every night talking for ages. We never shut up; we were always talking and planning.

Peter had a major heart attack in 1980, but he had two very good years after that. He left his job and decided he couldn't hang around doing nothing, so he took on my management. He turned out to be a fantastic manager. I was doing the work he got me for about five years after his death. We were very different people. He gave the impression of being light-hearted, but that concealed a person who absorbed stress and worry. When I got a write-up in the paper that wasn't very generous or very nice, it absolutely floored him. He couldn't cope with that at all, to such an extent that, three years before he died, we agreed that we would never buy another newspaper ever again. I find it hard to find any kindness in my heart towards those newspapers, because, if they were trying to get at me, all they did in fact was get at him.

I didn't sing for nearly a year after his death. I couldn't even go outside my door. It was terrible. I had to pull myself together for Hugh then, because he also was grieving. He was very close to his father, he was always with him. In fourteen years, he had more of his father than a lot of guys ever have in their whole life. A year later, when I went to New Zealand, I brought him with me. I said to Hugh, 'I don't know if I can ever walk out on the stage again, but let's have a go in New Zealand. If I can't do it, it doesn't matter, especially at the other end of the world.' I don't think I could have gone if he hadn't come with me. Although I have a most loving family, without whom I couldn't have had my career, I really felt he had to be with me at that particular stage. He had lost his father and, if his mother were to suddenly go off, even though it was to earn a living for the pair of us, it would never do for a child of nearly fifteen. So I took him with me and then we went to China the following year. A bond was established then. That was another thing I did right in my life. It was absolutely the right thing to do, and I have benefited from it ever since.

I suppose travel is one of the big pluses of a career like mine. I have been all over the world and sung with all sorts of conductors and orchestras, and life is full of concert halls and airports and hotels. However, a woman on her own is unacceptable. A man isn't for some reason, but society has ordained that a woman shouldn't be on her own. If you feel like having a drink, you can't go down and drink on your own; you are immediately something to be stared at. When I was younger, I couldn't stand that. I was often in a situation where I would be having a meal and the men would talk about me across me to each other. I wouldn't care now, I'd just laugh at them, but when I was younger and on my own, always on my own, I was more vulnerable. It is a very lonely life, so when you think of what happened to me, which wasn't part of our plan at all, my life as a solo singer has trained me to be a survivor on my own.

I am still being educated. Franz Paul Decker, a good colleague and conductor who I first met in Montreal when I was at the beginning of my career, has been a wonderful influence in my life. He was my conductor in New Zealand when I went back that famous year. He believed in my work and has got me a lot of very interesting engagements, doing stuff that wouldn't come up every day, like, for instance, in Barcelona we did the *Rape of Lucretia* by Britten, and we did *Dido and Aeneas* in the Palau de la Musica, which is an amazing hall. It is not a Gaudi creation, but it is by an architect of that period, so it's a bit over the top – with horses coming out of the wall! You don't need scenery, because it's all built in for you, so you can do the semi-staged operas, early opera, and we did all that. For a singer at my stage in my career, if you have about three conductors who like you and like your work, you can survive.

There are still things in music that I want to do and there is a good chance that I will get to do them. Over the next three years, I am going to do all of the Mahler song cycles and symphonies in Argentina with Maestro Decker. I've never been to South America, so that will be more education for me. Sometimes you begin to think that you have done it all and then suddenly something new comes along out of the blue. It recharges the battery and you just feel, this is extraordinary. Just when you feel they must all be sick of listening to you – here, there, thither and yon – suddenly you're going to a new place where they don't know you at all!

Charles Handy

Charles Handy was born in County Kildare in 1932, the son of a Church of Ireland archdeacon. He was educated locally and in Bray, County Wicklow, and later at boarding school in England ('a horrific experience'). He graduated from Oxford and worked in the Far East as an executive with a major oil company. He later studied management at the Massachusetts Institute of Technology before becoming Professor at the London Business School.

The death of his father was a turning-point in Charles Handy's life. He became warden of St George's House in Windsor Castle, 'educating bishops . . .' He became increasingly interested in 'the future of work' and eventually began to practise what he had been preaching – 'a portfolio life' – working (as writer, lecturer, broadcaster) part of the year, devoting another part to voluntary causes and leaving the remainder to travel and leisure. He has become a highly successful writer and broadcaster on such themes as the future of work, the nature of organisations and the changing pattern of how we live our lives. Books such as The Future of Work, Understanding Organisations, Beyond Certainty *and* The Empty Raincoat *have engendered debate and influenced thinking in those areas.*

Charles Handy lives and works in London and Norfolk.

I grew up in a Protestant rectory in Kildare where my parents ended up living for forty years. It was a very idyllic childhood in a way, even though a lot of it took place during the war. We all had ponies and we rode bicycles and so on, but it was a very small place. Everybody knew everybody and it was absolutely dominated by the church calendar and church services and so on. That was a very important influence on me, first of all in a negative way, because I was desperate to get away – to be somewhere where nobody knew my father, to be somewhere where I didn't have to go to church every second day and to be somewhere where maybe there was a bit more money around, which I felt I was lacking.

My father was the quiet counsellor, the wise man. My mother was the organiser, and she had great ambitions for her children – she wanted them to be very happy. She also had very simple rules of life, which certainly got embedded in me, though I tried to submerge them for a time. I didn't realise the influence those early years had on me until I was into my fifties, when they suddenly surfaced with a bang.

I went to the local primary school and then I went to a boarding school in Bray. When I was fourteen I was sent over to England, which was a pretty horrific experience. English boarding schools in those days were cruel places and I began to appreciate for the first time the cruelty of boys towards boys. I came away quite terrified of relationships, because on the whole they were brutal, so that was a very negative learning experience. It was quite a long time before I was able to trust someone.

The other thing I learned at that very traditional school was this strange message – that all the problems in the world had already been solved. The answer was known to the teachers and not to me and my job was to guess the answers, which the teachers knew. That may not seem very significant, but it crippled me for the first ten years of my adult life, because every time I met a problem I would look to the teacher, i.e. the expert or my boss. I didn't realise for a long time that lots of problems had never occurred before and some of them I could solve for myself.

I made no friends at that time, but there was one man in the school who became my mentor. He was my class master and also my house master and he taught me an enormous number of things, not just the subjects – Greek, Latin and ancient history – that he was teaching me. One morning after being in the school chapel, we returned to our class and were supposed to be translating Virgil or something terribly boring, when he said, 'Which of you can give me the name of the composer of the organ music that we heard this morning in chapel?' Dead silence. He said, 'This is disastrous. You are sixteen years of age. You have just listened to one of the most marvellous pieces of Bach that the world could ever hear and you don't even know it. We will not look at any Latin this morning. We will go back to my house and I will play you the kind of music that ought to be in your souls for ever more.'

This man opened my mind in a quite incredible way, and then he did something which had an amazing effect on my life. He made me sit the exam for Oxford, even though I was proposing to go to Trinity College, Dublin, where all my family had gone before me. In the end I went to Oxford and not to Trinity, thereby living in England and not Ireland. I don't know yet whether that was for good or for ill, but it certainly changed my life – and that man made it happen. In that desert, there was this wonderful prophet and I was very lucky that he latched on to me. He gave up his holidays, as so many dedicated teachers do, to take pupils on school trips, and in those days it was rare to go to the Continent, but he took us all off to the south of France, to look at Roman ruins and things like that. Not only did we see Roman ruins, but for the first time in my life I, a little Irish boy from the bogs of Kildare, began to understand the civilisation that exists in the Mediterranean – the smells, the scents, the wine and so on. I would not have discovered those things for many years but for him, because people didn't travel much at that time.

Oxford was an extraordinarily liberating experience, because in those days we lived like privileged young gentlemen. I had rooms in college – a sitting-room and a bedroom and a servant – paid for out of my college fees, which were minimal. I had two tutors, one for the classics and one for philosophy or history, which we also had to study. We would meet each of them individually for an hour each week, when we would read our essays to them. This has had a major effect on my life. If you have to read an essay out loud, you can't talk in convoluted sentences; you don't have enough breath to finish them. So you are forced to talk in relatively simple language, so that the other person can hear. Above all else, it taught me to write good English and, in the later stages of my life, that became absolutely vital.

'What Is Truth?' was the first essay I had to write in philosophy. 'You might like to dip into Aristotle or to look at David Hume, who has some philosophical thoughts on this, and John Stuart Mill and Locke, those traditional philosophers, have something to say. A J Ayer, a modern philosopher, also wrote a book called *Language, Truth and Logic,* which you might find useful, but, basically, I want your ideas,' the tutor said.

I thought this was dead simple, but I didn't sleep for about three days trying to work out this extraordinarily difficult subject, discovering of course in the end that I had no idea what truth was. The beginning of learning always turned out to be accepting that I was ignorant, even on things that I really thought I knew. Growing up in a rectory! Of course I knew what truth was! But no, I didn't.

That kind of experience became very crucial in later years, because it forced me to take things that appeared obvious and question whether conventional wisdom really was valid – for instance, the idea that a good society gives everybody a job for fifty years. My Oxford training would say, where did you get this notion from? What historical evidence is there that this is what a good society does? That became tremendously formative for me, though I didn't know it at the time.

After Oxford, I joined Shell, which promised to send me to some exotic place, pay me large sums of money and give me a wonderful lifestyle far away from England. Shell sent me off to the Far East, to Kuala Lumpur in Malaysia, for the next seven years. I had a wonderful time sailing out – three weeks first class on a P&O liner full of young ladies who were going out to marry British soldiers fighting in Malaysia and having the last fling of their lives. Gin was 4p a tot and the only decisions you had to take for three weeks was when would you start drinking and what would you eat for dinner. It was a wonderful voyage, a great learning experience in many ways.

I had been there for six months when they called me in and said, 'We've been asked by our London head office to appoint an economist for South East Asia, and you're going to be it.' That was quite a learning experience. When you throw somebody into the deep end of the swimming pool, they learn to swim pretty quick. And then they called me one day and said, 'Our man who manages the marketing side of Borneo has become ill and we've had to send him home. We have five depots there and tankers and things. That's it, you're in charge.'

The next day I flew off to my new empire. I was 24 and I had a territory about the size of the British Isles. I had 400 people working for me and 399 of them were Chinese or Dayaks, or Eurasians. There was one European. He was two years younger than me and he knew even less of what all this was about. If you want a learning experience, try going to another country to run an industry about which you really know nothing. There was no telephone line to Singapore. I was on my own. I didn't cope very well, but luckily nobody knew. One of the lessons I learned about learning is that, if you can keep your mistakes secret, you learn much faster. Private learning is quite a good thing.

In a funny way, I've lived my life backwards. The glorious, sybaritic part of my life, apart from Oxford, was in Malaysia. After Borneo, I became head of south Malaya. I had a beautiful house. I had five servants and a chauffeur. I had a tennis court and a croquet lawn and a private beach, and I had a separate house in the grounds for my guests, including staff. And I was a bachelor. I had allowances to cover all my entertaining and so on. My life has gone downhill ever since, in terms of materialism. It was very very good to have that sort of Californian lifestyle when I was only 26, because I didn't feel the need to do it again. It's all a load of nonsense of course, but they were heady days.

I eventually came back to Shell in England and that was very dull. It was an office job and I wasn't very good at it. But failure produces some extraordinary results. Because I wasn't very good at it, they shunted me sideways to help run their staff training college for all their managers. I did that for two years and in the process I discovered that teaching adults and managing the learning of adults was absolutely fascinating. So I said to Shell, 'This is wonderful, I'd like to go on doing this please.' And they said, 'Don't be silly, that's not what you're destined to do. You're actually supposed to be running the overseas companies. Your next job is running Liberia.' I vaguely remembered that Liberia was a state in West Africa run by a chap called President Tubman. It was the ex-slave colony of America. A most ghastly place.

I didn't want to go and my wife said she was certainly not going to follow me there. So I left Shell after ten years, wanting to be a teacher. I was introduced to the head of the new London Business School and he said, 'We'd love you to come and help design some of our executive programmes. But before you do that, you'd better discover what management education is all about, because we don't know in this country. Why don't you go for a year to the Massachusetts Institute of Technology and do the Sloane Program there, which is a sort of sabbatical programme for managers in their thirties, and then come back and start up the same thing in London?' And so I very soon found myself in Boston with my wife and three-week-old baby, a student once again, in the Massachusetts Institute of Technology, doing an MBA course at the age of thirty-one.

On my second day there, I had a meeting which, again, changed my life. I met Warren Bennis, who was Professor of Organisational Behaviour, a title I'd never heard before. He was the young rising star of this new field of human behaviour and organisations and he had gathered in his house that evening all the stars of the field, who, 25 years later, are still great people. They persuaded me that what really mattered in organisations was not the money or the market or the machines or the computers but the *people*.

I had a fascinating year with Warren Bennis, who is now one of my greatest friends and lives in California. He was another of those key people in my life at a key point in time who helped shape my world. That was still a slightly artificial world and some of my old upbringing in the rectory was beginning to come back to me. I was realising that what I really wanted was to help people who were worse off than me. I found myself very uneasy, sitting working with rather elitist, spoilt young men and women who were going off to earn huge salaries.

After ten years there, my father died. I went to his funeral, back in Ireland, at the old church that he had served for forty years. The place was packed with people crying and saying, 'This man meant more to us than anything else.' I suddenly realised that he had lived a rather special life, and the things that I had run away from, even despised, were actually incredibly valuable. So, in a way to apologise to him, I resigned my professorship, which was a crazy thing to do. It was a guaranteed job to 65, a comfortable life and long vacations. I resigned all that and went to run a small centre, which happened to be based behind St George's Chapel in Windsor Castle, which educated the new bishops and the up-and-coming clergy who might become bishops. In between running these courses, I also held rather high-level meetings of about twenty-five leaders of society, convened by Prince Philip, who was my boss ultimately, to talk about social justice in society, the changing nature of work, the changing distribution of incomes, and such things. So there I was, on a clergy salary, living in a rectory, helping people less fortunate than myself. My life had gone full circle.

I met six thousand people in four years. I sat at the feet of a hundred and ten theologians over that period. It was an amazing learning experience for me. I was bombarded with the ideas of very interesting people and it broadened my horizons enormously.

I had a five-year contract, but I always think that you should leave one year before it is expected. By this time I was actually talking and writing about what I call 'the future of work' and basically saying that a lot of people would have to spend a lot of their lives living what I called a 'portfolio life' – by their wits, bits and pieces of work, self-employed if you like, with a range of clients and customers and a range of skills. And wouldn't it be a very good idea if I actually tried to do that!

People thought I was crazy. I was forty-nine by then and at the height of my career. People expected me to go off and head a business school or a university – and that would have been an ambitious thing to do. Instead, I resigned from everything and went back to my flat in Putney in south London and my cottage in East Anglia to write books and do a bit of teaching. I had a £5,000 contract with the London Business School to do occasional bits of teaching and that was going to be my sole income.

It was frightening actually, but also incredibly freeing, because up until then half of me was Charles Handy but half of me was professor of this or head of that. I had to look over my shoulder to make sure I was saying the right thing. Suddenly I was all Charles Handy. I could be myself. I could say what I liked. I could arrange my life totally differently.

For instance, my wife and I decided to work 100 days a year on what you might call 'money-making things' – things that produce money – and 100 days a year on study; that is, writing books and researching them. We would give 50 days a year to charitable causes, my tithing to society, as it were. That's 250 days, which leaves 115 days for leisure, which is actually two days a weekend and a fortnight's holiday. By doing it this way, we could take two months off in the year, and spend one month in Italy and one month in America if we wanted. It looked extravagant, but then of course we would have to work on Saturdays and Sundays, which we would use for study time, which meant reading and writing in our cottage in Norfolk.

It seemed to us to be an example of what I call 'liberated upside-down thinking' – the old tradition I learned from Oxford: question everything. Why work five days a week and have two days at weekends? Why not parcel it out in other ways.

Economically, after a little while, we survived. My wife did something very important. Hitherto, she had been the mother of my children and the company of my bedroom and my social life and so on. She had her own interests. She had been an interior designer and a marriage counsellor. We decided to become full partners at work and that she would be my managing partner – she would be my agent, my organiser, and she would arrange my work. That was an enormously useful discipline for me.

When you are working on your own, you can be besieged by people. Some of them could be interesting, but a lot of them might not be. Elizabeth took over all the fielding of all that – she organised my life. She raised money for advances for my books and she took on several lucrative contracts, speaking and teaching in organisations. We very soon found that we only needed to sell 50 days a year of my time to produce enough money. We also took a very crucial decision – that we didn't want to be as rich as possible, we just wanted to be rich enough.

Now that sounds very privileged, but, if you think about it, most people really only sell 50 days of their time to other people and they clutter up the rest of the year preparing for that. We disciplined ourselves: 50 days selling, 50 days for preparation and 100 days of study.

In a sense, the place I ran away from is the place I have ended up in. OK, it's a flat in Putney and a cottage in Norfolk, but it's all about trying to discover the truth and helping other people to do that too; it's about preaching a little, which I tend to do now on the radio; teaching a little, which I do now through books more than anything else; helping people who are less fortunate to learn about themselves and to live out that truth. It's a little rectory in Kildare. I can't escape those first seven years.

Seamus Heaney

Seamus Heaney was born in Bellaghy, County Derry, in 1939. He was educated in St Columb's College, Derry, and Queen's University, Belfast. His first collection of poetry, Death of a Naturalist, *was published in 1966. A year spent in Berkeley University, California, in 1970 was important to him in 're-orienting towards Ireland'.*

He taught briefly at second level in Belfast and lectured at St Joseph's College of Education and Queen's University, Belfast, before moving to Dublin in 1976 as a lecturer in Carysfort College of Education. He has since been Professor of Rhetoric and Oratory at Harvard University and Professor of Poetry at Oxford.

After Death of a Naturalist *came a succession of acclaimed and award-winning poetry collections* – Door into the Dark, Wintering Out, North, Sweeney Astray, Field Work, Station Island, The Haw Lantern, Seeing Things *and* The Spirit Level. *That body of literature earned Seamus Heaney the Nobel Prize for Literature in 1995. With Ted Hughes, he has edited two poetry collections,* The Rattle Bag *and* The School Bag. *He has also published two prose collections* – Preoccupations *and* The Government of the Tongue, *as well as a play,* The Cure at Troy.

Seamus Heaney currently lives in Dublin.

A shadow his father makes with joined hands
And thumbs and fingers nibbles on the wall
Like a rabbit's head. He understands
He will understand more when he goes to school.
                                                    (*Alphabets*)

I was part of a moment of social history, and in this case I always quote Edmund Muir. Muir grew up in the Orkneys and had an almost medieval childhood, with open fires and horses ploughing the fields, water from the well and so on. He ended up in Prague, where he watched the twentieth century shift and change. He was present for the Communist take-over after the war and wrote that, even though his chronological age might have been about fifty at that time, his cultural age was more like four or five hundred. It was as if he had been born in a different anthropological era. In one sense I think that is also true of the people in my generation who grew up in the country in Ireland in the 1940s. We were at the tail-end of a steadier way of life that had persisted right through from medieval times.

The house I lived in was not a literary or a bookish household at all, but there was respect for books and for education. There was no tradition of secondary schooling in the family, with the exception of my Aunt Sarah. She went to school in the 1920s and got what they called a 'King's Scholarship' and trained as a schoolteacher. It was in my Aunt Sarah's house that I got a sense of books as an actual possession, as an element in a life. She had a set of Thomas Hardy novels, for example, and I have most of those now myself. Inside them is written 'S Heaney 1925', and my own initials are 'S Heaney', so I always had this little sense of identification.

Our own house was a farmhouse – not a book house – going about its farm business, but there was an education of a kind in that too. It was very, very close to the primal issues of life and death. I remember the instinctive distress I felt watching kittens being drowned. And yet you were being taught by the realism, the brutality of that custom of taking them immediately and drowning them before they grew; you were being initiated to some extent into the cruelties of human society.

> I was six when I first saw kittens drown.
> Dan Taggart pitched them, 'the scraggy wee shits',
> Into a bucket; a frail metal sound,
>
> Soft paws scraping like mad. But their tiny din
> Was soon soused. They were slung on the snout
> Of the pump and the water pumped in.
>
> (*The Early Purges*)

I think the same is true of going to school. I felt it when my own children were going to school for the first time. I took each of the three of them on the first day; Marie couldn't bear to do it. You have a very strong sense then as a parent that you are taking the little creature out of the nest life, out of the den life, and handing him or her over to the world of culture or the world of society. You tell children things which you want them to believe – like you will be very happy at school, you will enjoy it and so on. You suppress for yourself and for them the distresses, the sense of desertedness, the sense of crossing out from security into the aloneness of your own being. A couple of days after she went to school, our daughter Catherine said to Marie, 'A lot of girls cried and said they wanted their Mammy. I didn't, but my heart thinked it.'

I myself was part of a large family, so the opportunities for one-to-one intimacy with a parent weren't great. Also, the house we lived in for the first twelve years of my life was a three-roomed house with two bedrooms and the kitchen in the middle, so it was always full. The moments of stillness that I remember were during late Mass on a Sunday. I used to go to early Mass and my mother did too. The rest of the family went to late Mass and, in their absence, my mother and I would prepare the dinner. I was about ten or twelve and my job was to peel the potatoes along with her.

> When all the others were away at Mass
> I was all hers as we peeled potatoes.
> They broke the silence, let fall one by one
> Like solder weeping off the soldering iron.
> (from *Clearances*)

My mother was a woman of great strength and forcefulness, like many many women of her generation. Her religious faith, her identification with the suffering Mother of Christ, was the way in which she survived the biological penalty of child after child. There were nine of us inside of about twelve years. Women in those days were cornered in child-bearing, in exhaustion, in a kind of resentment of their position, both sexually and in every other way. Hence their intense devotion to the Blessed Virgin Mary, their devotion to the Rosary; that triumphant cry that you used to hear in country churches when women were answering the prayers. Within the realm of prayer there was a place for resistance; it provided a bracing other value that could be set against the penalties of the lived life. My mother had a very strong faith and it wasn't just a matter of religiosity or piety, it was a matter of fierce spiritual commitment. I think that I identified with that and I took it in too. I suppose there is always something oedipal in the boy growing up with the Mammy, but this was a process of osmosis from her spirit.

Then, too, there were the actual habits of the household, which were also deeply religious. In the Irish countryside of the 1940s, within the Catholic community in the North especially, the sub-culture was saturated in religious values. Added to that was the inner social bonding of the Catholic community. The chapel on Sunday, any entertainment run by the parochial committee or, indeed, any games played by the GAA. It was all separate from the Protestant side.

> *Learning's easy carried!* The bag is light,
> Scuffed and supple and unemptiable
> As an itinerant school conjuror's hat.
> So take it, for a word-hoard and a handsel,
>
> As you step out trig and look back all at once
> Like a child on his first morning leaving parents.
> (from *The Schoolbag*)

The characters, the aura of my first teachers remain in my memory, as well as certain customs of the school, the furniture of the school and so on. Catherine Walls, the infants teacher, was the surrogate mother for sure. The thing I remember from her class was fairytales. Also, the learning-to-write process. I think it must have been a transitional moment in the schools, because there were still slates around, even though they weren't quite used. You got them and you played with them in the 'baby infants'. I remember doing transcription from the board and also the Vere Foster headlines you had to write. I can still see the coloured lines in those copybooks with the pink and the very light duck-egg blue lines. I came across one the other day and it went to my heart. One of the joys of those early days at school was getting a new copybook, perfectly bound and perfectly clean, and just hoping that you wouldn't blot it.

Then we went up to the master's room and somehow life became more sombre with Master Murphy. He was like a figure from the nineteenth century. He had a wing-collar, a waistcoat, a slightly mottled face and an abrupt manner. When I did the 'eleven plus' exam, I was too young to proceed to the boarding school so I had an extra year in the primary school. What happened in this case was that the master took you under his care and prepared you for the first year of your secondary education. I used to go in early in the mornings for algebra and Latin and Irish. Latin was the one that I got the most grip on. After a certain stage in the algebra I missed the point. Master Murphy was what they would call in Scotland a *dominie*. What I remember best are the one-to-one moments with him, being brought up to the desk to do reading or to go through grammatical exercises. In *Station Island* I imagine meeting him on a pilgrimage, and he remembers the school, and, in particular, the gardening – that was a great thing in schools in those days. The boys did gardening and the girls did sewing and it was a great romance to get out into the open air and get the spades going. So the master turns up in the pilgrim's line of vision.

> His sockless feet were like the dried broad bean
> that split its stitches in the display jar
> high on a window in the old classroom,
> white as shy faces in the classroom door.
>   (from *Station Island*)

I was conscious at an early age of living in the midst of two traditions. There was a kind of forthrightness and robustness and confidence, culturally, within the Catholic group. I lived beside an AOH hall and on St Patrick's Day the banner came out. St Patrick was on the silk banner flowing down the face of the wind, a wonderful ritual. There was a mixture of religiosity and belligerence, people carrying pikes and playing hymns, *I'll Sing a Hymn to Mary* and *Hail Glorious St Patrick*. On the other hand, our neighbours, the Evans's, were Church of Ireland. I used to play with Tommy Evans. His uncles were in the British army; they came home after the war. Politics were never discussed, of course, but you knew the British army was the other gang. The Church of Ireland place of worship was 'the church', the Presbyterian place was 'the meeting house' and the Catholic place was 'the chapel'! There was a formulaic exchange of reassurances – 'Sure, it doesn't matter where we go on a Sunday as long as we can behave ourselves and people are decent.' I have to say also that our school had Protestants attending it. It was admittedly a Catholic school in ethos and by management, but the mixed religious element was at least some symptom of a good working relationship between the two sides. As I got a bit older, from my early teens, I began to be aware of the 'B Men', as they were called, on the road. You were also strongly aware that the government was not on your side, that you were excluded. One of the best examples of this in my own case was my birth certificate. I was christened Seamus, but on the official register of births at Magherafelt I noticed the name was wrongly spelled. I was registered on my birth certificate as *Shames*, which is a wonderful minority stigma!

> For he was fostered next in a stricter school
> Named for a patron saint of the oak wood
> Where classes switched to the pealing of a bell. . .
> (from *Alphabets*)

St Columb's College is called after St Columba (the dove of the Church) and is in Derry (the oak wood) and it has the oak tree and the acorn on its crest. I associate going to St Columb's among other things with learning languages, learning Latin and learning Irish. It was first of all a diocesan seminary; its primary function when it was founded and even when I arrived there in the early fifties would have been to supply vocations for the priesthood for the diocese of Derry. Gradually, though, from the early '50s through until now, it had less to do with furthering the spiritual life of the students and more to do with furthering their secular destiny – and my own generation would be an example of that. The teachers were terrifically devoted to academic excellence. We were first of all packed up like little cases full of the syllabus and then we faithfully distributed our contents in the exams.

I had a strong sense of the need to get through the exams –
there was very little sense of freedom and rejoicing in the subject
for its own sake. When I went into senior school, I played with
Latin verse and wrote parodies of Milton. And on and off
throughout that time you would be affected by single
experiences. I always remember hearing the English teacher,
Jack Gallagher, reading the whole of *The Rime of the Ancient
Mariner*. I think it took him two classes but it was quite a
daring thing to do. I often thought afterwards that Jack was
probably hung over when he started it, but that reading will stay
with me forever as a real experience. Later on, in sixth form, I
had an English teacher, Sean B O'Kelly, and reading Chaucer,
Wordsworth and Keats with him was also terrifically important.
But it was only after I left school for Queen's that I took to
doing my own writing.

> I tried to write about the sycamores
> And innovated a South Derry rhyme
> With *hushed* and *lulled* full chimes for *pushed* and *pulled*.
> Those hobnailed boots from beyond the mountain
> Were walking, by God, all over the fine
> Lawns of elocution.
>
> (from *The Ministry of Fear*)

I suppose somewhere at the back of my head was the
unadventurous idea that I would be a teacher. You didn't really
think very clearly into the future, it was always just the next
hurdle. And Queen's University was the next place after St
Columb's. I had a notion that I was going to do French there,
but, because of that English class and the teaching we got from
Sean B, I gradually proceeded to do honours English. In those
days it was a four-year course, so at the end of the first year at
university you began and you did nothing but English language
and literature for the next three years. That turned out to be a
genuinely widening experience, particularly the study of Anglo-

Saxon. I liked the history of the language and I actually enjoyed Anglo-Saxon poetry. I liked the fabric of it, the texture of the writing, the heft and thump of it.

At that point there were many things going on in my life. I was in the Irish Society, but I also attended the French Society's meetings now and again – I think I wanted to keep in contact with different parts of myself. I was also connected with a dramatic society at home in Bellaghy. I was performing in plays of execrable artistic merit in Bellaghy and then learning to exercise the highest critical standards thirty miles down the road in Belfast.

St Columb's College was devoted to turning out recruits for Maynooth and it had got that intense religious shape to the day – morning prayers, Mass, the Angelus, night prayers and so on. Going to Queen's, you met people from other schools and other parts, you met other accents, you met other *mores* and you met women, which was a huge development, because St Columb's was an all-male school. So there was a moving out from within your own minority grouping and over the years I became equally at ease with the people from schools like Methody and Inst. Amongst the English students in my year, those who graduated in 1961, sectarian differences mattered nil. They existed, but were well handled. It was a very lively group and it was friendly and open. I see the metaphorical shape of all this as an opening outward, a rippling out from centre. I love that bit in *A Portrait of the Artist as a Young Man*, when Stephen Dedalus writes his address in the back of the book – 'Stephen Dedalus, Class of Elements, Clongowes College, Clane, Co. Kildare, Ireland, the British Isles, Europe, the World, the Universe'. That has been my own experience too.

When I left Queen's, I made lists of the things I had to read. I got an award called the McMullan medal for distinction in the exams and could either take the medal or the money. I thought I'd take the money, because it was five guineas, but in fact it came in the form of a book token. So I bought a number of

books – Louis MacNeice's *Collected Poems,* J M Synge, Oscar
Wilde and so on. I'll never forget reading Synge for the first
time. I didn't read him in university – maybe because we were
taught English by English people. Anyhow, I remember
opening the old Everyman copy of *John Millington Synge, Plays,
Poems and Prose* in the APCK bookshop in Belfast and reading
the first lines of *In the Shadow of the Glen.* It was wonderful to
encounter the totally familiar thing in a book. A tramp at the
door, rain falling on the street . . .

After leaving Queen's, there was a gradual process of linking
in to a more specifically literary and writing life, which
culminated with my joining the group founded by Philip
Hobsbaum in 1963 in Belfast. Round about that time, too,
there was an anthology came out called *Six Irish Poets* and that
was very important reading to me. I also got wakened up when
I got the loan of Kavanagh's *A Soul for Sale* from Michael
McLaverty. All that started me off, and I had some poems
published in the *Kilkenny Magazine* by James Delahanty, and
by Terence de Vere White in the *Irish Times.* It is very very
important for a young writer to get the stuff that he sends out
accepted. I had no contacts, I had no literary milieu. I was just
testing. I was sending out the messages and the message I got
back was that these things were publishable – which was
enormously confidence-building. Immediately after that, Philip
Hobsbaum, poet and academic, came to Queen's. He had run
workshops in Cambridge and in London and he started one in
Belfast. That was another very good stage of confirmation and
another ripple outwards. It was at that group that I got to know
Michael and Edna Longley and various other people. Through
them I got to know Derek Mahon, so that was an opening out
beyond the Belfast thing into the Dublin thing, since they had
been to Trinity.

Encountering Kavanagh's poetry was enormously important.
It was like a woman discovering women writers. I was converted
and empowered and released into parts of myself through

reading him. You encountered in his work that which you thought was secret to yourself; he raised the sub-cultural life to cultural status and that is extremely enabling. The older I get the more I realise that Kavanagh's great power is in

> The lines that speak the passionate heart
> The spirit that lives alone.

There's a wonderful force and vigour, a mixture of solitude and courage in Kavanagh, a mixture of complete psychic impulse and honesty that whooshes through his poetry.

I only taught for one year in a school. I found it agonising. I found discipline a problem. I found I wasn't quite sure how to proceed, afraid of drying up in the course of a lesson. I managed, but it takes a long time to learn to teach. It takes a long time to learn the mixture of freedom within yourself and attention to the student in front of you that makes for good teaching. One of the things I really valued about getting into Harvard in the 1980s was the freedom to sit with groups of twelve students. One of the difficulties I had when I moved to the teacher training college in Belfast, and then later in Carysfort, was having to deal with very large numbers and the frustration of not having a closer and more nurturing relationship with individuals. It was conveyor-belt teaching, really, dealing with crowds of people.

When you begin teaching, you are your own pupil. I learned a lot through simply having to prepare courses. I widened my knowledge; when you do lectures, you get to first principles, you get clarifications. I still come back to the image of the ripple which moves outwards but in some way is still the same ripple. It contains other things, other experiences, other ripples, but there is a concentric element to it, as there is to human growth. Within yourself there is always the little self who was there from the beginning. I suppose the purpose of the writing I have done has been to make a wholeness out of all those moves and differences, to get the first place and the ultimate place into some kind of alignment.

In 1970, Marie and myself and our two boys, who were just babies then, set out for a year in California. It was possibly the most important year of my life. Marie and I had lived in Belfast and had been married for five years. We had never lived outside Ireland and this was a great time to go to the West Coast of America, when the Beat Movement was at its height. There was a tremendous sense of glamour about Berkeley; the free speech movement had started there, Ginsberg was still in full flight over the bay. It was a kind of a world centre. Another very important thing was that, for the first time in my life, I had enough money to live on. We had a wonderful year, great refreshment of the spirit, a sense that you were learning something.

It was very important to me also at that time to meet Tom Flanagan, whose book, *The Irish Novelists, 1800–1850*, is one of the great founding texts for Irish studies in this century. Tom Flanagan is a man with an intense intellectual life who is also a great raconteur. His whole thinking is Hiberno-centric. In Queen's I had been used to academics whose thinking was always Anglo-centric; the points of reference were Shakespeare, Wordsworth, Dickens and so on. Tom's conversation and his mental universe were wide ranging, but the normative thing at the centre of it was Joyce, Yeats, the sense of Ireland. This was a wonderful thing to encounter at that point because 1970 to '71 was a very political moment in Ireland, so I count that year of re-orientation in Berkeley an important one. It wasn't an escape from Ireland; it was a re-orienting towards it. Poetically also, I got a lot out of being there. I read William Carlos Williams' poems and that influenced my third book, *Wintering Out* – little poems about my most intimate places like Broagh, Anahorish, Toome and so on. A lot of those came out of reading William Carlos Williams. I don't mean the themes came out of it, but the form – the tentative, short-lined stanzas.

> *Anahorish,* soft gradient
> of consonant, vowel-meadow,
> after-image of lamps
> swung through the yards
> on winter evenings.
> (from *Anahorish*)

After I returned from the States, in the middle of 1972, I left my job in Queen's. Berkeley had unsettled me, loosened the soil around the taproot and got us all on our way – very important. I left Belfast because of inner shifts in myself. I needed to define myself and move on as a writer in some way. When I came back from Berkeley, internment had just started and so there was a huge influx of journalists and we were all being interviewed about identity. I wrote a number of letters to people in verse. These were first of all letters written for merriment to people I knew, but then they were all put together in a sequence of poems called *Whatever You Say, Say Nothing.* The title was totally ironical of course, although some dimwits think that it means what it says.

> This morning from a dewy motorway
> I saw the new camp for the internees:
> A bomb had left a crater of fresh clay
> In the roadside, and over in the trees
>
> Machine-gun posts defined a real stockade.
> There was that white mist you get on a low ground
> And it was déjà-vu, some film made
> Of Stalag 17, a bad dream with no sound.
>
> Is there a life before death? That's chalked up
> In Ballymurphy. Competence with pain,
> Coherent miseries, a bite and sup,
> We hug our little destiny again.
> (from *Whatever You Say, Say Nothing*)

The odd thing was that there was excitement and a sense of renewal in what was happening, but there was also a sense that it was repeating and trapping us into the sectarian syndrome again.

I read Nadezhda Mandel'shtam's *Hope Against Hope* in the early 1970s and found it a book of enormous power, very high voltage, partly because of the genius of Mandel'shtam himself as reported in the text. The great thing about it was a kind of passion, a passion that wasn't evident in the English literary texts that I read as a student, or indeed as a grown-up – the sense of the life and death importance of poetry, the sense of the demands made by the art, the sense of joy also, of rejoicing in the medium of language. Also, the crisis that Mandel'shtam faced was individual verity versus party demands or commands, and no writer could fail to find an echo of that in his life here during the '70s and '80s.

So I became entirely entranced by the Mandel'shtam thing, not just because of his situation, but eventually because of the rhapsodic nature of his prose in particular. *A Conversation about Dante* is one of the great statements of the century about poetry and creativity. I suppose the situation of the Russian writer in the '20s and '30s spoke to me. Ireland is divided in all kinds of ways and that same destiny of division was felt *in extremis* by the Russians in this century and by the Poles. So I found in them something I both recognised and admired, a tone of realism, an ironical sense that you had to keep going, that nothing much was going to change, that what mattered was the stoical maintenance of valour and good taste, good conduct. There was an aesthetic demand that had to be obeyed, in spite of the fact that vulgarity was going to triumph, tyranny and mediocrity were going to prevail in public life and so on. So, in those writers there was a 'plane of regard', as Joseph Brodsky would call it, which was very attractive; there was a kind of *hauteur* and a sense of being responsible for the culture of the past. Mandel'shtam has this wonderful phrase in that conversation about Dante where he talks about the 'steadfastness of speech articulation'. I remember reading that and being reminded of my own original joy in poetry, the exultation that had come from reading Hopkins, from the jubilation of sounds, the feeling of being played like some deep instrument by the actual poem, of being moved in a bodily way. And it was salutary to be reminded of that in the '70s, because poetry had then moved from being a sensuous transport to being an intellectual crisis, it involved some sort of stress about politics and content and so on. Mandel'shtam died in Siberia, that terrifically frozen landscape, and I think of him buried under the perma-frost.

> When the deaf phonetician spread his hand
> Over the dome of a speaker's skull
> He could tell which diphthong and which vowel
> By the bone vibrating to the sound.
>
> A globe stops spinning. I set my palm
> On a contour cold as permafrost
> And imagine axle-hum and the steadfast
> Russian of Osip Mandelstam.
>
> (from *M.*)

In 1981, I was offered a five-year contract to teach one term a year at Harvard. At that stage I had been at Carysfort for six years. I was very busy and didn't have as much time for my writing as I would have liked, so I jumped at the opportunity. Harvard was a further ripple outwards.

> The globe has spun. He stands in a wooden O.
> He alludes to Shakespeare. He alludes to Graves.
> Time has bulldozed the school and school window.
> (from *Alphabets*)

Nothing is ever quite settled in any life, but in a writer's life, and a poet's life in particular, it is as if you are constantly inventing the stepping-stones to carry you to the next point. That is why writers are particularly anxious and volatile; they don't have a very firm sense of security. They live in trust that they will conjure a next move, that a new circumference will be pushed out there. But there is also a great freedom. Oddly enough, one thing that the Nobel prize has done for me is to help my devil-may-care-ness. My work has been under scrutiny for thirty years now and has in fact been over-scrutinised, so I have got used to keeping going while being inspected, if you know what I mean. What I feel now is a freedom to proceed as before and that just means being true to your impulses and personality and trying to know as much as possible, to widen out and get a new perspective on yourself.

If you pitch your voice in a key that isn't part of your original tuning, then, poetically speaking, you are in danger. On the other hand, if you just keep to the vocabulary and the possibilities of your first given voice, you are also in danger – of repetition, of confinement. Credibility in poetry is very much a matter of intonation, of voice, of tuning your first speech to the larger literary voice that you learn through reading. Keeping some kind of echo and exchange, some kind of harmony or discord, establishing a living relationship between the first given and the ultimately learned – that still seems to me to be part of the effort at wholeness and *integritas* and *consonantia* that poetry requires.

Michael D Higgins

Michael D Higgins was born in Limerick in 1941 and reared on a small farm in County Clare. He attended St Flannan's College, Ennis, and studied at University College, Galway, where he graduated in English, sociology and politics. He later studied at both Indiana and Manchester universities. He subsequently lectured in sociology and political science in University College, Galway.

A former mayor of Galway city, where he now lives, Michael D Higgins represents Galway West as a Labour Deputy in Dáil Éireann. He was Minister for Arts, Culture and the Gaeltacht in the coalition government of 1992 to 1997. He is the author of a number of articles in political science, media and literary criticism. He has published two collections of poems – The Betrayal *and* The Season of Fire. *Much of his writing and his political thinking is influenced by his own childhood and a passionate conviction that people generally should be 'open to experience and development'.*

I was born in Limerick in April 1941. I left Limerick with my brother on 15 August 1946. My father had become very ill and it was felt that my mother, whose brother had died just a month or two earlier, wouldn't have been able to handle us all at that period of time. What became a temporary removal from Limerick city to Newmarket-on-Fergus, County Clare, became a quasi-permanent move and so I lived in Newmarket-on-Fergus until I was nineteen.

> When we set out together to find
> our new home,
> I suspect
> we cared less
> for the broken heart of our mother
> who had let us go
> than for the wonder
> of the journey
> in a black Ford Eight
> through fields at twilight.
>
> It is that wonder
> that brings me back
> to the age of five,
> not any great grief
> I should have felt
> or tears I should have shed.
>
> And then, we were
> together,
> a source of curiosity,
> a legacy from tragedy
> that had given a childless pair,
> an uncle and an aunt,
> two instant children,
> brothers
> so alike
> we could be twins.
>
>   (from *Brothers*)

I remember quite clearly the black Ford 8 car. Its registration was IE 3283. It had been bought by an aunt of mine who was a nurse and during the war it had been stored in a shed and kept in perfect condition. I remember being driven to the house in Newmarket-on-Fergus. It was a very interesting arrangement, because my father and his brother and sister had been involved in the War of Independence, and, in the Civil War, my father had been on the republican side and my uncle on the 'Free State' side and my aunt was in the middle as an ex-Cumann na mBan member. Both my uncle and aunt were unmarried and they had acquired two instant children. I was reared effectively by my aunt and uncle, with intermittent visits by us to Limerick city when it was possible, until the age of about thirteen when we were all reunited briefly again in County Clare. Then there was a kind of a scattering, with my sisters going to England and my brother and myself being educated at St Flannan's College in Ennis.

That parting was a tough decision for my mother and I was very influenced by it all my life. She had been reared in Liscarroll, County Cork, living over a shop and going away to secondary school. It was a quiet life with aspirations towards respectability and then there was the development of these aspirations in the early days of her life with my father in Limerick. My father's business collapsed and then came the encounter with poverty.

> She stood straight then, and, in a long leather coat,
> After her mother died she packed her case
> Left and joined him a full decade after
> The Civil War. And she had loved him
> In her way. Even when old Binchy placed a note
> Behind the counter in his shop
> In Charleville that when all this blackguardism
> Was over, there would be no jobs
> For Republicans in his firm, or anywhere else,
> For that matter.

Now bent and leaning towards the fire,
With blackened fingers holding the tongs,
She pokes the coals; and we knew
It best to leave her with her sorrow
For her lost life, the house she'd lost,
The anxious days and nights,
And all that might have been.

We ran outside and brought in turf
And did our lessons and vowed that we would listen
To what she said, of cities where always
There were voices for company, and churches
Close by, if never cheap.
We would listen to her story
And vow that, for her at least,
We, her children, would escape.
                              (from *Dark Memories*)

One of the most powerful things I learned much later was
that education wasn't just a series of years succeeding each
other – primary, secondary, third level, teaching or whatever.
I have spent my whole life learning from people, listening to
people, often very broken people and people with
extraordinary stories, not necessarily stories of success. There
is in the line, 'All that might have been', a sense of loss and a
sense of urgency, too; that you have one shot at life and that
maybe opportunities have passed. I know that my mother's
aspirations were for those respectable things, for a house, for
simple things, and that tells you something about her. I am
not interested in judging as to whether this was a form of
quiet snobbery, a desire for security, or a result of her
upbringing. It is more important to say that this was her story,
and I am interested in the democratic right of everyone to
have their story told. That is what makes me write poetry. In
that poem, when I said 'we did our lessons', I deliberately used

that phrase because it is the one I find buried in my own memory. Education was less about releasing anything in yourself than about getting these things done, but I had the extraordinary fortune of having a marvellous holistic primary teacher in a two-teacher school in Newmarket-on-Fergus, a man by the name of William Clune.

He defeated time because he was going back as well as forward. He knew the names of plants and bushes in Latin and Irish and English and, on sunny days, he used to take the whole school to the top of a hill to show them the history of the local area. He had an integrated approach to everything before that word was invented. He was a man with an extraordinary sense of history in his own life too, because his brother was Conor Clune, the Volunteer who had been shot just before the founding of the State.

He was a man who loved the wonder of children and he had some extraordinary ideas, which I am sure couldn't be proved. He had an idea, for example, that, if you tried hard enough and used your concentration, you could go back through not only your own memory but other people's memories to remember an Irish word. He was a Jungian. Everything that I was later to encounter about Jung and consciousness, he was in fact practising in his own way in the school yard. There was not one person who came into his school yard from any background, with shoes or without, who wasn't respected as a carrier of wonderment. It was the central value of his pedagogic technique.

We all went barefooted to school at that time, not because we didn't have shoes or boots but because that was what was done. It was before tarmacadam and I remember the sensation of the chippings on your feet as much as I remember the beet dropping off the backs of lorries, beet which we would then eat.

What I don't like is people romanticising these enriching physical sensations to the exclusion of the social side of things. I know the experience of grass between your toes and I know that a fern will cut you and I know where butterflies gather and I know about mosses. I can remember all these sensations very clearly, but I also remember when my aunt and uncle's house was caving in and youngsters going past the house saying 'We haven't broken windows in our house' and firing stones at the old couple and their nephews who were living inside. I remember the quiet cruelty of it and it is dishonest of people to take the quietness and richness and complexity of natural settings and use them as a mask for the cruel social divisions that prevailed in rural Ireland. I was very glad to escape from that poverty. It was only after a lot of healing that I was able to reach back through these memories and rediscover again the colour and sensation of a fern or moss or a grass. I really do not have much time for people who try to perpetuate a kind of pastoral nonsense about rural Ireland.

By the time I was able to relate to him, my father had been terribly wounded by life. He was a person who believed in a republic in this country. All his energy had been used up before I could know him. He had slept under reeks of turf and in dug-outs and he had developed a very bad bronchitis problem. He was on the run in the War of Independence; he was on the run again in the Civil War and had been arrested. He was unemployable; people didn't speak to him when he came home from the Curragh to Newmarket-on-Fergus. He started his business and was successful. What I got from him was a sense of how right it is for people to have both a dream and the courage to hold on to it, even at a price.

My mother was very different. She loved books and, on our visits to and fro, I read everything she had. I remember going through all the Annie P Smithson books and I got a love of learning from all of that. It has been my great love since about the age of twelve.

My mother played the violin, but I have no training in music and I have regretted that all my life. Even if you could get access, you have all these intangible barriers, like bogus critical categories, standing between you and the love of life and the world. Much I have encountered in criticism is of little value and yet, at the same time, when a great critic illuminates something I am so grateful that I could almost weep for his insight.

My uncle and aunt dedicated themselves totally to us. There was nothing they wouldn't have done for us, but they had difficulty explaining why we had come to them. I found it very hard as a youngster to deal with the illness of my uncle, who was bedridden. I looked after him a great deal and I often think about how insensitive very small children are to the needs of people in that situation. It was a one-room slated, two-room thatched house with no toilet and no running water. I am sure that if an Irish God had created the world he wouldn't have invented woman with a bucket at the end of each arm. My aunt was one of the women for whom electricity came too late to straighten their backs. Life was very hard for my aunt, less so for my uncle I think. In my book, *The Season of Fire*, I have a poem called 'Katie's Song' in which I give her the affection that I feel I should have given her then.

> Oh Katie, I remember
> when your writing carried a flourish
> and the lightness returned
> to your fingers
> as you smiled the magic
> on the schoolbooks you covered,
> satcheled ambassadors
> twixt home and school,
> our steps to the future.
> Your fantasy
> compensation
> for a life
> of lesser things.

Oh Katie, I would sing your song
if now I could recover
more
than your moments
of intimacy
and fantasy,
two threads that did not make
alone
the garment of your life.

On a sometime Sunday,
I recall
your playing with magic words.
You dressed yourself
with such unusual care
that the violence of my question
as to where you might be going
did not dislodge you from your dream.
You were not going to any haggard
that afternoon.
You were, instead, intent on strolling
in a pleasure garden
and you told us you had an appointment.
We, whose thoughtless demands
defined
your every action,
could not understand.

And, when you died,
after calling us for an hour,
your summons from the fields
not heeded
not perceived,
your anxious tones
faded,

alone,
at a distance
from children not your own
moved to an unbearable anxiety.

Oh Katie, I am making my way
along a lane of hazel.
I am stretching
for the fire of the senses
that will bring me back
to where I can stand still and shiver
and weep
at all the love
you earned
never paid
by a child afraid,
in iceberg times,
to throw his arms around
the plump frame
of the maker
of his bread
and magic.

(from *Katie's Song*)

I went to St Flannan's secondary school in 1955. We were all escaping. The teacher's children were heading for teachers' jobs, more were heading for the civil service and an odd one or two were heading for third level. There was a sense that you were on your way to someplace and you were grateful for it. The great aspiration within the institution was that it had been placed on this earth for three things: *one* to win the Harty Cup, *two* to win the gold medal in Greek and *three* to send priests to the diocese. These three great reasons for existence in the world tended to inform everything. As well as that, there were the usual single-sex brutalities and cruelties.

I met the odd wonderful individual teacher. There was a Canon Maxwell, who, if he hadn't given his life to the Church, would have been in the Royal Shakespeare Company. When he was teaching Shakespeare, he would act out all the parts – he was Iago one minute and Bassanio the next. There was another man, called Martin Kirwan, who loved English poetry as much as he despised Irish poetry, but even in his prejudices he was enthusiastic. However, there are subjects in which I was literally impaired, and I really think that this is a problem that must be addressed. If someone is not successful as a communicator of information, which teaching requires, we should find a different opportunity for that person within the education system. It is very wrong to leave such a person in the classroom year after year. Despite all that, I got over ninety per cent in seven subjects in the Leaving Certificate – 'a great Leaving', as they would say . . .

My brother and I worked in factories in Shannon and then there were different offers, culminating in the ESB in Galway. I remember going out on the road and getting a lift and asking where Newtownsmith was. I was a Grade 8 clerk there for six pounds, fourteen and twopence a week, paying three pounds ten for digs, living madly out of the rest of it and still sending some money home. I made my way through university and studied commerce and economics for one degree and English literature and language and sociology for another. I studied at Indiana University and Manchester University and then I came home and began teaching at third level.

I am pre-grant and pre-milking machine and that explains a lot about my life! I have enjoyed teaching, in terms of the communicating, but I have hated structures. I dislike the idea that we are 'processing' large numbers of people through the system. I feel wrecked as an educator and as a teacher by what is happening at the present time – the pressure, the strain – and for what? I feel violated by the suggestion that all of what I believe in about education should be thrown aside so that the transitory requirements of industry should be forced onto the educational process. I think it is an example of fatalistic and inferior thinking.

What influenced my choice to go into politics more than anything I read was the waste of humanity that accrues from stopping people from developing their potential. Nobody should have to struggle so hard for an education. Nobody should be without proper housing. Women's lives should not be shortened by poverty and need. There could be a marvellous humanistic endeavour around all the practical subjects in which I did my postgraduate work. I lectured in monetary economics for a while but I never believed that all the people for whom my father struggled to have independence existed for monetary economics, but that monetary economics was a technique that existed within economics to serve a social purpose. I met Dr Noel Browne in 1967 and I heard him give a talk in Galway. He spoke about the importance of those people who had had training giving back to society. I object to people saying you should have an amnesia about where you came from so that you can get on with your own personal mobility. We are supposed to wipe out all of what we have been trained to see and we are supposed to have some kind of vulgar individualism, but some of us see that as something people liberated themselves from in the eighteenth century.

At the age of fifty-one, I feel that my education is just beginning. I am beginning to see ranges in language that I didn't see before. I am re-reading existentialist literature. In these tough times, I regard it as very challenging to live within categories of constructive pessimism. We may need to paint with the colour black for a while before we earn the right to use the rich colours. I had no opportunity to study physics, yet I love debates about relativity and time. I get excited about new discoveries in biology. I would love to have several lives to pursue these things.

I can truthfully say that there are about a dozen books that have influenced me in my life, but there are so many *people*. I have been very lucky to meet people in different parts of the world – people who have been not only towers of strength in themselves but great sources of strength to other people. I think that my entire life was changed by my wife, Sabina Coyne, my partner, whose commitment to the Stanislavsky technique in her acting formation made for me a connection to the power of reflection, meditation and awareness. It was from her I heard for the first time the phrase, 'sense memory'.

I feel it is a very partial achievement to use the past to defeat the present. I remember when I was teaching sociology, looking at the Lenten pastorals of the old days and of the new days, one of the things that they had in common was the sense that, if you could march yourself out of the present and into the past, from the city into the rural areas and from industry into the farm, you would be in a kind of a golden age. I feel that I owe it to this alleged golden age to describe it as it was, with all its humanity, because it is the complexity of our humanity that is important.

The magical thing about being alive is the fact that you can weep as well as laugh, and there has been such little space for weeping and healing in Ireland. It is such a nonsense to say, 'I had a wonderful childhood'. Life is complex and I think that people should be able to release both the joy and the sadness that is in them, expressing the dark side as well as the bright side of themselves. I would be horrified to meet a street full of orthodontically cheerful people. I would say, 'Let me get a bus, quick . . .'

> You were better at all these
> practical tests
> of strength
> and judgment, too.
> For me, the image of escape
> distracted
> from the tasks of place.

The books I loved
were instruments
for the breaking of the bars
and a run
towards the light
and a new life
back
in the city.

At times, on the bar of a bike,
I vowed
to bring you
where I presumed
you wished to go.
It was through pain
I realised
that our journeys
would be separate,
alone,
requiring different skills.

And I sought my brother
in a hundred others
for whom
my heart warmed
at shared
hopes
and fears.

Every embrace a compensation
for the lost moments
of feelings
buried beneath
the boulders
of other expectations
of duty
and respectability,

of fear
and dust
and sweat
and a life reduced
to rehearsal
for the decency in depth
that was the legacy
of our family.

Back from the tomb,
Christ saw brothers
everywhere.
The stone rolled back,
he never returned
home
but embraced every stranger,
brothers all
in the light
out of the dark.
                    (from *Brothers*)

John Hume

John Hume was born in Derry in 1937, the first of the seven children of a shipyard worker who became permanently unemployed at the end of the war. He grew up through a period of extreme poverty and religious discrimination and the consequent struggle for survival was to have a major influence on his subsequent career.

John's generation was the first to benefit under the Butler Education Act, which enabled him to attend St Columb's College in Derry. He later went into Maynooth College to become a priest, but then decided he had not got a vocation and turned to teaching. All through his early years, he was particularly attracted to the notion of self-help and became strongly involved in the Credit Union and Voluntary Housing movements. The latter movement drew him into civil rights protests and ultimately into politics. He was elected as an independent MP in 1969 and eventually joined with others in founding the Social Democratic and Labour Party, of which he is currently the leader.

A tireless worker for justice and rights, which had been denied to Catholics for generations – 'people are more important than territory' – John Hume has also been to the fore in the quest for a peaceful solution to Northern Ireland's 'troubles' and was one of the principal architects of the IRA ceasefires in 1994 and 1997. He is also a member of the European Parliament and is strongly committed to the European ideal.

My first memories are of living in a single room with my mother, father, brother and sister until I was five years old, because the housing situation in Derry was appalling. From then on we lived in a two-bedroomed house – and I was the eldest of seven children. During the war, my father worked in the shipyard and, when the war ended, my father was out of work. I was eight years old and he never worked again. He was unemployed for twenty years when we were all growing up. Looking back, I wonder how my mother succeeded in rearing us. It is only in later life that you realise how extreme the poverty was and the sacrifices that were made, by my mother in particular.

I grew up in Glenbrook Terrace, which, at that time, was on the outskirts of the city on the road to Donegal. Out the road from us was what we called Springtown Camp, where the American navy was based during the war. When they left, the housing problem in Derry was so bad that people squatted there and it became a tin-town. It was only in later years, when we transformed the housing in Derry, that we were able to get rid of places like that. Housing has always been very central to me in my public life, because, when I came back from university, I got heavily involved with self-help groups and in the founding of the Credit Union. We set up our own very successful association for building new houses and, in my first election manifesto, I sought a mandate to take housing away from local government and give it to a central housing authority. Fortunately, Jim Callaghan, who was then the British Home Secretary, listened to me and he set up the Northern Ireland Housing Executive and, if you look at housing in Derry today, or anywhere in the North, it has been transformed – there is not a slum in our entire city.

I believe that all planning for housing should be done on a neighbourhood basis, because, in the neighbourhood that I grew up in, despite the fact that everybody was very poor, there was total law and order. There was total respect, because, if you stepped out of line in any way, you were taken by the scruff of the neck by your neighbour to your father. There was a certain pride in maintaining the house and the home, unlike these high-rise flats where nobody owns the common ground. The planners of the '60s have an awful lot to answer for in having built all these high-rise places. I think it is a major cause of urban violence today. The whole neighbourhood thing also gives you a sense of community, and that is a hugely important factor in growing up.

There was a burn – a small stream – at the end of our street. We used to build dams and swim in it. We went into the field and played football and cricket, because it was a mixed district as well. In our street there were three Protestant families and we were all extremely friendly. There was no question of any differences between us at all and, in fact, those families are friends to this very day. Other streets in the district would have been totally Protestant or totally Catholic and one became very aware of that. I used to be amazed when the twelfth of July or the twelfth of August came around – the marching season – and tension immediately entered the community. I remember going through one of the streets as a child and being stuck up against a wall by a young Protestant who, throughout the rest of the year, I played football with, but this week I was a papist. In those days, nobody had radios or televisions and the world you lived in consisted of your neighbourhood and your neighbours. The first time I left Derry, I was fourteen years old and I went to an All-Ireland final in Dublin.

You take your first steps away from your home or your neighbourhood when you go to school and I regard the first teacher I had as highly influential in my life. Her name was Mary Anne Coyle. She didn't just teach us, she got to know us; who we were, where we came from, who our family were. In other words, she understood the pressures on children, as well as teaching us to read and write, and that is a very important element of education. I was a teacher myself and I had learned from her that it wasn't enough just to teach the people in your class. It is also important to know them and know where they come from and what kind of pressures they are under, because then you have a better understanding and can teach them better.

I had a father who kept telling me the only way forward was with the books. I was very, very lucky that I was eleven in the very first year of the 'eleven plus' examination, which, for the first time, gave free education to everybody in the North. I was the first of my family to go to secondary school and, after that, I got a university scholarship. The eleven plus led to a huge increase in the size of St Columb's College and we were the first generation to go there, so we were a pioneering generation in that sense. It is a school I look back to with a lot of pride. It has a fantastic record of achievement. In my own time, the school produced Brian Friel, Seamus Deane and Phil Coulter, to name just three major figures in the literary and musical world. That says a lot for the nature of the school itself, without taking away from the genius and talent of those three people.

My father had beautiful copperplate handwriting and he was a highly intelligent man. A lot of people in the district used to come to him to write their letters for them, or to write letters to the local authority, so, from a very early age, as we didn't have a very big house, I was conscious of people and their problems. We had two bedrooms, one living-room and a parlour and people would queue up waiting for my father as he sat writing at the table. He was very committed to helping people solve their problems, because he had a very good knowledge of the whole system.

Without the dedication and self-sacrifice of my mother, I don't think I would have got anywhere in life. She was totally committed to rearing us in the best possible way, with very, very limited resources, and when I look back I just don't know how she did it. I am absolutely convinced that the major influence on any life is the parents and that this takes place in the early years of a child. Even though usually buried in the subconscious, these are the forces that create you and make you what you are and give you your attitude to life.

When I think back on those early days, I can see the roots of a lot of the things I later became involved in. I was founder of the first Credit Union in the North – in Derry – at the age of twenty-three. I learned about credit from my mother having to borrow to rear us and repay at a high rate. I remember thinking that, if she and her sisters got together every couple of weeks and pooled their money, they would have enough to go out, instead of this borrowing. When I discovered that these organisations existed, a group of us got together and set up our own Credit Union and had our first meeting with £5 1s 9d. Today, there are fourteen thousand members in that Credit Union branch and it has a brand new building and nine million pounds in savings. I became national president of the Credit Union movement when I was twenty-seven years old and I was president for four or five years. It is the most powerful co-operative in the history of Ireland and, if I did nothing else in my life, I would be very happy with that. It is the ordinary working people's own bank and it functions by pooling their resources.

I went to Maynooth to be a priest and spent three very formative years there. I had a French teacher there who spoke French to me all the time and French has become a major influence in my life. My history teacher was Father Tomás Ó Fiaich, later Cardinal Ó Fiaich, who really inspired his class with his lectures. When I left Maynooth and did a master's in history on the social and economic growth of Derry in the nineteenth century, he was my supervisor. Another major influence on me was Professor Dermot O'Donoghue. He taught logic and I took an enormous interest in that subject.

I have always taken life seriously. I used to think a lot when I was in Maynooth and I came to the conclusion that the priesthood wasn't for me. I decided to leave, but I was also taken ill at the time and spent a period of time in hospital, missing my final exams as a result. I took them a year later and, in the intervening year, I took a temporary teaching post in Derry. When I got my degree, I started teaching in Strabane. I taught French and history there for five years and then moved back to teach in St Columb's College for another five years.

In 1967, I left teaching and set up in business. We have the biggest salmon rivers in Western Europe, salmon which was sent away to be processed and then sent back to us. Michael Canavan said to me, 'If you can learn how to smoke salmon, I'll set up a company and you can run it.' So, I did this and it is now a very successful business, although, when I was elected into politics two years later, I ran down my involvement in the business because I don't believe that a politician should have business interests of any description.

There is absolutely no way that I could have done what I have done without my wife, Pat. I don't know how she coped with the pressures of it all, but she has done so very well. She is a major part of everything I do. In the '70s, for example, when Stormont fell, those of us who stayed in politics in order to provide continued representation – we described ourselves as constituency representatives holding on to the mandate of the fallen assemblies – received no wages at all, even though we were working as full-time politicians. In those years, the only income we had was Pat's wage as a teacher. Later on, when I was elected to the European Parliament, I asked her to give up teaching and run my office. That was one of the wisest decisions I've ever taken, because she is totally involved in everything I do. When I'm abroad or in parliament, the service continues in my office, Monday to Friday, led by Pat. Most of the people in my constituency know her better than they know me, for that very reason.

I was involved in civil rights in the early days, because I was heavily involved in the voluntary housing movement. The local Derry Corporation was a prime example of injustice in Northern Ireland. It was the worst case of gerrymandering, but, to make that work, they needed to control voting rights, housing rights and job rights. They controlled voting through housing – they built ghettos to house Catholics only – and when, in the early '60s, the Catholic ward in Derry was full, they built high-rise flats and, when they were full, they stopped building altogether, because they wouldn't put people into other districts in case it affected the voting balance. This put enormous pressure on the housing front and, when I was chairman of the voluntary housing board, we sought to build our own houses. However, the Corporation refused planning permission, because we would be building in the wrong area, and that was one of the major factors that brought me onto the streets in the civil rights movement.

It is often forgotten that, after three weeks of civil rights protests in Derry, Derry Corporation fell. Here was an unjust system that had lasted seventy years and, in three weeks, without throwing a stone, we brought it down and started the whole process of change. That brought me into politics and in my first election, in 1969, I stood as an independent and sought a mandate to found a political party based on social democratic principles. Even at that early stage, I was very conscious of what was going on in Europe and elsewhere. Social democracy, to me, was where I had came from and what I was all about.

After the election, we set up the Social Democratic and Labour Party. I wanted to call it the Social Democratic Party, but some of my colleagues wanted to include the word Labour and I had no objection to that. The SDLP was born, literally, out of the civil rights movement and out of the need to create a new organised approach to politics.

One of the major factors which brought success to the civil rights movement was the media, because, when we were being attacked on the streets by the police, among others, our message to our supporters on the street was, 'Do not retaliate. Let the world see who the real aggressor is.' We were marching for simple rights, like one-person-one-vote, fair housing and fair jobs. Those television images put massive pressure on the British government of the day, which had always held back from the Northern Ireland problem. Derry now has the best housing in the whole of Western Europe, because of the existence of the housing executive, which arose directly out of the civil rights movement and the foundation of the SDLP.

One of my first political lessons was learned from my father when I was a child. He took me to a nationalist meeting, where they were waving the tricolour and whipping up emotions. My father put his hand on my shoulder and said, 'Listen son, you see all that there.' I said, 'Yes, Daddy.' He said, 'Just you remember one thing. You can never eat a flag.' He was dead right, because politics should never be about emotionalism, and one of the great weaknesses of traditional nationalism – and it's still very strong with the Provisionals – is that it is all emotionalism and a sense of superiority, of looking down on people who are not as nationalist as you are. In problem situations, people are more important than territory for a start. The first priorities are bread on the table and a roof over the head, so employment and housing are key factors. Education, health, all the things that make life better for people – these are what politics is supposed to be about. In tackling our deeper political problem of a divided people, there has to be a planned approach and not a flag-waving approach.

Growing up in the '60s, the most impressive world leader that emerged was John F Kennedy. He was an inspirational leader and a lot of his sayings have stuck in our memories. 'Ask not what your country can do for you, but what you can do for your country.' In other words, patriotism is about spilling your sweat and building your country. Other sayings of his which remain with me are, 'One man can make a difference' and 'Every man should try'. Another person who strongly influenced me, and I quote him regularly in my speeches and articles, was Martin Luther King, the leader of the civil rights movement in the United States. His commitment and doctrine of non-violence as a positive thing was a very major influence on my own thinking.

I grew up in a walled city. Derry has still got the oldest walls anywhere in Europe. I have used walls a lot in getting my message across to people. Shortly after the Berlin wall fell, I was speaking in the Reichstag there and I thought of the Europe of fifty years ago. In the middle of my speech, I presented Willy Brandt with a piece of a wall, and you could see the astonishment in the room. I said 'It is not a piece of the Berlin wall, it is a piece of one of the Belfast walls – the last walls left in Europe.' These thirteen walls in Belfast, the highest church-going city in western Europe, built to protect one section of a Christian people from another, are an indictment of all of us. However, it was our past attitudes that built them and they are therefore a challenge to all of us – unionists, nationalists, British – to re-examine those past attitudes in depth, if we are to bring down those walls and solve the Irish problem.

At the end of the day, the lesson we have to learn is that every society in the world that is peaceful, stable and united is that way because it accepts its diversity. As we move into a new Europe, I hope people in Ireland will remember that European union is based on the acceptance of diversity and that, the day it stops respecting the diversity of its people, it will cease to be united.

Maeve Kelly

Maeve Kelly was born in Ennis, County Clare, in 1930 and educated in Dundalk, County Louth, where her family moved when she was six years old. She trained as a nurse in London and later did postgraduate work at Oxford. A voracious reader from her childhood days, Maeve was concerned that the women she read about did not represent the women she knew. She began to write herself and won the Hennessy Award for her short story, A Life of Her Own, *which was subsequently published in a volume of short stories with that title. Many of those stories were republished in a later volume –* Orange Horses. *Maeve has also published three novels,* Necessary Treasons, Florrie's Girls *and* Alice in Thunderland, *the latter being a satirical look at male-dominated society. She has also published a collection of poetry –* Resolution *– and she wrote a lot of poetry out of grief when her daughter was tragically killed in a road accident.*

Maeve now lives with her farmer husband in Limerick, where she has become very involved with various women's and social organisations. She has been particularly interested in the cause of abused women and was appointed administrator of a women's refuge in Limerick.

I was born in Ennis, County Clare, and spent almost six years there. I had two older sisters and two brothers who were younger than me. My father was from Dundalk and he decided that he wanted to go back there. One spring, he hired a taxi and – I presume all our worldly goods were sent on ahead – we travelled across Ireland from Ennis up to Dublin and on up to Dundalk and rented a furnished house there until we got a house of our own some months later.

My mother knew we were going to move, so she thought it wouldn't be worthwhile sending me to school in Ennis. At the time I was interested in words and reading, but I think she reckoned that I was getting enough at home. One of my early memories is of tugging her apron strings as she was standing at a sink, showing her one of my sister's copybooks and asking her the meanings of the words. She would take us for walks and she always told us stories as we walked. She was absolutely wonderful.

My father was a great man for reciting long poems, like *The Green Eye of the Little Yellow God*. He had been interested in amateur dramatics when he was young. My grandmother died when I was eighteen, so I knew her quite well. We used to travel over from Dundalk to Connemara on holidays and that was a great experience, just to see the landscape. My mother loved Connemara and she passed that love on to us. When we got to Oughterard and approached the Twelve Bens, it was like entering a magic country. It was one of the great treats of our young lives and I suppose that it had an influence on me.

I didn't like national school in Dundalk. It was a huge grey building and it had a large number of children attending. It was a very mixed school and was pretty rough. I don't know that I learned an awful lot there. I enjoyed secondary school. We had some good teachers. The principal was a scholarly nun and she used to teach us Latin. She used to take classes out in the yard in the fine weather and we would all sit around underneath a chestnut tree in the yard while we were doing our Virgil.

We had a very good English teacher, Sister de Sales. It was from her that I developed an interest in English literature. She taught me the value of good writing. She would always say, 'Maeve has style.' I used to keep diaries and I can see that there was a very definite change in them in that particular period, a particular style was emerging and she obviously picked that up.

When I was thirteen, I got a serious illness and was in bed for five months. I read everything that was in the house, including the Bible and poetry. I found poetry very boring in the beginning, but I was desperate, so I read any poetry books we had in the house. I had an aunt who sent me the collected works of Dickens in bundles of three or four in the post to keep me occupied.

After secondary school, I started going to art classes, but I thought it would be good for me to do nursing. I thought that it would toughen me up and improve my moral fibre, because I had been very scared of hospitals. I hated them and hated the smell of them. My parents weren't keen and they tried to stop me, but when I was twenty-one I said I was going anyway and I went and trained as a nurse in London. In some ways it was good for me, but I knew from the beginning that it wasn't the way I wanted to spend my life.

I didn't like the hospital routine and I didn't like the hierarchical structure of hospitals. I didn't think that nurses were given due recognition for their work. Before we went into the main hospital, we used to do three months' preliminary training in a small unit in Hampstead. There we learned basic anatomy and physiology and how to make beds and do simple dressings. Then, one day a week, we would go up to the hospital and on one of those days I was assigned to look after an old man who was dying. I had never seen anybody die before. That was my first experience of death, without any preparation at all. I don't think that young people should be put into that kind of situation.

My experience as a nurse ultimately influenced my writing. I wouldn't write in the traditional way about nursing – I would have rather a black view of it. I have a great admiration for nurses, but it is the system that I send up and I certainly did so in one of the stories in the collection, *Morning at my Window*. It is a monologue where a nurse is describing her day in a hospital. There is another look at nursing in the novel, *Florrie's Girls*, which is a funny book as well.

I finished my SRN and spent some time running a children's ward in the hospital and then I came home. I worked for a while in what is now St Camillus' Hospital in Limerick, because at the time my family had moved to Limerick. Then I went back to England to do a theatre course in Oxford and while I was over there I had to go in to a sanatorium with TB. It sounds odd, but in actual fact it was quite a pleasant experience. I was glad to be resting, because one of the effects of tuberculosis is a feeling of lethargy, so it was quite nice once I got over the initial despair of thinking that I was going die. I was reading Arthur Koestler, Chaucer – anything I could lay my hands on. I relied on people to bring me in books, because we had no library there.

I always kept a journal. I wrote from when I was very young through all my growing years and I would also write long letters to my friends and my family. I loved writing. It was just another part of my life. I never saw it as being a career or something that I would make money from.

Eventually, after leaving the sanatorium, I came back to Limerick and married a farmer. I was perfectly happy, even though it was tough at times. I wrote my first pieces for the *Farmers' Journal.* I think I had been reading something in it and thought I could do better. I was reading short stories in the *Irish Press* New Irish Writing page and I saw an advertisement for a competition for the Irish PEN. It seemed to me that something needed to be said about Irish life and about Irish women and it wasn't being said in any of the stuff I had been reading myself. I wasn't a great short story reader, but I had read a collection of Irish short stories which was published some time in the early '60s and had only one story by a woman in it, and that was

Mary Lavin. I just noticed the gap and I wanted to fill that gap. Women hardly featured in what I was reading and even when they did feature it was as if they weren't real characters at all. The women I met in my daily life were real people with great humour and strength of character. I wanted to write about ordinary women who had qualities of character that didn't seem to be portrayed by men.

Ultimately, I became involved with the women's movement. I had strong feelings about the way women were discriminated against in law and in society and in particular the way married women seemed to lose all rights when they got married. It was as if, by handing over your name, you handed over your whole person. This was certainly the view of the Church and I was very resistant to it. Married women lost their status and they lost even more status when, having been married, they were deserted. There was a real stigma attached to deserted wives at the time and that was why we started a group to help deserted wives in Limerick.

Initially, my friends used to laugh at me, because I would ask questions and I would reject the stereotyped view of women. When I met up with a group of women who were of like mind, I thought it was wonderful. At that time, I had been reading Simone de Beauvoir. She was the first and I would say the most important of all the feminist writers. At the time we didn't use the word 'feminist'. She made me realise that what I had been thinking was right, but she put a structure on it and slotted it into a historical perspective, so that I could see how this situation had arisen. It is the case, even today, that women who have really strong views on women's rights are still in the minority, because it is painful for both men and women to have to re-examine something as fundamental as how men and women view one another.

There was a tremendous dynamism about the women's movement in the early '70s. We were in the middle of a process of change – all of us in the women's movement were actually changing history. We would swap ideas, would argue, would disagree, and would have long arguments about what our priorities should be. Some women didn't want to be called feminists, some women were afraid of not being considered 'feminine', but the real debate was whether one should get involved in practical work, like changing or reforming, or whether one should go into something more radical, like politics.

Eventually, I took the more practical way. I agreed to be committed to helping battered wives, because not only are you helping somebody to a safe place or rescuing somebody from a situation of suffering and danger but you are also changing society. You are saying that it is not proper for men to beat women, it is not proper that women should be raped and that they should be dragged through the courts. There was a need to change the law in its attitude towards abused women and women who are the victims of rape. We were lobbying, with other groups, for changes in the law. We were looking for free legal aid, we were lobbying politicians to introduce family law in Ireland, because there was no such thing at the time. There was a famous court case in Cork that made me nail my colours to the mast. That was the case of criminal conversation which was taken against a woman's lover by the woman's husband. He got compensation for the loss of her company in society and the judge in his summing said that, in Irish law, a woman is her husband's chattel, like a horse or a cow . . .

The experience of meeting abused women in the shelter has been a major influence on my life. I was forty-one and it made me look at life in a different way. It was terribly painful. I always believed that human nature was intrinsically good. I had always had a very optimistic view of life, but for a number of years then I began to believe that human nature was in fact intrinsically bad, because I couldn't come to terms with the kind of abuse that these women suffered. It also made me look at men in a different way. I became much more sceptical of men and less accepting of them. In order to come to terms with that, I had to read a lot and I still read any feminist writers that I think will throw light on what is happening. I suspect it has a lot to do with people who have power being able to abuse people who have no power. There is something even more fundamental underneath it as well. Many men have a fear of women and a fear of women's power over reproduction and I would agree with the feminists who say that this is at the core of a lot of violence against women.

These are questions that men have to ask themselves sooner or later and, fortunately, men are asking those questions today, but they wouldn't have asked them without the women's movement. Certainly, the education of boys until recent times in Ireland left a lot to be desired. They were trained to be suspicious of girls and they had no understanding of sexuality at all. It was loaded with guilt and sin and that must have had a very damaging effect on them and, ultimately, on the women they married. I have always felt that, whatever else about our education with the nuns, we didn't have this sense of guilt. Things were simply not talked about. We were totally ignorant, but in a sense that was its own safeguard, because we were saved the terror of guilt associated with sex.

Some of this thinking began to find expression in my own writing. I was accused of being a propagandist in one of my novels – *Necessary Treasons* – but what I had attempted to do in that book was demonstrate the difficulties of a young woman coming to terms with the women's movement and the confusion and the ignorance that people have to face when they are trying to understand. I would regard my short stories as being, in a way, slightly subversive. On the surface they are stories about rural women and pastoral life, but they are saying something else at the same time. A lot of women who have read them have certainly picked that up, so, in a subtle way, my views filter through.

Everything has an effect on you. I have been married for thirty-three years. I suppose I learned tolerance from my husband. He would always be inclined to see two sides of a story, while I would be inclined to see the one side, so that was a useful balance. One's children teach you an awful lot. You learn more from your children than you teach them as they are growing up. When you stop learning, you grow old. I don't intend to grow old for a long time, but I am amazed at how much I am still learning. I learn a lot from the women I work with in the refuge – the women who are on the staff as well as the women who are residents there. I learn from the residents how it is possible to overcome what seem to be the most difficult of life experiences and come out at the other end. It is a long slow process, but I am continually amazed at the way women can come through it and change and take up life again in a different way, after going through experiences that would kill many another person.

In my early life, the Church had a powerful influence on me. I was very religious when I was young. There was a small Redemptorist church in Dundalk, a very pretty church set in lovely grounds, and every day, on my way home from school, I would go in and meditate, because it was so peaceful. I loved religious ritual too – high Mass, benediction – I loved all that ritual, the beautiful vestments, the candles and the flowers. I think it was our substitute for theatre. I am not too sure what kind of a mark religion has left on me. Christian education leaves one with some kind of a commitment to service and it is very hard to shake that off. I am quite sure that the kind of work that I am doing now owes a lot to my early Christian education. I couldn't deny that, but I don't believe in the religion itself anymore.

Again, I found the way the Church treated women totally unacceptable – it had no place for us in its structure. There were certain rules laid down for us and we were expected to play by those. Although Church men would say women have a special place, they are very careful to make sure that that place is not, for instance, to be a woman pope or a woman bishop –

anywhere where the power lies. Women would certainly change the Church if they were involved at that level. Then there is the Church's emphasis on married women having to stay at home, having to be the ones who make the sacrifices when it comes to raising children, its attitude to contraception and divorce; I find all that extremely repressive. One day, I was at Mass here in Limerick and a priest was preaching about vanity in life in general and to illustrate his point he spoke about the vanity of a middle-aged woman going to the mirror and using make-up. I looked up at him – he was a very handsome man with about twelve inches of lace on a beautiful starched white surplice and the hair beautifully done – and I thought, he didn't do that without a mirror this morning and some woman probably made the lace on the surplice . . .

I don't think that one's essential self changes at all, although, as you come towards the end of your life, you may begin to regress to the simpler stages of your early childhood. It is not so much that you come into a second childhood but that you get rid of all the dross that you have accumulated along the way and become simpler. I hope that is what is going to happen to me – that I will get simpler as I get older. I don't think I have changed an awful lot, but I think I am more tolerant. I don't get as angry as I used to and I wouldn't be so quick to take up the cudgels for a cause anymore. Maybe that is my husband's influence, but I definitely see the other side more than I used to. My father was a man who believed in standing up for what was right and my mother was a woman who believed in keeping the peace, so they were quite a good mix. Maybe, in my latter years, I am becoming a bit like both of them.

Brendan Kennelly

Brendan Kennelly was born in Ballylongford in County Kerry in 1936. He was educated locally and was fortunate to come under the influence of an inspirational teacher, Jane Agnes McKenna. He came to Dublin to work with the Electricity Supply Board but soon discovered that writing and the study of the English language were his real vocations in life. He pursued that study in Trinity College, Dublin, and went on to lecture there. He is currently Professor of Modern Literature in TCD.

Over the past thirty years, Brendan Kennelly has published in excess of twenty volumes of poetry, including The Book of Judas, A Kind of Trust, Islandman, Cromwell and Moloney up and at It. A Time for Voices represents his Selected Poems, 1960–1990. Brendan is editor of The Penguin Book of Irish Verse and is a frequent contributor to radio and television programmes. A noted footballer in his youth, he is a great fan of Gaelic football, which 'uses all your faculties, from roguery to opportunism'.

My primary interests are people and language. One of my earliest experiences was with a very interesting man who introduced me to a certain use of words. Father Langan was an old priest in the village of Ballylongford who, despite being known as a very tight priest, in fact had a very kind heart. He used to do the *Sunday Independent* crossword. I remember going to him for Confession one day. I told him my sins and he gave me three Hail Marys and then he said, 'Brendan, would you say that five down is "horse" or "house"?' We then proceeded to have a discussion on why it would be horse or house and that was my first introduction to the possibilities of words.

There was another wonderful man in the village and his name was Jim Carrig. He was a shoemaker and he used to philosophise at length about the origins of the GAA. I remember him telling me about Ballylongford playing Tarbert, who are great enemies still, on the football field. He said that the football would begin at the first Angelus, twelve o'clock noon, and they would kick the ball between the two parishes until six o'clock in the evening. When the second bell rang for the Angelus, whatever parish the ball was in lost the game.

The village of Ballylongford is in the form of a cross. There is a lovely old church at the left arm of the cross and out beyond the head of the cross there is Lislaughtin Abbey, about which there are tremendous stories. Father Ferris, another great old priest who used to translate Dante into Irish and get us to memorise history, used to send us out every April the sixth to clean all the graves of the parish, because, in his view, that was the day that Lislaughtin Abbey was destroyed by Cromwellian soldiers. Further down is Carrigafoyle Castle, which was occupied by the O'Connors and behind that there is a wonderful island called Carraig Island. About twenty years ago I went through a depression and I remember thinking – what is my life about at all? Into my mind came a man out of that island. He started to tell me things and I wrote them down. I wrote the poem, *The Island Man*, and worked hard at it for a year or so and I suddenly realised that he was helping me to express myself.

Father Ferris was a wonderful man who used to say a Mass for Jesse James who was born on the other side of the parish, in Asdee. Old men like Father Ferris come back into your mind and they help you understand yourself. That to me is learning – the inexplicable, irrational influences of the dead on your living character. I don't fully understand it, but why should I need to when it makes me happy.

Old people chuckle out of their own wisdom and perhaps even out of their bitterness and scepticism and they say things to a child in such a way that the child's interest is stimulated. It was a great experience for me in the late '40s when I was still at school to come home and go into the pub and draw pints for the fellows. That was my introduction to the curious freedom in conversation that marks a good pub. I think it was Yeats's father who said that every Irishman should talk as if he had just taken two large glasses of whiskey. After a few pints, men tell stories and release themselves and that to me has always been the peculiar delight of a public house. After thirty-five years, I still think of the men I met there and their names come into my mind and the way they sang their songs and told their stories. They were very kind fellows as well. It was a very poor time and they didn't have much money, but they really appreciated the drink and each other's company. There were a few of them that used to sing songs and they come back to my mind like ghosts, only they are like living ghosts.

> Richard Broderick celebrates
> This winter's first and only fall of snow
> With a midnight rendering
> Of *The Bonny Bunch of Roses O*
>
> And Paddy Dineen is rising
> With *On Top of the Old Stone Wall*
> His closed eyes respect the song.
> His mind's a festival.

And now *Ramona* lights the lips
Of swaying Davy Shea
In a world of possibilities
This is the only way.

His face a summer morning
When the sun decides to smile
Tom Keane touches enchantment
With *Charming Carrig Isle.*

I've seen men in their innocence
Untroubled by right and wrong.
I close my eyes and see them
Becoming song.

All the songs are living ghosts
And long for a living voice.
O may another fall of snow
Bid Broderick rejoice!
                    (from *Living Ghosts*)

The old should be treated with respect and should be loved and, above all, they should be listened to, because they have a lot to say and they say it with devilment! There is nothing as lovely as a smile on an old face and a bit of a twinkle in an old person's eye when he is telling you a lie, or when he is making up a story for you and you know he is telling you a lie. I remember Paddy Brandon saying to me one day, 'Take me home and wash my toes.' So I took him up to the little room where he was living and I took off the shoes and washed the toes. He began to say 'It's very hard now to wash your toes when you are my age, but I could tell you stories about these toes' and he started telling me these old yarns. That was wonderful and I never forgot it, whereas I have forgotten an awful lot of lectures about the ambiguity of philosophy!

I had many good teachers, including a very interesting footballer, Johnny Walsh, who taught me in fourth class when I was about ten years of age. He taught me how to memorise great passages out of *Agallamh na Seanórach*, the colloquy between St Patrick and Oisin. The postman's son, Bobby McGibbon, and myself did Patrick and Oisin at a *feis* and we had to memorise hundreds of lines in a dialogue of poetry. I think memory is a form of love, and things that I learned when I was ten years of age come back to me when I need them. There is something in the very nature of memory which should not be dismissed in preference to whatever is yielded by the power of analysis, deduction and influence and every other scientific method applied to literature and to life itself. I would say that children today should be taught to memorise so that they will have a private treasury to dip into in the years ahead. It is only when your father and mother, and other people you loved or that had an influence on you, pass away that they come back to you in memory and say things to you.

My mother was a nurse and there was no doctor in the parish for years, so, every Sunday morning, a lot of the sick people in the parish used to come to see her. She was greatly loved, a quiet woman. I had five brothers and two sisters, so she obviously spent a lot of her time dealing with six thumping brats and two girls, and she also worked in the pub. I have this memory of her just working non-stop and it has greatly influenced my own view of women – her compassion, her quietness, her calmness and her steady ability to continue under terrible pressure. She was a terrific example to me and to others as well.

My father was a fine, easygoing, intelligent, lazy kind of man who loved talking about football and politics. He would stay up until two or three o'clock in the morning after the pub was closed and he would talk all the night through. Then he would stay in bed in the morning – he would say that the streets weren't well-aired until noon – and he loved getting his cup of tea in the bed. He never put a stop to me. He was tolerant and he didn't interfere with my life. I remember when I came to Dublin and worked in the ESB, I decided to leave after two years and I wrote to him telling him I wanted to study the English and Irish languages. He wrote back and said, 'That was a fine letter you wrote. Good luck to you.' That was all he said, and it was his way of wishing me the best. I think I learned from that that parenthood is a strange blend. You must let children run free and at the same time you must watch them – it is a kind of standing on the sidelines of their feelings but keeping a watchful eye.

I came from a big family and I left home at seventeen. There was grief at my leaving, I remember, but I was glad to go as well; it would be dishonest to say otherwise. I wanted to shake my father off because he was big and powerful and lovable and I wanted to go away to find myself in the city. Once or twice he came up to see me. We used to sit in a little teashop out in Fairview and not say much. I would ask him about the lads and he would give an account, then he would go away and get the train back. If I had him back now, I would talk to him more of course, but that is the beautiful cyclical nature of life. You only get the one chance at it and life is full of lost opportunities. You learn from the chances you missed and the goals you didn't get and the moments of contact with your father and mother that you lost. I think there is a wisdom there.

Football is a lovely game. It is personal and intelligent and it uses all your faculties, from your roguery to your sense of opportunism. I had the dubious privilege of losing an All-Ireland minor final for Kerry. Bill Jackson of Roscommon pulled me up for a foul on the left-half forward on the Dublin minor team in 1954. I didn't foul him, but Bill gave a free against me and they got a goal. The ball was kicked out and Dublin got another goal. We had been five points ahead with three minutes left and they got two goals. I was responsible for the first one and that has been the cause of many a nightmare since. You could meet a fellow on the sports field and never meet him again, but you would remember him more after just sixty minutes than you would people that you knew for four or five years in an office. It is something about the intensity of the game and what they call 'marking' somebody, when you study his ways, his body, his mind – is he open to a conversation, can you deflect him, can you fool him, can he fool you?

I remember marking a fellow once. The ball was about to be thrown in and he said, 'Do you know anything about sex?' I said, 'I don't, Pat.' 'Well I'll tell you about it now. It is like Kelly's bull and Sullivan's cow and that's how it happens and that's how you came into the world. Would you ever think about that now?' The ball was thrown in and of course I was standing looking at Pat with my mouth open. He was gone up the field with the ball and I was left burdened with a sense of the origins of life! I was about seven or eight and I was just beginning to wonder and, of course, there was no sex education then. A lot of the confusion of adolescence was due to the fact that you weren't told. I think that is the reason for the dirty story, which is a perverse form of education for a lot of kids.

The openness about sexuality today is, to my mind, greatly to be welcomed. I am somewhat apprehensive about the idea of the 'expert' in our society, people who consider themselves expert in economics, in theology or in literature but who don't know much about anything else. Somehow or other we should relate to each other, not just as human beings, but as people who have ideas and feelings. The possibility of relating in a sexual way was withheld from me from an early age. I am not bitter about it but I can now trace my inability to relate to people back to that. I have tried to overcome that inability, but my generation were reared in fear, masquerading as morality, and we were not a generation of relaters.

I went to a second level school in Tarbert which was run by an amazing woman. Her name was Jane Agnes McKenna and she had two teachers, Pat and Alice Carey. She taught languages and some kind of commerce, but her emphasis was on words and on trying to tell the truth. She used to get very angry about telling lies and it was the only thing she would slap you for. Her love of literature was genuine and profound. She would get us all to say speeches from Shakespeare. It was great to hear the lads reciting *Macbeth*, *Hamlet* and *Othello* in north Kerry accents. The best way to experience words is to commit them to memory. As you walk along the street or sit down in pubs and talk to friends, you can allow your mind to be visited by words that you learned many years ago. Miss McKenna, as we used to call her, handed us this ability to be haunted, to leave our hearts and minds open to Shakespeare, to Latin, to French and to Irish. We had to write a lot at the weekend and then we would have to stand up in class and read it out, and read out other people's writing as well. It was a life of expression. Later, when I suffered from moments of depression, I learned that expression is the best way to heal depression and that it is necessary at every level to utter yourself. Silence is a great act of expression. Miss McKenna taught us to be silent every evening. I have kept that habit, particularly in the morning when I wake up and my mind is full of dreams. I can sit there and write, without trying to explain and, above all, without trying to analyse the dreams that have visited me during the night.

Trinity College is a small university and has the features of a village. It is gossipy, intimate, full of character and it has a great history, just like my own parish. Education nowadays is very utilitarian. There is a 'points mentality' that is quite dangerous. Education should give you the chance to know yourself, to lead yourself out of yourself, so that you meet yourself and see what part of life you should occupy, what job or vocation you should really have. That is a matter of instinct, as well as qualification, and you shouldn't brutalise a young person and say be a doctor, be a lawyer, be a teacher, when that child might want to be something else. I think it is very chilling for a man of about thirty-five or forty to think that he knows more than anyone else. He might know more technically, but emotionally quite a lot of academics have an awful lot to learn. Listening to people is one of the most crucial avenues of learning – listening to children, listening to drunkards, listening to people talking to themselves in the street, listening to radio, listening to your dreams, listening to your own silence, listening to the voices of the dead in you. That is true learning.

A lot of the rigid direction of the young by middle-aged parents is a form of neurotic egotism – the father taking out on the son what he didn't fulfil in himself – and this is sometimes true of the mother also. People should not see themselves as being finished or written off when they are forty-five or fifty. We should be like the person the Dingle man spoke about when he said, '*Tá sé ag dul in óige*', he is going into his youth. That is what old age should be – we should perish of youthfulness and die of enthusiasm. I would love to see more people of my own age coming back into the universities. Of course there is a terrible shortage of staff, shortage of money, shortage of space, but I have a dream that in the future this will happen and that the wisdom of people who have passed through the difficulties of life will be passed on to the young people who are just starting out. Can you imagine young fellows of sixty and sixty-five years of age retiring from banks, businesses, RTÉ, the Church and passing on what they have learned from life to the young people? That is an awful lot better than what you would get from most lectures, which are to be found in books anyway. There is nothing to beat the value of human experience, well expressed and transmitted, and we have no channels for doing that.

Alice Leahy

Born in County Tipperary, Alice Leahy has spent her working life as a professional carer. She qualified as a nurse in Dublin and worked with various voluntary groups that cared for people in deprived areas of the city. Alice became particularly involved with the homeless and eventually set up, with others, the organisation TRUST, which offers practical care and rehabilitation to homeless people.

She traces her own commitment to the homeless to her upbringing, where she was always made to feel confident in her world. 'A lot of people end up homeless because there was no one to encourage them or inspire confidence in them at an early age...'

I grew up in Annsgift, just outside Fethard in County Tipperary. My father and mother were two great people and I suppose it is only now I realise how powerful and how marvellous they were. We were very close to the land and in fact five generations of my father's family lived on that land. They didn't own it, but they tilled the soil as if it was their own. We didn't feel bitterness because the land wasn't ours. My father loved every blade of grass and every animal on the land as if they were our own. I remember, as we walked through the fields, my father looking at the animals, encouraging me to respect nature and saying that one didn't have to own it to respect it, that we were all part of the world.

The land belonged to the Hughes family; Olivia Hughes was a driving force in the country markets, the ICA and the League of the Blind in the early days. They certainly had a great influence on my life. They owned the land and had what we would call a 'big house' there, but we depended on one another. We were never made to feel they were superior and we were inferior. We treated one another with great respect and care. In fact, we looked forward to their visits when we were small. They would come and see us and bring us presents and tell us about the parts of the world they had come from. Through them, we were in touch with professional people like doctors, dentists and eye specialists – people who can often be seen as aloof, but who we saw as real people who were part of our lives.

I went to school through the fields – and there was nothing romantic about going to school through the fields. If you got wet, you were wet for the day. I liked the national school and I remember my own national school teacher with great affection. Julia Ryan was a woman from Kerry whose husband had died when she was young. I think the mixture of boys and girls was very healthy. We had to go to the well for our spring water for whatever we had at lunchtime and we had to collect *cipíns* from the ditches to light the fire.

Secondary school was something I just passed through. It was the first time I noticed any kind of class distinction in our society. We didn't play tennis and we didn't play music. Some of that could have been due to the fact that, geographically, we were so far out from the town, but money was also a factor. I didn't find any great challenge at secondary school, although credit is due to my teachers for helping me to get through my exams.

A lot of my real education was taking place outside the school, anyway. Olivia Hughes played the cello with the opera society in Clonmel and she always took us to the opera – something a lot of people would have been excluded from, even in those times. There was also an amateur dramatic group in Fethard and my parents would take us to that. We were also involved in *Macra na Tuaithe*, and the Hughes family gave us part of their house to do up as a youth club. It was a very active youth club, where we had debates, question times and visiting speakers. We did weaving, collected sheep's wool from the ditches and carded it and made long ropes. We knitted squares for the refugees. We also ran the youth club ourselves, with Olivia's help and encouragement, with a chairman, a secretary and a treasurer, and taking minutes at a very young age.

At one time, we had to think of a project for the Young Farmer of the Year contest. My project was rearing guinea pigs and I was allowed to keep the hutches under the Hughes's apples trees and rear them there. It was a very interesting experience, because I had to document every penny I spent and every penny I made. My father and mother were great believers in keeping diaries and accounts, so had I learned all of that at a very young age. I had a contract with Professor Stewart of Trinity College and he bought the guinea pigs from me for research. When they were ready for sale, I had to pack them in a special box and take them on the back of a bicycle to the railway station, then I would go into the local post office and get the postmistress to send off a telegram to Professor Stewart in Trinity. He would send someone to pick up the guinea pigs at Kingsbridge, as it was then, and that went on for years. In fact, I was awarded the runner-up in the Young Farmer of the Year contest – I couldn't get the Young Farmer of the Year because we didn't own land.

My father was a very resourceful man and, in many ways, was ahead of his time. He was into things like recycling before the word was even invented. Everything we had was used and re-used. A family near us used to give us a goose every year and the goose feathers were kept to make cushions and pillows. We embroidered old canvas bags to make the cushions; we used all the raw material we could get. We grew our own vegetables; we kept hens; we got milk from the Hughes family; we always had access to a good supply of fruit; we used tea leaves to sprinkle on the floors to keep the dust down; we collected all our firewood; we had to sew and iron and knit; we preserved eggs and made jams and chutneys; we used eggshells to keep the water in when we were painting – we were always encouraged to paint and draw and to make puzzles.

My mother had three old aunts: one lived to be 100 and the others lived into their nineties. One of them was a nurse and we used to love visiting her. She had worked in Daisy Hill Hospital in Newry and I suppose she gave me an insight into nursing. We grew up caring for the elderly and visiting the old county home, so it was probably inevitable that I should become a nurse. I didn't want to go to England, so I wrote off to different hospitals in Ireland. One of the eye specialists at Baggot Street Hospital introduced me to the matron, and I got an interview and started in Baggot Street.

It was hard. We had to do a lot of the work that would now be done by domestic staff, as well as going to lectures and studying. When we were on the wards, we had to light the fires and clean the wheels of the beds. We had to be very resourceful. There was nothing disposable in those days, but there was nothing new in all of that for me.

I went on to work in the Rotunda and it was there that I got involved with Voluntary Service International, a voluntary group that was involved in very practical work in deprived areas of the city. There was an old complex of flats in the north inner city and there I made contact with VSI, which ran workshops with the mothers and children and the older people there. It was a most interesting time of my life in the city. I got very involved with VSI and the adoption society in the Rotunda and a lot of the mothers I met there I would meet again later outside in the community.

I was very taken with a quotation from the founder of VSI which I suppose is now a part of my own philosophy – 'The world is a poem, an immense poem which people have no time to read because they are busy in their offices.' That was written many years ago and I think it is still true today.

I worked in the Rotunda for a few years and then I worked in Germany for a short time before I came back to Baggot Street as a night sister. I had an interesting experience at that time. One night when I was on night duty, a woman who died shortly afterwards called me and said, 'Do you mind if I tell you your fortune?' She told me many things that came true, including that I would be asked by the hospital board to go abroad and do something completely different that would dramatically change my life. She also told me I would meet a widower and get married. About a month later, Matron invited me to the office and said the hospital board wanted me to go to London to look at intensive care units with a view to setting one up in Baggot Street. I set up the intensive care unit and ran it for two years and then decided I would move on. And, later, I did meet and marry a widower!

I felt intensive care was very important, but at the same time I was constantly reading and questioning the whole area of technology in medicine. It is very high-powered work and I felt we needed more staff and a facility to discuss what was happening. There was no opportunity in nursing for groups to get together and look at the stresses and strains involved in that kind of work. The only time I saw such a thing was when I was in the London hospital, where doctors, nurses, social workers and the various disciplines got together and were addressed by an outside speaker. One of those was Sally Trench and the other was Cecily Saunders, who was involved in the whole hospice movement. I had no time to do voluntary work, because you were constantly under pressure, hadn't enough staff or you were just too tired when you got off duty. So, I decided I would give up my job in intensive care.

When I said I was leaving, there was absolute consternation in the hospital. One of the consultants said to me, 'Well, Sister Leahy, I've made an appointment for you to see a psychiatrist,' and he really meant it! I applied to the Simon Community and was accepted as a full-time worker. At that stage, the philosophy of Simon was very important to me. The idea was that very broken people and people who are deemed not to be so broken live and work together in a community. They had an old building down on Sarsfield Quay. I thought it was an awful building – the smells, the dirt, the chaos – especially having come from a very clinical setting. But in the middle of all of that there were very powerful broken people who really inspired me to think about politics and such things, what we are doing about medicine and health care. The people who ended up living there were absolutely marvellous.

We live in a society where you are judged by your dress and your status in the community, but many of the people in Simon would really be the philosophers of the world. For instance, on a wet day you may be wet and annoyed and everything's going wrong but you can go home, lock your door, have a shower and a hot drink and do what you like. But, when you have absolutely nothing, only the clothes you stand up in. . . A lot of the people who end up in places like Simon are there because they are so sensitive and aware of what is happening in the world that they have just withdrawn.

Very often, there is a kind of a elitism about helping these people and very often people who may have a lot to offer get pushed aside. At that time, Dr Gerry O'Neill, who is a child psychiatrist in Dublin, used to go down one night a week to visit people who needed help and sometimes he could be left outside the door because nobody even knew who he was. I felt he was doing great work.

When you leave Simon, you either never want to see a homeless person again or you feel you should do something. I had no money, so I went over to England to do some private nursing with my best friend from my nursing days. Around that time, CHAR, a campaigning group in England for the homeless, produced a report on medical care for homeless people and I thought it would be useful to do something like that here. Also, when I was there, Dr Philip Kennedy, who is now a neurosurgeon in Newfoundland, wrote telling me that some of the people from Simon were asking about me. So I came back and, when I got there, Christy, one of the residents then and now, was outside the door very drunk and he was crying. He put his arms around me and kissed me and said, 'Alice, you're back.' In a way, that encouraged me to do something more.

I got a job in the national office in Simon and I drew up some questionnaires. I enlisted the help of Tom McPhail, who was a journalist with the *Irish Press* group, and we took the questionnaires round to hospitals, casualty departments, GPs, gardaí, hostel workers and homeless people themselves. The questionnaire was based on how we see other people, how we react to them and how we react to one another, because at the end of the day the quality of our services depends on how we react to one another. The report was published in 1974 and, as a result, I was appointed by the health board to work as a nurse with homeless people. I must give credit to Fred Donohoe who is one of the inspiring people I have met along the way. Fred was later to become programme manager with the Eastern

Health Board and he had great courage in seeing that I was employed by the health board.

Dave McGee, who is now a psychiatrist, spent a year working with me for absolutely nothing when I was appointed as a nurse. We were visiting the hostels regularly as Alice and Dave, and we were getting to know the people who were homeless. Anne Rush was a woman in her forties who suddenly discovered she had cancer and hadn't long to live. She had £11,000 that she felt her family could do without. Anne and Brian, her husband, used to do a soup run once a week. They were a very caring couple. So she decided that, as she was dying and she had this money, she wanted to spend it to help homeless people. A group of us got together, people from the health board, Simon, the Vincent de Paul Society, Anne and Brian and myself. Robin Webster was our facilitator and eventually it was decided that a private charitable trust would be set up and that a doctor would be employed by the trust and a nurse would be employed by the health board. It was very much the barefoot doctor kind of project that at that time was very fashionable in places like China, its purpose being to make sure that a health service would be available to everyone. I think it is as relevant today as it was then.

It was Anne herself who came up with the name TRUST, which is a powerful name because we all need to trust one another, whatever our colour, religion or politics. TRUST was set up then, with the use of the old health centre in Lord Edward Street. Both Dave and I were great believers that health care isn't just about giving out tablets or putting on bandages, it's more about involving people in their own health care. We have a very important group of trustees, very challenging people like Justin O'Brien, John Long, Dermot MacMahon, Fred Donohoe and our chairman is James McCormick, head of the Department of Community Health in Trinity, a very inspiring man in his own way.

Eventually we got the basement of the old Iveagh hostel, built by Guinness in the early days, and we still operate from there now. We no longer employ a doctor full-time, as most of the people we know are entitled to medical cards. In fact, we have a lot of services in this country that we take for granted. I feel we have a lot more going for people who are homeless and poor here than in any other city in the world, but the reality is that a lot of those people can't avail of the services because of their own personalities or difficulties.

The whole area of rehabilitation has to be one that isn't too structured. An example is one man we work with who lives in a hostel and is tremendously talented. A few years ago, I asked him to come with me to the Dublin fruit and vegetable market. I wanted him to carry the fruit and vegetables I bought for a start, but I also wanted to get him out. He said, 'Nurse Alice, would you walk on the street with me?' and I said, 'Of course I'd walk on the street with you.' Over a period of time I have got him to come to different places with me. For instance, one day I took him into Arnott's and he went into the men's toilets and came out telling me in glowing terms how nice the toilets were – things we all take for granted. I think it's all about inspiring people to be confident. I suppose, at a young age, I was made to feel by my parents that we were all important, that we were a part of the world, but so many people that live outside of things, in this hidden Dublin, feel they are only part of poor places or dirty places and they are only fit to go to food centres. I think we all have to encourage people to feel they are part of a nicer Dublin.

There is a side to our work that is very disturbing; there is terrible violence and there is dirt. I always make a point of looking well and feeling well. I meet people who are just very, very cut off. I wouldn't continue to do the work if I didn't get some encouragement and inspiration from it and I do. There is a lot of job satisfaction. We work in a very practical way. Very often I just have to put on a man's shirt and get on with the job, but when I see somebody coming out of the bath and they look well and they see themselves in the mirror and say, 'Oh, I look well' – there's great satisfaction in that. It's hard, but it's worthwhile.

It all goes back to my childhood, feeling confident in my world. I wouldn't be as I am if I hadn't had people along the way who encouraged me. One of the reasons why a lot of people end up homeless or down and out is that there was never anyone to encourage them or inspire confidence in them at an early age.

Patrick Lindsay

1915–1993

Patrick Lindsay was born in Dublin in 1915, but moved to County Mayo with his family at a very young age. He was educated at St Muredach's College, Ballina, and University College, Galway, where he pursued a master's degree in classics. A brief and unsettled career in teaching followed (he taught in seventeen schools in three-and-a-half years!) before Patrick reached his real objective – Dublin and the study of law at UCD and King's Inns.

A master of oratory and a keen student of the English language, Patrick Lindsay embarked on a glittering legal career, rising to the position of senior counsel and eventually to master of the High Court. His other great interest was politics and he first stood for election at the age of twenty-two. He eventually made it to Dáil Éireann in 1954 as a Fine Gael deputy and became part of the coalition government. He became the country's first Minister for the Gaeltacht. His wit and classical background made him a formidable opponent, both in court and parliament, and he had many memorable jousts with his opponents, notably Donogh O'Malley.

Patrick Lindsay published his memoirs, Memories, shortly before he died in 1993.

My father was a great reader and my earliest learning experience was reading the books in our house. The first one that I remember really getting stuck into in a big way was *Old Moore's Almanac*. It provided a great deal of general knowledge, with anniversaries for every day of the year. Many years later, when I was a practising barrister on the western circuit, I always carried *Old Moore's Almanac* in the car. It was a staple diet in many homes where books weren't readily available, as were the local papers. *The Western People* probably started my liking for law, because of its great and detailed publication of court cases. Then there were little religious periodicals, like *The Far East* and *The Messenger*, all of which contained lovely short stories. I remember with great affection the questions at the back of the *Messenger*, which were so innocent that they would put Madonna to shame!

My father was certainly a book lover, but my mother, although she would read a book, was extremely limited by reason of time. She was a woman who reared seven children, did her own washing by hand, did her own shopping and baking and cooked on an open fire – it wasn't easy and there was little time for reading. My father, who did nothing in the house – never even lifted a kettle off the crane – was always reading. He was a very adventurous man in all respects, in fact he was the first man in the parish to have a racing bicycle with dropped handlebars and cane rims on the wheels. He had been deprived of a monitorship at the national school by a local teacher, but he took some kind of examination and got into the Department of Posts and Telegraphs, where he worked for some years before eventually moving to Mayo.

I was eighteen months old when my father purchased a smallholding in the village of Doolough. My father was a great fisherman who had no pretensions about flies – he used worms as bait. He could sole and heel shoes, give you a haircut and cure milk fever in cows with a bicycle pump. He was an extraordinary genius altogether and a very diplomatic man. I remember, years later, when I was working out how to frame parliamentary questions, he would know how to word them far better than I would so that they did not give offence to anybody. He was a mighty influence on me. He provided me with books. I had read an awful lot before I went to boarding school – Charles Kickham, Canon Sheehan and virtually all of Dickens. I read Lord Macaulay's essays and I had come across poetry too, mainly the works of Oliver Goldsmith.

When I went to St Muredach's College in Ballina, that reading was both an advantage and a disadvantage. It allowed me to doss, but, there again, mischief is largely built on ingenuity – how to get into trouble and, better still, as the old LDF books used to say, how to retreat from it. There were two notable examples in Ballina. On wet days, there was very little to occupy people's minds and we had to invent our own fun. We used to congregate in the second- and third-year classrooms and somebody would do his party piece. Mine was imitating the then bishop, Dr James Naughton, on prize day before the Christmas holidays and I could do his accent perfectly. One day I noticed a considerable lack of appreciation for my performance and something prompted me to look round. Behind me were the bishop and the president of the college. The president sent me up to his room, which meant at least twenty strokes, but the bishop said a better punishment would be to make me do my impersonation again. I did and it wasn't a bad performance!

The second incident is well known to many people. There were two prizes that I won every year in Ballina. One was, and this will surprise many people, first prize in catechism and apologetics. My real interest in it was that it wasn't a book prize nor was it any kind of religious token – it was a full-sized, genuine five-pound note. There was another prize of five pounds on the annual school sports day for the bicycle race, which I had won the four years prior to my final year. When sports day arrived, in my last year, I went to ask permission to go into town and borrow a bicycle. However, I was *persona non grata* with the authorities and I was told by the president, who later became Bishop of Killala, that I couldn't go into town that day or any other day, for that or any other purpose, and he banged the door in my face. As I was going downstairs, a little hurt but not beaten, I saw the reflector of a bicycle sticking out of a little alcove near the oratory door, so I went over and took it. It was a huge, three-geared green Raleigh bicycle, not the racing type, but I was a fairly strong fellow and I knew I could win on it. I did win the race and then had to go over and stand with the bicycle between myself and the president, who was giving out the brown envelope with the fiver in it. He was a great gentleman, because he never adverted to the fact that it was his own bicycle . . .

I got a county council scholarship to the university and an entrance scholarship on the results of my Leaving, a separate thing altogether, and so I arrived in Galway in October 1932. I went up to the Aula Maxima and there were forms to be filled in stating the subjects of your choice, the faculty of your choice, choosing your dean of residence and things of that kind. Nobody advised you what to do. I went after my favourite subjects – Latin, Greek, English, logic and Irish. It was extremely fortunate that I chose the classics and English, although I was unlucky with the English, as the professor, William Byrne, died at the end of my first year. He was a native of Kildare and he spoke English beautifully, not with an accent, but clearly and concisely. When he died, I dropped English and stuck with the classics. My classics teacher was one of my great mentors, Father Tom Fahy. He could bring the classics to life by drawing analogies between things that were happening during lectures and things that had happened in Athens or Sparta. We weren't professor and pupil, we were friends.

In my first year at university, whenever I passed the courthouse, I would notice the people going in and out. I attended every criminal trial in the courthouse for the five years I was at college. That began my interest in law and that interest was strengthened by this wonderfully attractive man, Judge Charles Wyse-Power. Later, I practised under him and he was very kind to me and taught me a lot of things. However, I couldn't do law at that time because there was no recognised law school in Galway, so I finished at Galway in 1937 with a master's degree in classics and a Higher Diploma in Education – and the only use I ever got from that was as a sort of status symbol, because in my part of Mayo they called it the Highest Diploma in Education, and I never corrected them. I never benefited from it anyway, because, although it allowed you to get increments, I never stayed long enough in any school to qualify.

I taught for two years in Cavan Royal School. It was my first experience of co-education and also of meeting Protestant people *en masse*. I taught in seventeen schools in Dublin in three and a half years before I went to the Bar. I was never sacked – I was out by a short head each time. There were a lot of things I didn't agree with and that was my trouble. I had no respect for inspectors, principals or anybody else. If a view had to be expressed, I would express it and that was that.

I got into law through a man who had tremendous influence on me. He had been a TD for north Mayo in the '20s – the late Professor Michael Tierney, ultimately president of UCD. He and my father were great friends and my father wrote to him when I abandoned ship in Cavan and went to Dublin with nothing. Michael Tierney made me tutor and guardian to a very brilliant lad, now dead, called Eoin McWhite. He died in a motor accident while he was our ambassador to The Hague. Mahaffy of Trinity used to say that Oscar Wilde was the only guy who understood the middle voice in Greek, but I was fortunate to meet another, and that was Eoin McWhite. Teaching him helped to pay the rent on the flat and I did grinds as well. Then Michael Tierney asked me if I would edit book twelve of Virgil's *Aeneid* for Browne and Nolan's, for which I received what was, in the 1940s, a massive fee of one hundred guineas. I paid law fees, I paid outstanding digs money and everything else and I finished up on Saturday with nothing but dirty fingernails and coppers and memories. I would say I was a rake with a touch of class and making progress all the time!

The man on whom I modelled my own career was the late James Fitzgerald Kenny. His family were landed gentry from near Belcarra, outside Castlebar. He was a member of the Dáil in 1927 and was appointed Minister for Justice after the O'Higgins assassination. He was the kind of man you would respect for bravery as well as clarity of thought and of expression. He had a tremendous command of the English language and he could use words and inflections which were extremely powerful. Whenever, in a country court, he referred to the senior counsel on the other side by saying, 'Here, strenuously to defend, is Mr Ernest Wood from Dublin', Wood, or any counsel that came from Dublin, would be finished in the eyes of the jury! I was to use that same ploy to great effect in several cases afterwards.

We never learned anything practical in either UCD or King's Inns. I was fortunate because I had Paddy McGilligan, Michael Ryan and Dan Binchy as mentors. I was lucky in the King's Inns to be taught by the late Frances Moran, Regius Professor of Law in Trinity. She was a lovely person, very strict. For some reason I had made up my mind that I wouldn't answer any questions in class (we were asked questions at every third lecture about the previous two). She got fed up with me saying 'I don't know' and would pass over me altogether. One day she came in and said, 'I have often thought that Justinian would not have been half the man he was, were it not for his beautiful wife, Theodora. Does anybody know anything about Theodora?' I shot up the hand and told the story of Theodora, which I'm sure shocked a good many people, and she looked at me and said, 'Accurately if indelicately told'. From that day, we became friends.

I went for election for the first time in 1937 and, to my surprise, saved my deposit down in my old north Mayo constituency. Ultimately, at the sixth time of standing, I was elected in 1954. When I reached the Dáil, two things occurred to me. One was that, when I was first defeated in 1937 I had thought it was a national catastrophe that a man of my talents had been kept out of parliament, but here it was still functioning, albeit badly. The other was that I was horrified at the lack of attention that was being paid to legislation; it was all letter-writing and clinics. I have never actually held a clinic. Clinics, you see, are a fraudulent operation – fraudulent in the best sense of the word, in that everybody, of whatever political persuasion, comes to them. I was more of a community person. I was interested in local drainage, land reclamation, rural electrification and the provision of these everywhere. It was I that started the Tidy Towns competition. I remember making an almost violent speech against that monstrosity called An Tóstal. I said that bunting or bowls of light would not bring tourists to this country if we did not tidy up our towns and get rid of derelict sites.

I never wrote a speech. I would be travelling from one chapel to another on the political scene and I would make a different speech at each chapel, because I would make it up as I went along in the car, talking aloud to myself. I did the same thing with law later. I always had a tendency to speechifying and declaiming. Our professor at St Muredach's, the late Father John Murphy, was a brilliant man who inculcated a love of language in us by the way he read poetry to us and the way he got us to read to him. He never corrected an essay – you had to stand up and read it out to him. In February of my Leaving Cert year, he had given us a freelance essay. We could choose any literary or historical character and write about him or her. I chose, for better or worse – worse as it happened – Catherine the Great of Russia. What my attraction to her was, I don't know, because she wasn't very attractive, but I stood up and said my little piece. He told me to read the last sentence again. I repeated it, but it was obvious that I had changed it, so he said,

'Show me that. It's not the same as the first time.' I handed him the copybook and there it was – 'Patrick J Lindsay, 4 September 1927'. I had never written an essay; I had spoken them all. Father Murphy went mad, but he apologised years later when I was addressing a meeting in his parish in Lacken, north of Killala. He said he had been quite wrong not to have given me full credit for having performed so well for nearly five years!

I eventually became parliamentary secretary for Education and the Gaeltacht. John Costelloe's idea at the time was that, after a respectable lapse of a few months, he would slip me into education as a full-time minister and let General Mulcahy go into the Gaeltacht, but it didn't work out that way. I was in the secondary-education branch in Hume Street with the late Seamus Breathnach and a girl called Betty Hunt. We were in this rather dark room and nobody came near us for three months. Nobody. I said to Seamus Breathnach, 'Maybe they think we're photographers developing pictures in this room!' We did nothing, absolutely nothing.

Eventually, I became Minister for the Gaeltacht and I went up to Earlsfort Terrace. I didn't get on too well with the secretary, who had been appointed by Mulcahy. I should have been given my own appointment, but he had forgotten to appoint an assistant secretary, so I appointed a fellow called Sean Glynn from Cong who had been a land commission inspector.

A very interesting thing happened in 1969. I decided to leave north Mayo and stand for election in Dublin. I thought the worst thing that could happen to me would have been to be elected to a Dublin constituency, because I was not a Dublin man. I was a country guy. I loved to look at the houses on the side of the hills and recognise whose they were. There is great philosophy in the country home and the country pub. I had a famous set-to in the Dáil with Donogh O'Malley about country life when I was defending the small schools. I was singing the joys of watching the frogs jumping out of the ditches, which is a well-known phenomenon – frogs leaping out onto the road after heavy rain. There were a lot of country deputies who thought I had a lot of drink taken when I made that speech.

I was arguing for the retention of the country school, because there was a different kind of education to be got, going to and coming from the school. You could enjoy the seasons, whereas now children are all locked up in a bus or a Hiace van. They see nothing. Even stealing carrots or onions out of someone's garden is an education in its own way. It was the law of survival and, of course, what grew in somebody else's garden was always sweeter than your own . . .

I have enjoyed everything I have done in my life, even the forbidden things. I have met lovely people and I firmly believe that the greatest thing anyone can achieve in life is the making of good and sincere friends – and keeping them.

Patrick Lynch

Patrick Lynch was born in Dublin in 1917. He worked in the Irish civil service before entering academic life in 1952 at University College, Dublin, where he rose to the position of Professor of Political Economy. He was director of a major survey of Ireland's educational needs, which culminated in the influential 1965 report, Investment in Education. *A former chairman of Aer Lingus and deputy chairman of Allied Irish Banks, he has acted as economic consultant to the Department of Finance, OECD, the Council of Europe, etc.*

Patrick Lynch has written extensively on economic planning and is generally recognised as one of Ireland's most distinguished economic thinkers over the past forty years.

I remember, as a child of four, being taken for a walk past Christchurch, down Winetavern Street, and seeing the name K Hare over a secondhand clothes shop. Outside the shop there was a donkey and cart and I remember being mystified by the juxtaposition of the donkey and cart and the hare. I think 'hare' was the first word I ever remember reading.

From there on I began to acquire an interest in words. There were some books in the house, but my family were not widely read. The first book I ever read was Rider Haggard's *She*. I recall it being a very good novel. I remember dipping, at about the age of ten, into Walter Scott, where my interest in books really began.

My father owned a pub in the Liberties, at the corner of New Street and Kevin Street. It was a Victorian building, very spacious and very ugly. It didn't really have any redeeming features. I would not wish to romanticise the Liberties in any way; they were in a state of squalor when I was young, but I could escape to St Patrick's Park along by the cathedral. My father had come from Tipperary and had bought that house around the turn of the century. He had served his time as what was called a grocer's curate in the pub patronised by Skin-the-Goat in what is now Fenian Street. Skin-the-Goat was the cabby who drove the Invincibles on their journey to the Phoenix Park, where they killed the Chief Secretary and his colleague Mr Burke. I remember my father often speaking about customers in that pub who had actually known Skin-the-Goat.

My main memory of the Liberties is of seeing survivors of the First World War, unfortunate creatures who had lost arms or legs. Another memory is the pungent smell from O'Keefe's, the knackers, which was located in the Liberties and which killed off unwanted horses. The third very vivid memory is the smoke from the burning Customs House darkening the sky all over Dublin and another equally vivid memory is of a platoon of the British army marching down from Portobello Barracks for the last time, as they left Ireland.

My first school was the convent school in the Coombe. There was a plaque on the door: 'Select School for Young Ladies', but young men were also accepted up to the age of eight or nine without reference to whether they were carefully selected or otherwise. I remember an elderly nun there, Sister Bonaventure, who had a great love for books. I still remember her reading an extract from *Gulliver's Travels* and saying, 'Pay attention now. It could well be that the chapter I am reading was written just a few hundred yards down the road at the Deanery where Dean Swift lived.'

Later I went to the Catholic University School on Leeson Street, where I had the good fortune to meet a number of teachers who played a very important part in my development. There was a remarkable man called John Lyons, who had come from Cork. He had started studying medicine in Cork, but he had abandoned that for literature and philosophy. He was one of Daniel Corkery's friends. Corkery introduced him to classical music and, above all, to the Russian novel. Lyons was an extraordinarily widely read man. He observed the ordinary school curriculum, but he had much wider interests. He talked a good deal about philosophy and about German and French literature; he introduced me to Pascal and to Montaigne; he talked about the influence of Buxtehude on Bach, about Scarlatti's Portuguese period; and then he introduced me to a very odd book, *Fabian Essays*, which, I suppose, induced my first interest in economics. I remember him giving me a good piece of advice about the difference between examinations and education. There could be a conflict between education and examinations: a good examinee is not necessarily a well-educated person.

There was another remarkable teacher in CUS at that time. He was Alexander Darragh and he taught mathematics. He believed in teaching the principles of mathematics, the foundations. He concentrated mainly on algebra; he felt that you could learn geometry from the textbooks and you could learn arithmetic as you went along, but that real mathematics was to be found mainly in algebra.

I think that I acquired the larger part of my education in Rathmines Public Library, in Capel Street Public Library and, later, when I came to the university, the National Library. Some of the most worthwhile hours of my life were spent in libraries.

In due course I came to University College Dublin. The outstanding influence for me there was the Professor of Economics, George O'Brien. He had been a lawyer – jurisprudence was his original interest – but he settled down to teaching economics and had enormous influence on students, not merely students of economics but students from other faculties as well. I remember the late Myles na Gopaleen telling me that he frequently went in to George O'Brien's class to hear him lecturing. He was one of the best lecturers that I have heard in any university. He took lecturing very seriously and was very, very fluent. His technique was to begin by telling the class what he was going to tell them, then to make eight points and the final point was to summarise what he had told them.

It was sheer chance that led me to economics. I was not able to start in UCD at the beginning of term and so I was informed that arts was the only faculty in which I could have a place. I took a number of subjects in my first year, of which economics was one, and then I think it was the attraction of O'Brien's lecturing that led me to concentrate on economics.

There were other people who played a fairly influential part in my college life. In those days Colm Ó Lochlainn was lecturer in Irish. He used to illustrate his lectures by giving us parts of a song; he was an authority on ballads. There was Tomás Ó hAilín, to whom I owe a great deal. He was lecturer in Irish and he gave me a grind in Irish for the oral examination for the civil service and I am quite certain that, without that teaching from Tom Allen, I would never have got in.

I entered the civil service and spent about ten years there and eventually came back to the university as lecturer in economics.

Of course, my colleagues had an influence on me too, contemporaries such as Desmond Williams, Martin Sheridan, Ben Kiely and Tommy Woods. The student societies played a very important part in my life – the literary and historical society, at which I learned to do some public speaking; the English literature society, of which I was auditor; *An Cumann Gaelach*, of which I was a member; and then there was the college magazine, of which I was editor for some years.

I certainly enjoyed college life. Talking to people, and especially mixing with people from other faculties, had a real beneficial interest for me. There is a great deal to be said for the arts faculty rather than for the professional faculties. Professional faculties are of course essential, but there is very much more to education than mere vocational education. I think it was Maritain, the French philosopher, who said that the trouble with utilitarian education is that it is not utilitarian enough. There is a great deal to be said for being able to read widely in literature, in history, in politics, in philosophy and preferably, if you have the opportunity, in classics. One can specialise later on. I don't know who it was that said that professional qualifications should lapse every five years, but the more we advance in technology, the more relevant I think that observation becomes. I am convinced that, if one has a liberal education, one can adapt, and experience has shown me that adaptation is essential in the life we are enduring today.

I graduated in 1939, which was the fatal year of the outbreak of the Second World War. We in Ireland escaped the worst of that appalling experience. The only minor inconvenience that I can recall was that foreign travel was impossible, even if we could afford it. It is said that travel broadens the mind, but I wonder is that a valid cliché. I believe that travel is best for young people who know what they want to see, know what they want to do, know what they want to find. It is beneficial for adults as well, but I'm not an enthusiast for aimless touring. It seems to me to be a mindless occupation. I don't have much regard for busloads of tourists who can't distinguish between Bantry Bay and the fjords of Norway. It is a different issue if you want to go to see the pyramids of Egypt or the source of the Nile, something specific. I don't regard myself as a great traveller, and to tell you the truth I have learned much more about places from books than from casual visits.

I had the good fortune in the '50s to spend some time in Peterhouse College in Cambridge. It was a very lively time. Some of the great minds of the century were teaching there then, people like Dennis Brogan, the historian, the wittiest lecturer I have ever heard; Postan, an economic historian; Butterfield, the historian; the great economist Joan Robinson, who was perhaps the best exponent of Keynsian economics. I had the good fortune of meeting John Vaizey, who subsequently became a close friend. People have had an enormous influence on me as well as books, people like Owen Sheehy-Skeffington, Thomas McGreevey, and Conor Cruise O'Brien.

I would be making a critical omission if I did not refer to the influence of radio. I would find it impossible to exaggerate the power that radio played in my development. I think first of all, of course, of the old BBC, especially the third programme, which was extremely good, and the old Radio Éireann. I'm thinking of the tremendous part that Roibéard Ó Faracháin and Francis McManus played in such things as the Thomas Davis lectures. The late Theo Moody and McManus between them conceived the notion of the Thomas Davis lectures, which have made a contribution to Irish written history which has not been officially recognised even to this day. I remember, too, the *Sunday Times* in its great days, when Desmond McCarthy was literary critic – you could quite clearly see that he had spent the whole week writing the long review of the one book he reviewed each Sunday; when Ernest Newman was music critic and James Agate was drama critic. One learned a great deal from writers of that calibre. The old *Listener*, the official journal of the BBC, frequently reprinted BBC talks and I think it was a very formative influence in my development as well.

I enjoyed my period in the civil service. I like work; I dislike idleness. Not all the civil service work was exciting, but a good deal of it was in my own area, in economics. I met some civil servants who were making a distinguished contribution to the development of the country, people like Leon Ó Broin and J J McElligott.

It is worth recalling here, too, the books which have had most influence on me and these are not necessarily great books. For instance, one of the books that certainly changed my way of thinking was Arthur Koestler's *Darkness at Noon*, published just before the Second World War, dealing with the trials under Stalin. It is quite an extraordinary insight into the Stalin regime. Events thirty years later demonstrated how right Koestler's concept of Stalinism really was. Another great book was *The Open Society and Its Enemies* by one of the great modern philosophers, Karl Popper. His approach is interesting and original. He is concerned more about falsifying concepts than verifying them. Another book – not a great book, but a book which had an immense influence on many people – was *The Treason of the Clerks*, by a French writer called Julian Benda. The clerks were the intellectuals who were politically corrupt. He demonstrated that intellectuals, who should in fact be leaders in society, became instead agents of corruption and were either bought off politically or bought off financially.

Another writer who was an outstanding person was G H Hardy. He was professor of mathematics at Oxford and he wrote a book called *A Mathematician's Apology*. He dealt with the difference between useful mathematics, which he regarded as merely trivial, and creative mathematics, which he regarded as artistic. Oddly enough, Graham Greene agrees that Hardy's exposition of creative mathematics is as near to a discussion of the artistic method as anything written by Cardinal Newman or Henry James. In an age of technology, it is extremely important that we do whatever we can to liberalise technology, otherwise we become its prisoners. Bertrand Russell used a phrase which went something like this: 'technology advances like an army of tanks that has lost its drivers and is heading blindly towards the abyss'. He went on to say that this is because technology has lost touch with humanity and that we cannot survive unless we humanise it. I'm afraid events today in many parts of the world demonstrate the correctness of Russell's predictions. My conviction is that limited technical skills grow stale and become obsolete, whereas, if one is genuinely interested in technology, one finds that it is inseparable from the society in which it is developed.

I went back to university as a lecturer in 1953 and then later I was promoted to be professor. It was a major learning experience for me. One did acquire knowledge from colleagues, naturally, but there is a special satisfaction in teaching students. In my experience of life, questions are much more important than answers. It is much more difficult to ask the right question than to give the glib answer. One of the jobs as an economist which I was given to do was to undertake a study which was eventually called *Investment in Education*. This brought me into contact with a number of ministers for education. I don't want to be invidious mentioning names, but I cannot help but mention one. Dr Hillery was Minister for Education during part of my time spent working on that task and I must say that I regarded him as one of the most thoughtful people I have come across. He used to discuss the project that we were engaged on, but he very rarely made a direct contribution. He confined himself to asking a very awkward question, with the result that one went away and spent the next week thinking out the implications of that question.

Twenty-five years after the report *Investment in Education*, I still consider education in this country to be very much a matter of privilege and class. It is true that we now have free post-primary education of a sort. It is also true that the more money you have the better the post-primary education you can acquire. It is when you reach third level that the trouble really begins. There is no doubt that third-level education in Ireland is provided on an economically selective basis. It is quite inequitable that one should be debarred from third-level education on economic grounds. The so-called lower income groups are not much more represented at that level today than they were twenty-five years ago. The State must provide more scholarships. Education is increasingly becoming not a luxury but a necessity.

History is for me an important educational influence. I think that history and economics are very closely related. I don't believe one can be a competent economist unless one has a good knowledge of history. It is nonsense to imagine anybody teaching economic theory without having a very good knowledge of the Industrial Revolution and the background which produced so much of the economic theory of the nineteenth century and the early twentieth century. The remarkable historian Simon Schama produced a vast book on the Dutch republic of the eighteenth century, *An Embarrassment of Riches*, showing how a small country can create such wonderful art. Some of the greatest European artists emerged from Holland in the seventeenth and eighteenth centuries. Last year, when the French Revolution was being widely commemorated, Schama produced a book called *Citizens*, which does a great deal of revising of French history. The revision of French history does not mean a distortion of French history, any more than a revision of Irish history means a distortion of Irish history. It merely corrects some misleading claims that have been made. I was shocked in reading Schama's book on the French Revolution to discover that there was a higher level of literacy in France before the French Revolution than there is in the United States of America today. He gives the actual figures.

Economics continues to enthral me. I think that the more we know about economics, the more we realise how inexact a science it is. There have been three or four great names in economics, but they weren't purely economists. Keynes was not purely an economist. Adam Smith was not purely an economist. Marx was not purely an economist. I mention only three great figures, whose economics perhaps can be questioned today but nevertheless whose influence is very, very considerable. Without doubt, Keynes has influenced me most, as political thinker and economist and as a historian. His book, *The Economic Consequences of the Peace*, displayed remarkable foresight, in that he indicated that the conditions of the Treaty of Versailles were unduly harsh towards Germany and that the consequences of that harshness would be incalculable – and indeed they were, producing Hitler two decades later.

John McGahern

John McGahern was born in County Leitrim in 1934. He became a primary teacher and taught successfully in Drogheda and Dublin. His teaching career came to an abrupt end when he was dismissed, on the instruction of the Archbishop of Dublin, following the banning of his novel, The Dark. *He subsequently taught in England, at first and third levels, before returning to his native Leitrim, where he now lives and writes. He has written five successful novels, the most recent being the much-acclaimed* Amongst Women. *He also writes short stories and has published three well-received collections.*

I remember very vividly a certain day in school when letters on the page that until then had been a mystery – just signs – suddenly started forming into words and making sense. I experienced a feeling of triumph, or the coming into knowledge. I suppose I was four or five at the time.

My mother was a teacher and I went to school wherever she taught, which was a lot of schools. She had a permanent job, but it was in a small school and the numbers fell. She always had to go to where there was a vacancy at the time, because of a thing called the Panel.

In one school, I remember there was a very wicked teacher called Mrs McCann and I thought I'd pacify her, maybe, because my own mother was a teacher. I decided to bring her flowers, but the only flowers that were growing around our house were thistles. I thought these purple flowers were quite beautiful and I brought her a big armful. She took it as an incredible insult and I got an extra biffing for that!

I think that nearly all the children of that generation went to school in fear. The war was going on in England and there was always the hope that one of the bombs would be dropped on our school.

My mother was a very gentle sort of person. She came from a very clever family, but they were poor and they came from the mountains. She was the first person from that mountain ever to take up the King's Scholarship, but I think that it was a hard thing for her, in that she was uprooted from her own class and sent to boarding school in Carrick-on-Shannon. She had seven children in nine years, and then she died. We had a farm as well, because in those days it was easier to buy a farm in the countryside than it was to buy a house – you had to buy the land with the house – so she had a very busy life.

My father was a garda sergeant and again it was a very strange house in the sense that we used to go to the barracks in the school holidays and he would come to the farm on his days off. He was stationed about twenty-two miles from home and of course there were no cars then. He often used to come on wet nights and I remember still the blue glow of the carbide lamp on his bicycle and its strange hissing noise.

I had a distant relationship with my father. He was an only child himself and didn't relate very easily with people. To a certain extent I suppose he was, with the great influence of the Church at the time, very much a kind of symbol of God the Father. My father was very conventional in the sense that he would do whatever would be approved of. He was exercising the law and he was going to see that he set an example, first and foremost.

There was a lot of superstitious talk then. For instance, we were told that the sun danced in the heavens for the joy of the resurrection at Easter. I was always getting up early to see if the sun actually danced. I heard so much about heaven that I went in search of it. We had an old rushy hill at the back of the house and I remember climbing it and being terribly tired and thinking I would never get to the top. Eventually I reached the top and there was a valley and an enormous disappointment to find another hill at the end of the valley. I remember falling asleep and alarming everybody because they couldn't find me.

My mother died when I was ten. When news of her death came, I was shattered. Our farm was sold and we went to live with my father in the barracks. There was a succession of maids, as they were called then, or servant girls that looked after us.

The barracks was a very interesting place. We lived in the living quarters and all the activities of the police station actually happened in the house. It became part of our domestic lives. We would see the few prisoners that were there and we would witness the routine of the barracks. Nobody had anything much to do. They used to cycle around the roads and they used to write reports, which I think were one of my first glimpses of fiction. They used to call them the patrols of the imagination! On wet days they would hole up in some house, but then they would have to pretend that they had cycled and had to dream up what they had seen along the way. These reports were quite long, often a page and a half of the foolscap ledger. Often in the evenings the policemen would be bored, because one of them always had to be in the barracks. They would come up to play cards in the living room. We would hear them thumping up the stairs with their bed in the morning and taking it down again at night, where they slept beside a phone that never rang.

There would be enormous excitement on a court day, when they would all be polishing themselves up. They had to go into town to the court and they would put a few bets on the horses. There would also be great excitement when the superintendent came on inspection. He used to line them up and comment on their dress and that sort of thing.

They also had to measure the rainfall. There was a copper rain gauge out among the cabbages in the garden and that was one of the daily rituals. There were a whole lot of pointless ceremonies. They had to put out the thistle, ragwort and dock posters and notices about dog licences too.

I got a scholarship to go to secondary school in Carrick-on-Shannon. It was a very good school and the Presentation Brothers were marvellous people. I taught for the Christian Brothers myself afterwards, in Drogheda, and there was certainly a difference between the Presentation Brothers and the Christian Brothers. The Presentation Brothers were much more liberal and they encouraged reading. A lot of people got scholarships to university, from what was a very poor part of the country. Brother Damien was quite snobbish and he used to say that the people of this country are remarkably ignorant. 'If you tell them that you're going to "the Brothers", they'll immediately assume that you are referring to the Christian Brothers. Add to their little knowledge by informing them that you are Christian in the sense that you are not pagan, but that you are not Christian in any other sense!'

There were no books in our house, but I discovered them in the house of friends of my father, a family called Moroney.

There is a wonderful portrait of them in that good book *Woodbrook*, by David Thompson. Old Mr Moroney was a beekeeper and he was very eccentric. Father and son lived together and they had 180 acres of good limestone land. In fact, David Thompson says they were landless, but in a way they were landless in spirit. They had a farm that they never looked after and in fact they gathered apples and sold them for half a crown a bucketful. I remember being sent to buy a bucketful of apples and falling into conversation with the old man about books. I was interested in books and when I was about eleven he gave me the run of his excellent nineteenth-century library. For about eight or nine years, I would come every fortnight returning five or six books in my oil-cloth shopping bag and taking five or six more away.

One reads with an incredible intensity in childhood. You really believe everything you read. My sisters still remember one time when I was reading and was completely lost in the book. I was so lost that eventually they unlaced my shoes, put a straw hat on my head and they were moving the chair away from the window light when I woke up from the book and found that the whole household was howling with laughter at me.

Often it is the book that you wouldn't read now that you remember most. I remember there was a lot of Zane Grey. I would have read every Zane Grey book in the library, which would be thirty or forty novels. Somebody in that nineteenth-century house was fascinated by the Rocky Mountains, so there was an endless amount of books about them, with bears and all sorts of adventure stories. Then there were Scott and Dickens and Shakespeare. I don't think I differentiated between Zane Grey and Dickens. I just read for pleasure.

I imagine the Moroneys had once been ruled by women, but at this stage the two boys were on their own. They would run through all the cups and plates and every month they used to have a big washing up. They lived on tea and bread and jam. Willie Moroney was a great beekeeper and he had an enormous beard which was stained with all sorts of colours of food and drink – you could smell him at quite a distance. When he was talking about books and the raspberry jam on his bread fell into his beard, it set off a buzzing noise. Without interrupting his conversation, he extracted three or four bees from his beard, cast them off into the yard and went on with his conversation. His son was interested in astronomy and so they did practically no work on the land at all. He was also interested in unusual breeds of sheep. I remember going with him in a van with five or six special sheep that they had imported from England to sell at the Dublin market. He wanted to see the stars, so we went out to the top of the Sugar Loaf mountain and were absolutely frozen sleeping in the van. We sold the sheep in the morning and had breakfast in the big hotel at the cattle market. They were both lovely people, so gentle.

At the end of secondary school, a lot depended on how well one did at the exams. If you did well, you had choices. If you didn't do well, you didn't have choices and you went to England. I got a number of scholarships, including the ESB and the civil service, but I went to the training college and trained as a teacher.

It was quite a shock going from Carrick-on-Shannon to the training college, because the Presentation Brothers were much more civilised than the people that ran the training college. We were not trusted. I don't think they seriously wanted to educate us. In fact you could get into trouble for reading books in the study hall. It is amazing to think that we were going out to parishes as teachers, but we were only allowed out from two to six on a Wednesday and I think from two to seven on a Saturday. You had to be in for all meals on a Sunday and you had to be in by ten o'clock at night. If you broke any of these rules, or if you didn't go to daily Mass, you'd find yourself expelled.

I received most of my education from the other students and by going to the Gate Theatre. There was a marvellous boy who was in the same class as me called Éanna Ó hEithir. He was a nephew of Liam O'Flaherty and a brother of Breandán. He was envied because he had the use of O'Flaherty's flat in Paris. He knew a lot about books and he would lend them to anybody interested in reading them or talking about them. But the whole atmosphere at the college was anti-intellectual. There was a small group of boys that came from some of the better colleges like Rockwell or Blackrock and they formed a debating society. They were nicknamed Oideachas Éireann and were hounded mercilessly. You would think debating would be a normal activity for any third-level college. Also, if you didn't unlearn your table manners, you would absolutely starve there! There was a crowd from Donegal I remember that used to work in tunnels in Glasgow during the summer holidays, big fellows, O'Donnells and Gallaghers, and they were quite formidable at the table.

You had to be academically bright to get into college. You had to get eighty or eighty-five per cent to get in, but you only needed forty per cent to get out, so there was really no examination pressure. One had leisure and one learned how to obey the rules – and use them for one's own purposes.

In 1955, I came out of Drumcondra and I started teaching the same year. I went to the Christian Brothers in Drogheda and I spent a year teaching there. I then started to go to university at night and got a teaching post at a school in Clontarf and of course that was a great help to one's income – I think we were paid six pounds a week then.

I didn't enjoy teaching. I'm very suspicious of people who say they do. I think that if you do anything well, or even if you try to do anything well, it's hard work and it's painful. It means taking attention from yourself and giving it to the children, in the same sense that writing is simply giving it to the words; there is a certain discipline that is pleasurable, but I wouldn't call that enjoyable. I think that teaching is very honourable work, but it is also very hard work, and I don't think it is appreciated as much as it should be in society. They say about writing that, if the writer has a great time writing, the reader has a bad time reading. I think that, while people that enjoy teaching might be having a ball, the children may not be learning much. The real work is quite a hard struggle and out of the struggle you get moments of satisfaction, but you're really just working in order to put something across for the children to learn.

My teaching career in this country came to an abrupt end when my book, *The Dark*, was banned. There was enormous pressure on me to be the decent fellow and resign. I was determined that I wasn't going to do that and I turned up at school even though I wasn't allowed into the classroom. I had taught with all the teachers for seven or eight years and we were a very good school. We had got the 'Carlisle and Blake' award the year before, which meant that every teacher had to be highly efficient. They were friends and colleagues and I am still very close to one of them.

When I turned up at the school, everyone was in a worse state then I was and we must have made endless cups of tea that morning. The headmaster was in an awful state. He had informed me that I wasn't allowed into the classroom. The parish priest couldn't face it – he had gone on his holidays and could only see me when he came back. I think he was hoping that he wouldn't have to see me at all. I met him when he came back off his holidays and he told me that he was very happy with me and why did I have to go and write that book and bring all this trouble down on him. He told me that he had nothing against me but that the Archbishop, John Charles McQuaid, had told him to fire me. Everyone was strangely pleasant about the dismissal. It seemed as if nobody else wanted it and he was more or less saying that it wasn't his fault, that he was well disposed towards me.

It was unpleasant, but I suppose I was lucky in that I had been writing and had had two books published already. I certainly was interested in writing as much as in teaching, but I couldn't afford to live off my books. So I went and taught in London.

That was a very different experience to teaching in Clontarf. Where you have the father and mother interested in education, as most of the people in Clontarf were, it makes teaching much easier, but in the East End of London they couldn't care less. I remember teaching a class that couldn't read, but the beginning of teaching was to get them to believe in their lives. You didn't teach them formal English, you got the *Evening Standard* and taught them about football. I had about fourteen kids in that class and I think I taught about twelve of them to read. I remember getting a marvellous sentence from one of the kids: 'My granddad used to roll barrels at Whitbread's Brewery at London Bridge, but now he's puffed when he comes up the hill after his dinner from the betting shop.' I thought 'puffed' was a marvellous word.

Eventually, Professor Gordon at Reading liked my work and gave me a research assistantship at the University of Reading, so I left teaching in London. I had been four years teaching in London after the Dublin débâcle. I have taught at university level since but never again at primary level.

I am back in the rushy hills now, back in my own place. Life is the same everywhere. I think that the quality of feeling that's brought to the landscape is actually much more important than the landscape itself. It is the light or passion or love, if you like, in which the landscape is witnessed that is more important than whether it contains rushes or lemon trees. A writer knows that he is only as good as the next day's page. In that sense I think of a writer as being always a beginner, and the day you cease learning is the day that you're finished.

T P McKenna

T P McKenna was born in Mullagh, County Cavan, in 1929. At the young age of fifteen he was bitten by the acting bug but adhered to the advice of the distinguished actor, Anew McMaster, who told him only to try acting when he was sure he could do nothing else . . . T P pursued a career in banking for six years, before deciding that acting held far more attraction than balancing the books.

After some initial lean years, he eventually got regular employment with the Abbey Theatre. His big break came with the role of Cranley in the London production of Stephen D, *Hugh Leonard's adaptation of* A Portrait of the Artist as a Young Man. *Doors began opening for the man from Mullagh and for the past thirty years his acting career has flourished, on stage, screen and television, with a variety of acclaimed and distinguished roles.*

The woman I knew as my granny was, in fact, my grandfather's second wife and she was an extraordinary lady. She had no Irish blood in her at all; she was born in Louisiana in America and was part German. She arrived in the village of Mullagh, County Cavan, in 1908, when my father was a child, and she helped bring up the children. I was the first grandchild and she used to read to me from a very early age, maybe two or three. She would read a great deal of Dickens and other writers of that kind. All I can remember is that she used to sit me on her knee and that she had a lovely southern lilt to her voice. Then she had a stroke and I missed this business of hearing stories every evening so much that I started reading myself at a very early age.

My source of reading was the Cavan county library, but my earliest readings tended to be Zane Grey, Sapper and *The Saint*, and that kind of thing. I remember a little later moving on to more ambitious writers like Canon Sheehan. I had a morbid fascination with a book of his called *The Success of Failure*. It intrigued me as a title at the age of about thirteen or fourteen, because I had a dread of ending up in the gutter. Failure was in some way more attractive than success, just because the challenge was too much.

My father was an auctioneer. He was a very warm man, but he was quite stern as a father. He gave me a few clips around the ear in my time and he had a very strong personality. I remember a well-known lawyer describing him as the last of the Brehon judges. In those days in the village of Mullagh we had no solicitors and he drew up more wills in his lifetime than any man I know. He would travel down long country lanes of mud to visit the houses of dying men and advise them about who to leave the land to. He was trusted in that way by local people. People would come from all over the area for advice from him. He was very wise.

My mother had twelve children, of which I am the eldest. Only ten of us survived; two babies died. God help her, from the age of twenty-three she was all the time bearing children, like so many women of her generation. I wasn't very close to her. My Auntie Angela brought me up, so my mother wasn't that much of an influence on me, really.

I suppose the main occupation we had was football, football and football. Cavan were in every All-Ireland semi-final for as long as I could remember right through my youth and so we kicked a ball up and down the main street, because cars were scarce in those days. We would have one goal in one archway and the other goal in another archway. We made a ball out of paper tied with string and we would spend whole hours of the evening just kicking this ball around.

I was fairly useful at the football. I was on the junior team that won the Ranafast Cup when I was about fifteen and then I was on the senior team and won a McRory Cup Medal. I played in the All-Ireland Colleges final in 1948 and a lot of that team formed the basis of the 1952 Cavan team that went on to beat Meath in the All-Ireland final in Croke Park.

I am essentially an auto-didact. I didn't get any academic training. I didn't go to anything past secondary school, so whatever educational scope I have has been picked up along the way. I went to secondary school at St Patrick's College, Cavan, in September 1942 and if my father ever made a mistake it was that he made me feel that this was an enormous big deal and they were making great sacrifices. I felt a great weight of responsibility on me and I collapsed under it. The end result of this was that I wouldn't study. I spent my study periods reading poetry and English literature. I used to sit up in my room late at night looking out into the dark with a sense of despondency. The result was that I would never, never put any pressure on my children and say 'get down to that book there and study'. That was the effect it had had on me. I was very good at English and for some reason very good at sums, but geometry and algebra were a struggle and Greek and Latin were worse. I got to know Irish a bit better when I went to the Abbey.

Unquestionably, the biggest influence in my life was Father
Vincent Kennedy, now dead, God rest his soul. Looking back,
having met many, many eminent people, he was really one of
the most sophisticated men I ever met. He was a very stylish
man. He was small and dapper and everything he did was very
graceful. He had a rather lovely room in Saint Patrick's College,
with a Bechstein piano and a very nice library. He used to
produce operas. I was a boy soprano. My first appearance on
the stage was in *The Yeomen of the Guard.* I had an
extraordinarily powerful boy soprano voice, something I
inherited from my father. When my voice broke, we used to go
up to Father Vincent's room and he would play us a wide
variety of music. He also gave us classes in school in general
music education and the history of music. He would
demonstrate the difference in structure between the work of
Beethoven and Chopin, for example, and the development of
the piano as an instrument. This was very, very fascinating and
unusual for a secondary school. We would listen to the Proms
on BBC in his room and follow it with the score. He had a
wonderful range as a classical pianist. He could play the Grieg
concerto from memory and he had hundreds of scores as well.

We were the chosen few – just three or four of us – like Jean
Brodie's *crème de la crème.* We would knock on his door after
night prayer and if he was in a good mood he would let us in.
We would have coffee and talk and he would play the piano. If
he was in a bad mood, he would just sit there and puff smoke
in the air very elegantly. I remember one Leitrim fellow saying
to him, 'Are you bored, Father?' There was a long pause.
'Haven't I the right to be bored in my own sitting-room?' he
replied. We had the good sense to get up and leave.

His influence was all-pervasive at that time. I had moved on
from Gilbert and Sullivan and into drama; the plays of Louis
D'Alton for example. I had got the acting bug as young as the
age of fifteen. Anew McMaster was visiting Cavan and he had
brought his usual repertoire of Shakespeare. We saw *Hamlet* and

Macbeth and Father Kennedy then brought us backstage to meet McMaster. Myself and another chap decided to go down and talk to him in The Farnham Arms. He was very nice and he bought us tea. He said, 'Don't be an actor, my dear boy, until you are absolutely sure there's nothing else in the world you can do.' I took that very literally, so I decided to set about getting a job when I left school and then maybe get around to the acting sometime later.

Before I left St Pat's, one strange and amazing thing happened. The vice-president came into the class and said, 'The manager of the Ulster Bank in Cavan has written to me looking for young recruits for the bank. There is a great future in it, because during the war years they didn't recruit anybody and they lost some young men in the war.' What he didn't, in fact, say was 'young Catholic men', because the Ulster Bank had sixty branches in the Republic and they needed staff very badly. We had a chat about it among ourselves and three or four of the lads said it was a great idea. I laughed at them all as they went up the stairs to his room. I went to the college chapel, genuflected and, without any rational process, turned and walked out the chapel door and back behind the last person into the vice-president's room . . .

So I went to Belfast to do the bank exams and, for good or ill, I was called to the bank at the end of May, which meant I didn't sit for the Leaving Cert or matric. This came as an enormous relief to me, because I was going to use the bank for a year or two and I was going to become an actor, and what was the point in going back and doing my exams? My first posting was in Granard and after a year I was moved to Trim and I spent a year there. Trim had a good musical society and I was very active that year. When the bank decided to move me to Dublin, the people of Trim signed a petition asking the bank to leave me in Trim, as I was invaluable to the town and its amusements. The bank wrote back saying that they couldn't stand in the way of the brilliant career that this young man had in front of him in the bank. So I moved to Dublin in 1950, but it was very nice of the people of Trim, all the same.

My banking career lasted six years. I had moved into various amateur dramatic societies, the Royal Shakespeare Society and the Rathmines and Rathgar Society, and performed in the Gaiety in the Gilbert and Sullivan shows. All through my life decisions have been forced on me rather than being great independent gestures, until the day a bank inspector arrived unannounced and said to me, 'You haven't done all the exams you're supposed to have done and I believe you hang around with actors and that's keeping your mind off your work. We're going to transfer you to a country branch, where you'll have nothing to do but think of your banking.' I couldn't face that and I resigned.

I wasn't a member of Equity when I left, but, through the friendship and generosity of people like Milo O'Shea and Godfrey Quigley, I eventually got parts in plays and became a member of Irish Actors Equity. A year later, I ended up in the Abbey Theatre. In terms of education, the bank taught me very little except one thing, and that is order. In those days, before all this technology, everything was done by hand, and the volume of work was quite enormous. You had to learn to cope with vast amounts of paperwork at great speed. If you look at my table, you will find that it's very tidy to this day and I can put my finger on anything I want. That's the only thing I brought from the bank – an ability to keep things in order and be able to find things immediately when I want them. I'm very good at filing.

The decision to give up the bank caused mayhem at home. My cousin Paddy O'Reilly, State Solicitor, was called in and I was given the full drill – put on a chair and hauled before the judge, which was my father!!! 'Don't you dare come back here. There'll be nothing here for you!' However, I persisted and it didn't deflect me.

The early years were very lean times indeed. The Gas Theatre Company was run by Godfrey Quigley and, as we were on shares of the profits, things got very bad. I was down to two pounds a week, which was exactly my rent, so I had nothing to eat. I couldn't approach people at home for money. A radio programme called *The Kennedys of Castleross* did bring in a little bread on the side. I went to Mr Blythe of the Abbey and gave him a long spiel which I had prepared about how I felt that continuity for some period of a young actor's life was essential for him to learn his trade. He brought me in to the *Geamaireacht*, which was a yearly Irish pantomime in the Queen's. I had Padraic O'Neill to polish up my pronunciation and various things. A vacancy came up just shortly after the *Geamaireacht* finished in January. An actor failed to turn up for a show and I came down and read in for him and spent the next eight years there, without a contract.

The repertoire at the Queen's was dominated by the fact that the theatre held eight or nine hundred people. There was a need to fill that building and therefore the standard of plays was pretty awful. I've forgotten so many of them. I became deeply unhappy, to the point of almost clinical depression, around my thirtieth year. I had been married four years at that time. Then Frank Dermody was brought in to the theatre and we did *Long Day's Journey into Night*. It was a revelation to me, because suddenly here was a play with dimensions which I hadn't come across in the other plays we'd been doing and that set me back on my feet a bit.

The Dublin Theatre Festival put on *Stephen D*, Hugh Leonard's adaptation of *A Portrait of the Artist as a Young Man*, and, in 1963, I was invited by Norman Rodway and Phyllis Ryan to come to London with it. It was a huge critical success in London, not a great commercial success, although it could have been. I made some sort of mark and I did my first television plays for the BBC in that period and decided not to go back to the Abbey. I have been a freelance actor ever since and that was thirty-one years ago. I had employment at the National and the Royal Shakespeare Company for periods of more than eight or nine months.

You become educated in a strange sort of way in the theatre and in films. I did a film called *The Charge of the Light Brigade*, which involved a huge amount of reading the history of the period. I was playing George Russell, an Irish man who was the *Times* reporter on the Crimean War and in fact was one of the great war reporters of that time. His reports were responsible for changing the structure of the British army. I also made a point of reading about the history of Turkey and how Mustafa Kemal insisted on moving the capital, the old Ottoman Empire capital of Constantinople, into Ankara in central Anatolia. I learned a lot about the politics of that era in Turkey and its revolution and Kemal's bringing the Turkish people into the twentieth century and into Europe out of the East. I also learned a great deal when I played Robert Emmet. You can't play Robert Emmet without reading the history of the period. One remark made about him was for me the key to playing the character, the fact that Robert Emmet was totally ingenuous as a person and trusted everybody. On his way from France to Dublin he met a very cultured gentleman who asked him why was he going to Dublin. 'I'm going to start a revolution,' he said. The chap he spoke to went straight to the Castle and they let him go ahead with that revolution, knowing they could quash it, as they did in a matter of hours.

I am still, of course, being educated. There is always the quest for self-knowledge and the discipline of the profession. At this moment in time I am in Brian Friel's play, *Molly Sweeney*, which is the most challenging thing I have taken on, because it is a series of monologues. On my way to the theatre on the first night, I had to work hard to exercise enormous self-control over my fears. I could have run away and said, 'I don't need to go through this', but it is important to put yourself through that pain barrier. It's a question of don't take the easy way out. I always call it getting behind yourself and giving yourself a good kick in the backside and saying 'Get on with it there, for God's sake!'

In my youth I really had a morbid feeling that I wouldn't be able to make it in life, considering that, when pressure was put on me going through school, my response was a negative one of saying 'I'll throw in the towel'. I'm very lucky that I have found in life a talent, going back to McMaster's advice. My years in the bank were useful in that I discovered that I was no damn good at that kind of job, which was mundane and boring and unchanging from hour to hour and from day to day and week to week and year to year. I was lucky to find just a simple little string of talent which provides an enormous variety of challenges. I am, in a sense, the success of failure.

Frank Mitchell

Frank Mitchell was born in Dublin in 1912. He was educated at the High School and at Trinity College, where he was diverted from his initial pursuit of an arts degree into the area of the natural sciences, mainly through the influence of a number of mentors who crossed his path. His distinction in a number of fields – zoology, geology, archaeology – ultimately led to his appointment as Professor of Quaternary Studies at Trinity College in 1963. He was president of the Royal Irish Academy from 1976 to 1979.

Frank Mitchell has written extensively on his studies of the Irish landscape, notably The Way that I Followed *and* The Shell Guide to the Irish Landscape, *later revised and expanded (with Michael Ryan) as* Reading the Irish Landscape. *A scholar of international renown, Frank continues to work in his mid-eighties ('I have this incredible curiosity, I can't leave a thing alone . . .'), his most recent concern being the study of a unique pattern of agricultural use in Valentia, County Kerry.*

I was born and bred in Rathgar and lived all my early life on the periphery of Rathgar. We were real Dubliners. I had a colleague at school, Alec Mason, who was the son of the famous Tommy Mason, the photographer and archaeologist. Alec had inherited his father's interest in natural history and I can remember as a boy going out with Alec to Rathfarnham and climbing trees looking for rooks' nests and that sort of thing. I think it was that association with Alec that started off my interest in the natural sciences.

My father and his brother had a firm called Hodges, which was on Aston's Quay where I think the student travel bureau is now. My uncle dealt in furniture on the first floor and my father dealt in hardware on the ground floor. It was hoped by my father that either my brother or I would succeed him in the business.

My mother was very keen on education and my brother was a fast learner as a schoolboy and he carried exhibitions and prizes before him. I was very slow to get off the mark and it was only really by the offer of an exhibition that I entered Trinity College at all, which my father obviously saw as time out of the apprenticeship in the business.

My mother was born before it became common for women to go to university, but she certainly was of the calibre that would have profited from a university education. So was my father, but he left school prematurely, following the death of his father, and his schooling wasn't of the same high level as my mother's.

There couldn't have been two more devoted or well-meaning parents. They were very simple people, unaware of the complexities of life, and they certainly spared themselves no effort to look after myself and my brother and sister.

We had a nursery school at home, run by an aunt of my mother's, Mrs Hewson, and she was a very formidable instructor in the three 'R's. I can still see us sitting there, using our hands to demonstrate what a preposition is – my hand is *above* the table, my hand is *beside* the table and my hand is *under* the table – and by dint of repetition she gave us a good grounding in reading and writing and elementary arithmetic.

I proceeded from there to the High School. I think we were a pretty rough crowd and perhaps the masters reacted to that, but I don't really feel that the teaching was of the highest quality. Then again it was largely our fault, because, looking back on it now, I can see we were very boorish in our behaviour. The High School was a classical school and we slaved away at Greek and Latin texts. Nobody ever conveyed to me any feeling of poetry or drama in what we were doing, but I persisted. I even took the paper in Greek verse at the Trinity exhibition. There was always the hope that you might get a couple of couplets right and get a mark or two, which would be very valuable in the long run.

The High School was one of the Erasmus Smith schools and there was a special exhibition for the boy from an Erasmus Smith school who did best in the junior exhibition examination. My friend came out first. He was above me in the list, but he elected for a career in the Bank of Ireland and didn't go to college, whereupon the scholarship fell on my unworthy shoulders. Trinity College has certain very valuable scholarships which give you a free dinner and free rooms in college and a modest salary as well. It hit me that I could get one of these, so, for the first time in my life, I started to work. I stopped lying on the floor with the radio on.

I spent a brief period doing arts. My father had decided that, if he had to forfeit me for another four years from coming to work with him in the business, I had better do something that could be of some use. So it was decided that I would do English and French. Basically, I wasn't really very interested and certainly Sam Beckett wasn't interested in me. It was his first term as a lecturer and doubtless he was ill at ease and not confident, but he was just rude to anybody who seemed to him not particularly bright and then they went away and didn't come back to his lectures anymore.

Throughout my long career, there were a number of mentors who came into my life and influenced me greatly. One was Arthur Stelfox. He was a very curious man, who had come from Cheshire to Belfast. He trained as an architect, but he was always deeply interested in natural history and his wife, too, was a botanist of distinction. After various wanderings, he ended up as an assistant in the natural history department of the National Museum in Dublin. I used to go in to look at mounted groups of birds and that sort of thing and he used to wander through the museum and chat with any interested youngsters. It was in this way that he got to chatting with me and arranged for me to go out on excursions with friends of his and it was really through him that my interest in natural history was greatly fostered.

Stelfox was a man of habit. Every day had its pattern; he would get on his bicycle and go down to the museum to work, come home later, have an evening high tea with Mrs Stelfox and the children and then immediately move over to a corner of the room, where he occupied the winter evenings mounting the numerous insects he had collected over the summer months.

My family was very strict and my father was a strict Sabbatarian. The Dublin Naturalist Field Club had what they called an active service unit, which was a group of three or four people with different scientific interests, and they would go out on a Sunday and stravaig the sides of Lugnacoille or climb Kippure, or something like that. But they always met on a Sunday, so that was ruled out as far as I was concerned.

An important member of the field club was Mr Brunker, who worked for Guinness. He had a passion for the flora of County Wicklow and, indeed, before his death succeeded in publishing a very valuable *Flora of County Wicklow*. He took to taking me out with him on Saturday afternoons. He had an old bull-nosed Morris car in which we would go down to Kilcoole and he would look out for rare clovers and identify the various birds that we saw. Brunker was unmarried and lived with several of his sisters. He was meticulous in his time-keeping at the brewery, but he looked forward to his Saturday afternoons and Sundays. He would be out in some part of his beloved Wicklow every weekend.

Both Stelfox and Brunker were very formative influences for me, but they paled into insignificance compared with the Danish man, Jessen. That was another of those chance occurrences. It was a time coming up to the war when peat cutting was greatly emphasised and enormous quantities of peat were cut by hand. Marr, who had recently arrived as director of the National Museum, was faced with a flood of bronze implements and other things being brought in from the bogs. Tony Farrington of the Royal Irish Academy was interested in how Ireland's climate had developed after the ice age and Praeger was interested in anything that would throw light on the history of Irish flora, so they combined and got generous government support, largely due to Mr de Valera's personal interest in the matter. Jessen was brought with his assistant to Ireland for two seasons to visit bogs from which archaeological objects had recently come to the museum and take a series of samples through the top to the bottom of the bog. Then, by studying the succession of pollen grains trapped in these samples, he worked out the history of forest development in Ireland and so placed the discovered object at an appropriate point in history.

Louis Bouvier Smith had succeeded Professor Joly as Professor of Geology and he encouraged me to give up zoology, in which I was specialising for my degree, and turn to geology. I did that and, in due course, became the assistant in the department of geology. He heard about the proposed visit from Jessen and how guides were needed to accompany Jessen, both to show him around the country and to pick his brains. He suggested that I should apply for one of these posts as a guide, which I did and was fortunate enough to be appointed.

Jessen was a most attractive personality, one of the most engaging people I have ever met. I rapidly realised what a

privilege it was to be working with him – his assistant was also
an interesting man – so we had a tremendous time touring the
country. The tour, which would last perhaps two months,
would result in enough specimens being taken for more than
two years' subsequent study in the laboratory. The counting of
pollen grains embedded in the deposits was a laborious and
time-consuming process, but it gradually revealed how the
proportions of the trees had changed with time – how some had
expanded and others had contracted. In those happy days we
were not aware of the profound effect that prehistoric farming
had had on the woodlands, so, to a certain extent, our early
work was superseded very rapidly when it was realised that we
were not just dealing with nature's effect on the woodlands but
also with man's effect. This, in turn, made it possible to make
more precise archaeological correlations, because we were now
matching forest change with agricultural activity rather than
just seeing a general drift of forest change over time.

Our studies were of the crudest nature compared with what
would be done now. We started off by just counting the tree
pollen only. Then it was realised that the pollens of a great many
herbs and grasses could also be identified, so that was another
whole range of material that had to be studied with the new
techniques. Pollen grains themselves are composed of a most
remarkable substance which practically defies chemical attack,
so that, if you have a bog comprised partly of pollen grains and
partly of decayed plant material, you can oxidise and acidify it
and do all sorts of things to it to get rid of all the other debris
and leave only the pollen grains.

In those days we believed that the whole of Ireland had been
covered with one kind of woodland from end to end and that
therefore you could extrapolate from one part of Ireland to the
other. Now it is known that the forest growth was very
intimately related to soil conditions and so the forest around
Killarney would have been wildly different from the
contemporaneous forests in the Boyne Valley, for example. So

the whole thing has become more precise, everything is so much more detailed. Where we just looked at the crude surface of the pollen grain – how many pores it had, how many slits – now, with the electron microscope, you can actually see the surface of the grain and see that it carries a minute pattern which varies from species to species, meaning that you can make identifications with infinitely more precision.

In my travels around the country, I have visited many, many sites, but, if asked to pick out the site that has given me the greatest insight into the way things were, I always come back to Goodland in County Antrim, which is just a few miles from Fair Head. At one time in the geological past, a thick sheet of white chalk covered the vast bulk of Ireland. That has all been eroded away, except in north-east Ireland where it was largely covered by a later sheet of basalt which protected it. However, at Goodland there is a small area where there is no protective covering, giving an expanse of chalk downland which is absolutely unique in this country. We used to think that there was a very small number of farmers in Ireland in early times, but now I think there were probably great armies of them, because we can see evidence of intense agriculture all the way from Fair Head to Valentia Island in Kerry, from at least three thousand years before the birth of Christ. At Goodland, there was extensive Neolithic occupation and then, for some reason, peat began to form and these Neolithic settlements were buried. At a later date, people came along and laid out a field system and cultivated the area, and then, still later, people came and built huts there. Some of the huts are situated on top of the field banks, so the field banks must have been abandoned before the people who made the huts came along. Estyn Evans of Queen's University thought that these were huts used by people who went up there in the summer time with the herds, when the flush of summer milk was on, and they milked them there and made cheese. And all the time the bog was expanding and swallowing the whole thing up. From aerial photographs, you can't physically see the Neolithic site, but it's definitely there under the bog and you can see the field banks buried by peat, with huts lapping over on top of them. That's the place where I get the most vivid impression of the continuity of man's occupation of the Irish countryside.

I now live at Townley Hall, near Drogheda, County Louth, which has an interesting history. At the time the National Health Service was introduced in Britain, everybody was going to be healthier, so it was thought that there would be less need for hospitals. There would be a gross surplus of doctors, so the universities were told that they had to cut down on their intake of medical students. Trinity College sought to expand in other areas and, with agriculture and engineering in mind, bought this property – 800 acres in the Boyne Valley – with the idea of developing one part for research and another part for demonstration purposes. The project was originally supposed to be in co-operation with the Agricultural Institute, but, for various reasons, it never really got off the ground. When Donogh O'Malley announced his famous merger scheme, which of course never happened, it became clear that there would not be sustained support for agriculture at Trinity College and so the college pulled out. But, for about twenty years, it was a very active place of work.

I had been very interested in the agricultural project and worked hard at it and it was disappointing when it failed. I certainly enjoyed the running of the farm. We had a very able and dynamic manager, Pat McHugh, who came from the Department of Agriculture. He was a great taskmaster and he would turn me out on a Sunday morning to move the electric fence or give a general hand with the milking. I enjoyed it very much indeed, as did my wife, who was also city born and bred. She, too, took to the country life with a vengeance.

When Trinity pulled out, my wife and I took on the main house and we ran it for a number of years. She ran it as a place for extension courses, chiefly weekend courses, and there were no holds barred as far as the subject was concerned. We had groups from archaeological departments all over England, we had religious groups, socialist groups; you name it, they were there. This really provided a service which was enormously appreciated and she conjured it up out of nothing. We were running a two-man show and we were both getting older, and it became clear that we would have to withdraw sooner or later, but she died before that could happen, so I moved across to the gardener's cottage.

After four score years, I'm still active and still learning. I just have this incredible curiosity. I can't leave a thing alone. I have now discovered that if a calcareous spring oozes out onto the surface, a spongy white deposit of calcium carbonate will form. I realised that this was extensively used in church architecture, at least on the eastern seaboard of Ireland. I am hoping to visit as many ruined church sites as I can to see how many of them have got blocks of this white material built into them, because there is no known local source for it. It is light, you can cut it and carve it anyway you like, a wonderful building substance. Is it imported or is there, somewhere awaiting discovery, an abandoned quarry? I have just stumbled on this and, for me, a nice afternoon's excursion is to potter around a few churches, and it is surprising the amount I am discovering.

Maire Mullarney

Maire Mullarney was born in 1921. Her father's long periods of absence from home (he worked as an accountant with the British Colonial Service) left her very much under the influence of her mother and her aunt, who, together with books, were her real educators.

She trained as a nurse, married and became the mother of eleven children. She and her husband, Sean, taught all eleven children at home. Maire later wrote about this experience in her book, Anything School Can Do You Can Do Better. *She has also written a book on* Early Reading, *based on her experience of teaching reading, and an autobiography,* What About Me?

A doughty campaigner on a wide range of issues – family planning, corporal punishment, compulsory Irish, the environment – Maire has been active in local politics as a Green Party County Councillor. In recent years, she has passionately promoted the notions of a basic income for all and the adoption of Esperanto as the primary language of international communication.

Maire Mullarney lives in Dublin.

My father was an accountant in the post office here in Ireland and, after Independence, he had the option of staying in the British Colonial Service or staying here in Ireland. His friends stayed here, but he went to Nigeria for the experience. It suited him and, on the whole, it suited me. He would be there for a year and back here for six months, and the understanding was that wives would go out for six months at least. My mother managed to dodge the first six months, but the second time she was able to leave me with her sister. I had a marvellous time with her. She used to tell me stories about Teddy every night.

I was an only child living in a house where I had the complete run of everything. It was in the Glen of the Downs, just facing the Sugar Loaf mountain. My only worry was that they had told me that the Sugar Loaf was a volcano. Otherwise, I hadn't a worry in the world and I was given a great feeling of affirmation.

My father had very authoritarian views. I was living with my mother and Teddy, but, when my father found that that was the way things were, he was jealous of Teddy and had some story about a nun saying that it was very wrong for children to spend their affections on inanimate creatures. I remember him putting Teddy up at the top of a wardrobe and breaking my heart.

I calculated that, by the time my father died, my parents must have had forty years of marriage but only about twelve years under the same roof, so I didn't do too badly.

The real nightmare in my life was the second time that my mother went to Nigeria, when I was just turning six. My father insisted that he didn't want me under the influence of my mother's family. I would have to go over to the north of England to his mother or go to boarding school. I don't know which would have been worse, because they were a very puritanical family, but boarding school was desperate. It was a convent boarding school and nobody meant me any harm, but it was a frightful shock, after having been with adults who treated me like a person, to find myself in this crazy world where you had to have the right veil for going to chapel – black for Confession and white for other things. I was completely lost. When I went up to bed at night, Teddy was the one hope of the day, the one bit of real life. One night he wasn't there and I spent three days going around the school crying. I don't think it was an unnatural attachment at all. He was just part of the family. Anything that you can feel affection for is a good thing. My mother used to tell me stories about him and I believed that he got up and walked around and had a life of his own at night.

My little brother was born when I was seven, but in a sense I could feel for him the way I did for Teddy, because he was a Down's Syndrome child and therefore didn't respond in the way that other kids would. I was very fond of him and it was an awful shock when he died when I was twelve. Possibly the habit of feeling affection for Teddy also explains why I had absolutely no problem getting on with people when I went to school.

When I was nine, my father had the opportunity to transfer to Gibraltar and it was there that I had another valuable experience. He didn't like the idea that I would spend all the summer swimming and fooling around with my mates, so he insisted that, before I went swimming, I must spend one hour teaching myself Spanish. When that hour was up, I was to go down to the garden and pick stones for an hour and throw them over the wall. He didn't want an undisciplined child and that worked quite well, because it left me with the feeling that, if you want to learn something, you go off and do it. I had no resentment and I thoroughly enjoyed it.

I spent a couple of terms in the national school, which was futile. It was one long stretch of boredom, because I was reading well by then anyway. The important thing that my mother was able to do was something which I now know is called mediation. It is essential that a mother mediates for small children what life is about. If nobody tells them that something is beautiful, that music is something worth listening to, that flowers should be respected, they will miss out and will be very defective. My mother did all her own gardening, she pumped water from the well and sawed the wood and so forth – all of which she was positive about. I remember discovering that, when she chopped a worm in half with the spade, the two halves would survive, but she wouldn't have dreamed of chopping a worm in half just to show me. Worms deserved their share of life as well. My mother, a care-for-nature countrywoman, wasn't at all unusual among Irish women of her time, but she certainly gave me her full attention when I was a child, which I know she enjoyed too. I feel that is probably the most important background to the rest of my learning.

Karl Popper says that the only things we need to be taught are how to read and write and, even then, not everybody needs to be taught – some pick it up for themselves. The kind of thing I learned from my mother was one half of my education and the rest was books. Chesterton and Belloc were part of family life and when my father had me learning Spanish he told me I could buy any books in Spanish that I liked. I had an account with the local stationers. I read a lot of historical fiction and, indeed, I went on to read through Spanish literature right up to fairly recent times. In the library, I made a mental rule that, for every two Edgar Wallace books, I would read something more solid – if it was in five volumes I felt it was solid. I remember reading the memoirs of Tallyrand, for example. It was quite advanced reading for teenage years. Perhaps the most influential of the lot at that time was a thick, five-volume Boswell. That gave me a feeling that conversation was what life was really about.

I went to school with the Loreto nuns. They did a lot of good, but not a great deal academically. Loreto convents at that time held internal debating competitions between them and that gave me a lot of experience and it was also very good fun.

My father's view was that there were only two things a woman was entitled to do – nursing and teaching. I had a short, pretty horrid experience of teaching in my own convent for three months, so teaching was not going to be for me. I went to

Baggot Street Hospital, which was a useful experience, if only to ease my conscience. I had been to the college of art for a term or so before that. I was always hoping that, when I got nursing out of the way, I could get back to drawing and painting, which I had done since I was an infant. Somehow the nursing thing took over and I moved into physiotherapy then, which I found very interesting. I have no interest in illness, so that I was pretty sceptical about the hospital system as a whole. I still am, but it was a good thing at that age to meet death from time to time. I often sat with people who were dying and it was a very reassuring thing for the rest of my own life to know that dying is not frightening, but that it comes smoothly and is welcome enough.

Eventually I got married and we had eleven children and achieved some fame, I suppose, by teaching our own children. This was due to my husband's habit of picking up secondhand books. We found and read something about Montessori and it sounded very sensible. We also knew we were so far from any school that we weren't likely to be able to send the children until they were quite big, so we decided to have a bash. We started much earlier than the Montessori age. When Barbara was about eight months old, we started doing roughly the kind of things Montessori was offering at two and a half – geometrical insets and so forth. The next boy began to read when he was two and I have done the same sort of thing with the others.

Because of that chance experiment, I was learning all the time. I was watching what they were doing. The first thing I learned was that human beings like learning. That was one reason I was involved in setting up Reform, which aimed to get rid of corporal punishment. I was very, very shocked to find that they were actually hitting children in school if they didn't know something. I learned two things. I learned something about comparing methods and experimenting and also to be quite sceptical of authorities. I was already sceptical in the health field and now I am also pretty sceptical in the official educational field.

I enjoyed teaching the children and it took very little time or effort because I did not just sit down with them and tell them things. I showed them how to do something and then they would go and do it themselves. It just seemed so natural. We had a game we played with plants. We would pick several different varieties of leaf in the garden to give to each child and they would have to go and look for a leaf to match it and come back with it. We might just casually talk about which one was spotty and which one was hairy and which was smooth and which was prickly and so on. One of the children turned into a plantswoman and she is now a landscape gardener. She went to the Botanic Gardens and did very well there. Most children, certainly in the primary years, if they are given a chance to follow something of interest, will teach themselves.

When our own children eventually went to school, they were always first in the class for a term or so, but then they would assess the temperature of the water and settle down, in order not to be outstanding. There was one occasion when my eldest son was asked why he never recited his tables and he just said, 'Well, Brother, did I ever get a sum wrong?' He was working well below his capacity all the time. Teachers are tremendously handicapped by class size. Most children are working years below what they could be doing, simply because of the numbers in each class.

When I was about twelve, my father gave me a missal with Spanish on one side and Latin on the other, so, almost without noticing, I moved backwards and forwards between the two. I can read Church Latin with ease, but when I applied to do a degree in Latin later on they wouldn't let me because I hadn't got classical Latin. It was all for the good, though, because I found Esperanto instead.

My husband and I educated each other. He used to write me lovely postcards in Latin when I was in the nurses' home. People were baffled, because I was receiving postcards every day with beautiful small writing all in Latin. I had met him as a patient there when I was running the outpatients department. We used to read philosophy and Latin. We have diverged a little now, because he has gone more and more towards history and the past and I have moved more and more towards the future, but we meet in the present and we meet with the children.

I went to extra-mural lectures for quite a long time, when Dermot Ryan, our late archbishop, was still a professor. He was a marvellous lecturer on the Old Testament and, after that, he got us studying a Greek New Testament. That was a revelation, because it was so much easier to follow, not to write but to understand. So we had a grounding in theology in general and, to some extent, in moral theology. When the controversy about family planning broke, I could prove that I was a dutiful Catholic because I had eleven children, but it was only on philosophical grounds that we had followed the rules, never out of obedience.

We set up Irish Family Planning and I was the Irish delegate to a couple of meetings of International Planned Parenthood. There were about forty nationalities there who were all using English and I could see many disadvantages in this, particularly when one brilliant Polish professor gave a paper with such wretched English that it did not do him justice. At that time I didn't think there was any alternative, but then I discovered Esperanto when we were on holiday in Vienna. I had excellent opportunities to learn Spanish, but I always knew that it was not my own language. I always felt I was looking over my shoulder, thinking how would the Spanish say it. Then I found this language that I could have complete control of, saying exactly what I wanted, expressed accurately with no problems of accent, and I could also understand people – Chinese, Albanians, Russians and so forth. I am quite clear that it is something the world badly needs now. I could read it the first day I encountered it. I gave my mother, at ninety-two, a Chinese magazine, to look at the pictures, and when I came back to her she said she had been able to read and understand most of the articles. The Chinese write the purest Esperanto, and they do it in a very big way.

I got into the Green Party through Esperanto, incidentally. When I wanted to learn Esperanto, I was put in touch with

Christopher Fettes, who, shortly after, proceeded to set up the Greens. When I have been Irish delegate to the European Greens, I could see how badly we need a language that we can all speak competently, without having to spend enormous sums on translation or rely on English or French. For instance, one Bulgarian delegate, last year in Budapest, discovered he really hadn't understood anything, but he could speak perfect Esperanto.

Reading Boswell early on had some kind of permeating influence on me, but then, a good many years later, I read de Chardin's *The Phenomenon of Man*. That was an opening out for me on a much larger scale – Europe, the universe and people's role in the world. Teilhard de Chardin was the eleventh in his family, and when I found out I was going to have an eleventh child I was quite pleased. I can still remember, at about five one morning when the sun was shining, reading a crucial part of that book where human intelligence becomes incandescent. Another book which follows on from that is *The Ascent of Women* by Elaine Morgan. I found one nearly as impressive as the other, in the sense of trying to know who we are and where we are, our place in the planet and in the universe.

I think I am an ordinary person who just didn't happen to be pushed through the murder machine – I wasn't what they call socialised. I have a great dread of the idea of school as a socialising agent which preaches to people who they are and where they fit in, even though most of those doing the preaching are not very competent. This is Ivan Illich's considerable argument against school – that it is really meant as a sort of sieve to sort out the people who can be top people and let the others understand that they have had their chance and didn't take it, so they are no good. I have never felt that it was particularly important to be doing what other people are doing or to be doing something different. I was allowed, as a child, to do whatever presented itself as being interesting.

Brendan O'Regan

Brendan O'Regan was born in Sixmilebridge, County Clare, in 1917. His father was a hotel proprietor and businessman whose motto was 'The best is the best'. His mother's motto was 'Love is all that matters'. Both mottoes were to have a profound influence on Brendan's career.

He was educated at Blackrock College, Dublin, and studied hotel management in Germany before taking on the management of family hotels in County Clare. He then took charge of the restaurants at Foynes and Shannon airports. Shannon airport would be the 'airport of the future' and, with incredible zeal, Brendan O'Regan built up the catering business there, pioneered the duty-free shops, created the tax-free industrial zone and the School of Hotel Management, leading ultimately to the development of the Republic's only 'new town' – Shannon. In many ways, Brendan O'Regan was 'Mr Shannon'.

In later years, Brendan turned to peace strategies for the seemingly intractable problem of Northern Ireland. He was founder-chairman of Co-operation North and chairman of the Irish Peace Institute. 'The key to peace is management.' In retirement, he has become active in the renewal of community in his native Clare, focusing on the strength of the parish.

I was born in 1917 in the village of Sixmilebridge. My father was a very strong character and my earliest memories are of the influence that he had on me. He was the chairman of Clare County Council when I was just a young fellow and he was filled with the possibilities of accomplishing things through the democratic system in his time. My earliest recollections were stories that he would tell me of what was going on in Ireland in those days, such as the ambushes, which were led by Micheál Brennan, and how the Black and Tans and the Auxiliaries at that time would take retribution on the village.

When I was ten years of age, in 1927, my father had purchased what he called the bones of the Old Ground Hotel. He had decided that he was going to educate his family in how small hotels were run in France, so the whole family of seven, my mother and an aunt were all taken to northern France. We spent about three weeks there, during which time my sisters Maire and Jenny had to do all the translation from their rudimentary French. They came back then and were the first management team in the Old Ground in Ennis, which was a very progressive hotel from the very beginning.

That was the beginning of a lot of other visits to the Continent with my father. Apparently he had picked me out at an early age to pass on many of the things that he knew, a gift I greatly appreciated. He was a very dominant influence in my whole life. He was very much of the belief, from the Parnell–Redmond days, that we could get what we needed by democratic methods and this certainly played a part in my enthusiasm when the peace movements began. We began the southern movement for peace in support of the women's movement in the North and I have my father to thank for encouraging me to join with others in the creation of Co-operation North, which I believe will have a great part to play over the next twenty years.

My mother was one of the Ryans of Kilrush, who were a strong merchant trading family, and it is her I have to thank for sending me to Blackrock College. Blackrock was a tremendous school at that time, with Dr McQuaid as president. We had both rugby and hurling teams – I was on the hurling team, which was a great experience.

My mother was a very big-hearted lady, very religious, and she succeeded in convincing me that human relations were probably the most important thing – good human relations, loving people and acting correctly towards them. That had a big bearing on whatever success I had in Shannon, because, from the beginning, the Catering Services operated on respect between management and staff. At a very early stage, we had a staff management council which met monthly and which was one of the driving forces behind the great enthusiasm which eventually led to Sales and Catering being given the task of setting up the Shannon Development company.

At one particular stage, there was some suggestion that I had a vocation for the priesthood and I remember Dr McQuaid saying to me, 'It's a very very lonely life.' My father's influence and the Old Ground made me decide that I was going to follow what he had started. I ran the Old Ground until I decided I had to give all my time to the Shannon job, and I then sold the hotel.

At nineteen I went to work under the famous Toddy O'Sullivan, who was running the Rock Park Hotel in Wales. He and his wife Niamh initiated me into the hotel industry and I am always grateful for that. When I got back to the Old Ground, I found that my father had set up an exchange for me with a young German – he came and worked at the Old Ground and I went to his hotel in South Germany. I was there when Hitler was coming to power in 1937. It was an exciting time and I must admit that I couldn't see the evil that was to come at that stage, and I am sure a lot of Germans couldn't either.

I couldn't stand the 'Heil Hitler' – it seemed a very stupid salutation and I never used it. In Southern Germany it was quite acceptable to say 'Grus Gott', which is a little bit like *Dia Dhuit*, so I always said that to somebody who Heil Hitlered me.

I was working in the buffet of the hotel when six or seven Brownshirts came in and all together they gave me a 'Heil Hitler'. I thought that was far too much altogether, so I said 'Heil de Valera'. They were aghast and thought I had said something very insulting about the Führer, but I was rescued by the proprietor, who said, 'Er ist nicht Deutsch, er ist Engländer!' and I said, 'Nicht Engländer, Irlander.'

After Germany, I went to work in the Carlton Hotel, one of the best hotels in London, when my father sent me a wire to come home. He had leased the Falls Hotel in Ennistymon and he wanted me to come back and run it – and in those days you did whatever your father told you to do. I came back, even though I was very disappointed, because I had succeeded in getting a job for the winter as a steward on the SS Narconda, which was going to South Africa.

When I came back, I found that my father had leased the hotel from Francis McNamara, one of the great Irish aristocrats of the time, who had converted the hotel into a first-class place with a very bohemian atmosphere and had run it for two years at a considerable loss. I ran it for five years and I just about made the equivalent of a salary while I was running it. A lot of the bohemians continued to come and there were great jokes about pyjama parties and so on, so I was soon educated into that kind of thing. On hearing that I was running the place, Dr McQuaid wrote to me and said that, on the way to visiting the Bishop of Galway at the weekend, he would like to call in and see the hotel. I was horrified, because at that time there was a Mrs Winterbottom staying and she had an escort of several young men with her. I would have done anything to get him to change his mind about coming. A guardian angel must have stepped in, because, at the last moment, he cancelled. However, 'bohemian living' was harmless in many ways. It wouldn't be regarded as high living now at all.

The Falls Hotel was patronised in those years by members of the professional Dublin elite, many of them members of the

Stephen's Green Club. In my fifth year there, when the hotel was closed for the winter, they asked me if I would help them remodel the catering in the Stephen's Green Club. That brought me to the attention of people in Dublin, particularly Sean Lemass and John Leydon, because I got a call from Tim O'Driscoll to say that he wanted to see me, at the request of Mr Lemass. I was offered the job to set up the restaurant in Foynes. So I found myself, at twenty-five years of age, being offered a contract to take over the small restaurant from the BOAC, or British Imperial Airways, as they were known. I am told that de Valera had gone there in the early days when it was still run by British Imperial Airways and he wrote on a file, 'We should run this.' The restaurant was a vital ingredient in presenting a new image of ourselves to the people from America and Europe who were using the restaurant at that time. British Imperial Airways had three hundred staff there and when I first went there I felt it was almost like a British colony. One of the things that drove people like me and Joe Lucey and some of the other people who worked with me there at the beginning was the attitude of 'we'll show them what the Irish can do', because people had a very serious inferiority complex in Ireland at that time *vis á vis* the British.

We had no management institutes and we were operating on an import substitution experiment, which wasn't working very well because you cannot industrialise in a small space. The department, under John Leydon in those days, had purchased the Mount Eagle Arms and it had to be remodelled in the winter of 1942. Fortunately for me, I got to know John and Putzel Hunt, very cultured people who eventually donated their great collection to the nation. When I saw their house I said, 'This is what I want the restaurant to look like.' The British had appointed Lord Headford as their station manager. 'That was an astonishing meal,' he said to me one day. 'You Irish are very good at doing things once or twice, but you never keep things going.' That was of tremendous advantage to me, because I repeated it every year at our annual general meeting. Young people should know that the biggest driving force for the Irish in those days was their love of Ireland.

John Leydon was special – he had a great sense of idealism and of sheer patriotism. I met a lot of civil servants over the years and they do an awful lot behind the scenes. They must share a lot in our success in the sales and catering service, because they gave me the freedom to do what I had to do. I would not have had that freedom without the backing of Lemass and Leydon, who regularly came to Foynes. John Leydon would ring up on Christmas Day to find out how things were. He was quite extraordinary. He was secretary to the Department of Industry and Commerce and, during the war, he and others in that department would have been the brains behind helping Ireland survive, despite the fact that we couldn't get many supplies. He and his colleagues were men of great vision. They saw clearly that the manner in which we had been cut off from the rest of the world would be eliminated by the age of air travel.

I had only been in Foynes a little over a year when the battle between the sea plane and the land plane was won by the land plane. At that stage the Irish government were backing both Foynes and Rineanna and had begun to build the terminal building at Foynes. I ran that for about three or four years until it became a children's hospital. We called it the Foynes Country Club and it was filled with people coming on sea planes from England and booked for five meals a day, all through Lunn's travel agency. One can imagine how important that was to people who had been living on rations!

For a period I found myself running both the restaurant at Foynes and the new restaurant at Rineanna. The new Rineanna was really an extension of the Old Ground Hotel, because we didn't have equipment there and it was run with supplies sent from the Old Ground, with Maggie McArdle, the cook from the Old Ground, being the behind-the-scenes chef.

The duty-free shop idea, which has spread around the world, began out of necessity. One winter, it began to look as if the

catering service was going to lose money and there was a fierce
necessity to find a new way of bringing in money. The idea had
been initiated by the government at an international conference
in San Francisco where, in order to draw attention to Ireland's
willingness to act as a major link on the way to Europe, they
declared Shannon a free airport – not quite knowing what a free
airport would be. The fact that they had done that made it
possible for me to come up with the idea of selling duty-free
liquor and cigarettes. The Bunratty Castle and the Rent-a-
Cottage ideas came as a result of a six-week visit I paid to
America in 1950 as part of a Marshall Aid invited team. When
we came back, there was some difficulty in the department
about our making a report recommending what should be
done, because this might have looked as if the Americans were
telling us what to do. I made a separate report, recommending
a whole series of things which included the Bunratty Castle
complex, the hotel school and the Rent-a-Cottage scheme.

Shannon new town was also born out of necessity. We had
to find a way of stopping the overfly and there were two ways
of doing it. One was by promoting disembarking traffic. It was
all transit traffic up to then, so the idea of the industrial free
zone came out of the necessity to create payload for the aircrafts,
so they would have to land for it. The town had to come to
balance the industrial estate. We promoted the idea with each
of the airlines and told them that they would miss out if they
left us out of their schedule, which encouraged them not to
overfly. I think that the possibilities that exist now are at least as
great as they were in those days. The whole vision of aviation is
one of expansion, as the population of the world is increasing.
People are getting richer and there will be more and more
tourism and more and more use of aviation, and Shannon is a
vital link in this.

The Shannon story is worth studying, because we were the
first generation of free Irishmen who had a chance to do
something at an international level. We have a great need to do

exceptional things *now* at an international level, because of the frightening crisis of unemployment. We should be able to show what happened at Shannon as a challenge out of which the Irish imagination began to work. We now have the opportunity of working together with the people from the North, who I know from my work with Co-operation North are very talented people, as they need to make a go of it on this island with us.

At the end of the '70s, a group of women in Belfast protested against violence and I, with Colonel Keane and Dorothy Cantrell and others down here, was involved in doing something to support them. We set up the southern movement for peace, but, when there was a Nobel peace prize given in the North and somehow or other the peace idea got a bad name, we looked for something different. Gerry Dempsey suggested a new peace role for the south and out of that suggestion came Co-operation North. That has been in existence for over fifteen years and it has been spending over a million pounds a year on north–south co-operation in what we call track two diplomacy. I only hope that the politicians involved in track one realise the power of track two diplomacy. It carries no threat, it has no political strings attached and I believe it is the fastest way to bring about what we all desire – that we will live and work together on this island, recognising our differences and accepting that we are comprised of two great traditions.

The key to peace is human co-operation, but it has to be skilfully managed. It won't come about just by wishing it. This country has to learn the lessons of Europe. When wise men in Europe said they would never again let Europeans slay one another, as they had in two great wars, they didn't look for a political solution, they looked for an economic solution. They set up the OECD and skilfully managed co-operation. Forty years later they are talking about political co-operation. But the economic work has to be done first.

At one time, Lemass and O'Neill came up with the idea of co-operation without political strings. I know that well, because

I was given the task, as chairman of Bord Fáilte, to bring the two tourist boards together. We agreed with the British and the northerners to have one brochure for the whole of Ireland and one good brochure for the two islands together which would be held in all the British offices. We insisted that it would be called Ireland and Great Britain, not Great Britain and Ireland. Just after that the violence began, but the idea should be revived. Quite evidently, if the two islands are sold vigorously together, and the British have many more offices than we have, we lose nothing. It's just like selling the Iberian Peninsula!

It is now quite clear that community development is our greatest hope, because unless the people get into the act, the State alone is not going to be able to overcome the tragedy of unemployment. I am now involved, at their invitation, with the people of Newmarket-on-Fergus – one parish, three thousand people – who are going to prove that it can be done parish by parish. Parish precedes county. We all have a sense of belonging to a parish, not just in a religious sense, although the religious link has to be there because we are not going to get out of this tragedy without help from the man above. Eliminating as far as possible the agony of unemployment and the fear of it for young people can be done, but only if management skill is introduced at the lowest level. That particular parish in Newmarket-on-Fergus set an example because many of the people there saw what happened in the airport. A lot of the people in Newmarket-on-Fergus were employed in the airport and they know that, if you have the determination and the will and you give it the time, you can accomplish anything. Co-operation is the closest thing to the great virtue of loving one another, so there is something spiritual in the word co-operation. It has to be done in every parish throughout the country, and management companies like Shannon Development and FÁS have got to ensure that they do not dominate the situation. They must work very closely with the communities, give them the skills, do all the things they should do, but as far as possible let the focus be on the people themselves.

I have a great sense of incredulity from time to time at having been involved in so many big things and I recognise that it puts me under an obligation till the end of my days to try and do anything I can to pass on the benefit of the extraordinary experience that I have had. It is an exciting time for the young in Ireland, because we have a great country and we have a lot of well-educated young people. They need to understand that we haven't had our independence all that long and we are moving fast. We have got to make the south an efficient, effective, organised community, so that we will win the kind of co-operation we need from the north to really make the whole island a magnificent example to the world.

Tony O'Reilly

Tony O'Reilly was born in Dublin in 1936. He was educated at the Jesuit Belvedere College, University College, Dublin, and the University of Bradford. A brilliant rugby career, which saw him rise from schools level to playing with the British Lions in South Africa within the space of eighteen months, was mirrored by an equally meteoric rise in his business career. He was appointed chief executive of An Bord Bainne (Dairy Board) at the age of twenty-five and considers the launch of Kerrygold butter in 1962 the 'greatest personal satisfaction' in his business career. He became managing director of the Sugar Company and Erin Foods in 1966 and, two years later, became managing director of H J Heinz in the UK. He went on to become chairman and chief executive of the H J Heinz company. He is also chairman and largest stockholder of Independent Newspapers, chairman of Fitzwilton plc and Waterford Wedgewood plc and major shareholder in ARCON.

I think probably the earliest learning experience I can remember is a certain idolatry of my mother, who, after all, is the most fundamental and important teacher all of us have. I can remember living in Portrane with her when I was probably three years of age and following her everywhere. She seemed to me to be the incarnation of everything that was good and beautiful in the world. She taught me how to make pastry cakes and I watched her pickle onions and do the beetroot and cook and all those things which are immensely exciting and interesting to a three-year-old. So she was the first great teacher I had and I have to say she remained one of the great forces in my life until her death.

My father was rather a more formal influence in that he was himself quite academic by disposition. He was in the customs service and, while actually serving as a customs officer, he put himself through the King's Inns and became a barrister. He also studied to become a chartered secretary at home through a correspondence course, so he always seemed to be reading a book, enveloped in a cloud of cigarette smoke. He became more important in my life when I started school and there were problems and conundrums set by the academic world that he could help me with.

School seemed to be forever Belvedere. I went to Belvedere when I was six years of age and I was the youngest boy they'd ever taken in, which I think owed as much to my mother's attractiveness as any particular need to bring in boys one or two years younger than anyone else. I had a very joyful twelve years there. I stayed until I was eighteen, did my Leaving Certificate a year early and then went back to do what they rather coyly called philosophy. It was in fact a concealed attempt to turn me into a professional rugby player and win the Leinster Schools Cup, which sadly I failed to do.

I had immense admiration for the Jesuits and I think that all of the great influences in my life – sporting, academic and cultural – have been either directly or indirectly related to the

Jesuits. I was a keen rugby player, as well as being a keen tennis and cricket player. I played soccer also, so my life essentially revolved around sport. But the Jesuits had the notion of *moderatio in omnibus* – the all-rounder was prized by them – so we had very substantial musical training, through Gilbert and Sullivan operas; we had an excellent chess club, which I enjoyed; we had cycling clubs and camera clubs and of course the inevitable debating societies, plus the academic world. But the Jesuits didn't emphasise the academic and I would describe my academic career at Belvedere as quite average.

I suppose I showed some early signs of being an entrepreneur there. I ran a penny library, which taught me a little bit about inventory control, in that nobody ever returned the books! We had an initial spurt of prosperity, as people paid us a penny for the loan of the book, so it did teach me a hard lesson that the initial success of an enterprise doesn't confirm its longevity.

In Belvedere there was one particularly profound influence on my life, Reverend Father Tom O'Callaghan. He was a mathematician of distinction, a theologian of great merit and probably the best rugby coach that I ever experienced in my entire rugby career. He was a theoretician, a hard taskmaster, a lover of the game – although he had never played it himself – and, because I was on what is called the Junior Cup team from the age of twelve, I had his influence for virtually all of the final six years of my rugby career in Belvedere. That was an extraordinary experience, because it brought an intellectual dimension into the game that I think stood by all of us who experienced his training for the rest of our lives.

I have always felt that rugby football was the great tutor, because it is really a template for life. If you don't train, you don't get your rewards. So there's a risk–reward ratio established clearly in your mind at an early stage. If you don't participate collegially with the other boys on the team, you are isolated. One learns about winning with grace and, more importantly, losing with grace. I call to mind Rudyard Kipling's poem, *If.*

> If you can meet with Triumph and Disaster
> And treat those two impostors just the same. . .
> Yours is the Earth and everything that's in it,
> And – which is more – you'll be a Man, my son!

My father had given me these lines and he reminded me of them before we went out on the field to play in the Leinster Schools Cup Final. We lost to Blackrock by an intercept in the very last moment, when it looked as if we were about to win. I went behind the line, they took the kick and converted the try. The intercept was achieved by a very brilliant Blackrock player, Tom Cleary, who, funnily enough, had done the same thing the previous year against Clongowes, but this was more mortal, since it was against us. He scored the winning try, the full time whistle went and the sky was a blizzard of blue-and-white Blackrock scarves. He was festooned with his team-mates and I went over and waited until they disengaged. I shook hands with him. We had lost the cup. My mother had bought a new hat, as she had for the previous nine years, but, yet again, she had no opportunity to present the cup. It was a moment of very acute sadness in my life.

About twenty-eight years later I was president of Heinz and we had a major technical problem which could have led to a product recall and could have cost the company about 30 to 35 million dollars. It required the support of a company called Del Monte. I flew to California to meet the president of Del Monte, who luxuriated in the extraordinary name of Jim Schmuck. I went to see Mr Schmuck and said to him, 'I'm O'Reilly, president of the Heinz company. We wonder if you could help us in this.' He then related to me a story of how his parish priest in Santa Barbara was a man called Father McCarthy who was a scholastic at Blackrock College in Dublin when, as Schmuck rather poetically put it, 'you were engaged in the Superbowl while a schoolboy. At the last moment, when you had lost the game, you showed some grace under pressure by shaking hands with an opponent from the side which had won the game. He thought you were a pretty good guy and advises me so, and so the Del Monte company will vote with Heinz on this issue.' That was the famous thirty-five million dollar handshake!

I was very fortunate in that one of my colleagues at school was a boy called Peadar O'Donnell, the nephew of the great Peadar O'Donnell, the writer. He used to invite me to Donegal where the family home was, between Meenmore and Dunloe. I have vivid memories of wonderful summers between the age of seven and twelve spent in Donegal pottering around in boats round Arranmore Island and the waters of Burtonport. Peadar O'Donnell was very much a *paterfamilias* to me during those years. He had a great love for the islands and he felt particularly passionate about the exploitation that was so evident in Donegal in the early 1900s, when the unfortunate potato pickers had to go to Scotland. It was he, of course, with Canon Hayes from Galway that led the agitation on the land annuities, an issue that de Valera was to adopt as a central theme of the Fianna Fáil party in the 1932 election, ultimately leading to the famous economic war with Great Britain.

I was thinking I would like to be a barrister when I finished at Belvedere, but my father advised me, 'You look like the sort of person who would need time off. I advise you, therefore, to be a solicitor, rather than a barrister.' I think that was probably very good advice and I greatly enjoyed studying to be a lawyer.

I went to college in 1954, although intercepted by a bewildering rise in my rugby fortunes, in that after only five games of men's rugby I was on the Irish rugby team and five months later was in South Africa with the British Lions. Despite that major distraction, I became quite purposefully academic when I went to University College, Dublin, and most particularly when I joined the Incorporated Law Society, because it was extremely competitive once you got into a professional examination like the solicitor's examinations. I think in those years approximately fifty per cent of all examinees failed. At the end of the football season, I would abandon all contact with the outside world – no papers, no phones, no travel, no contact with anybody. I would work a twelve-hour day, four hours till lunch, four hours in the afternoon and four hours to nightfall, and I'd do that for five months.

I think my experience with the Lions in 1955 was more educational than even that twelve-year experience of being at Belvedere, because it was a pressure cooker of almost epic proportions. Suddenly, in a period from November 1954 to January 1955, I went from being one of the most distinguished players from the previous year's crop of good football players that 'should not be rushed into men's football' to a player who went through club games, a final trial, four internationals, was selected for the Barbarians, selected for the British Lions and, on 1 May, flew to South Africa. The very first time that I'd been in an aeroplane was to fly with the Irish team to Scotland that year, so it was an extraordinary, accelerative thrust in my whole life.

In South Africa, we had an intensely competitive group of thirty players, only fifteen of which would get onto the test side. I played in the four tests. The first test was probably one of the most famous tests ever played, 23–22 to the British Lions, the first defeat for South Africa in this century on their own soil before 105,000 people. It was an epic tour with great players like Cliff Morgan, Jeff Butterfield, W P C Davies and my great mate Cecil Pedlow from Northern Ireland. We split the series 2–2; I dislocated my shoulder – an injury that came back to haunt me for the rest of my career – all very dramatic.

I learned a lot about myself and also about mature adults and their conduct under intense conditions during that six-month period. As the baby of the British team, my early scoring feats became very much a matter of public discussion. The intensity of the games increased and I found the going very much tougher and so any proclivities one might have had to swagger around the place were firmly knocked out of one at the first tackle on the next Saturday. But I came back and kept my place in the test team and I would say that possibly the best game I played was that last test in which I dislocated my shoulder in the last minute. So I learned something about fighting back from adversity.

On that particular tour, the colossus was Cliff Morgan. Eloquent, passionate, insightful and totally brilliant as a player. Just to play with him was an experience that I will always treasure.

In my business life I have always said that An Bord Bainne, the Dairy Board, was the most exciting job I have ever had. I became the chief executive of a State Board at twenty-five years of age, so that in itself was fairly remarkable at the time. I was relatively innocent of many of the problems of the co-operative movement, but I might say I was quickly informed of some of the dynamics when Pat Power, the old Chairman of the board and General Manager of Ballyclough Co-op, said to me on the first day, 'Tony, let me tell you one thing about the Irish co-operative movement, and that is that you can expect shag-all co-operation!'

He was absolutely correct. There were titanic struggles at the time between the co-operative movement and between the two great dairy organisations, the National Farmer's Association, headed by Rickard Deasy, and the Irish Creamery Milk Suppliers Association, headed by John Feeley. Two wonderful men, but united in one thing, which was their dislike of one another. All of these forces were at work on the board, which was a nine-man board with four farmers, two government representatives and three manufacturing representatives. The function of the Dairy Board, as the Dairy Produce Marketing Act of 1961 stated in that wonderful bureaucratese, was 'to export or to provide for the exportation of such class or kind of milk products as the Minister may from time to time decide in writing to the board'. We were fundamentally the financier to the entire dairy industry in that we provided the subsidy mechanism which has helped the exportation of cheese, milk powder, chocolate crumb and other products that were in development. And so, at the age of twenty-five, I found myself with 110,000 farmers, direct producers, and all of the co-operative movement (we had 157 co-ops at that stage). There were probably 600,000 people involved in the milk industry when you took into consideration the families of all of those people. This was a mighty responsibility for a young man. I was also just married and we were starting our family. It was in that year, 1962, that I hit upon the idea of Kerrygold, which I launched on 7 July 1962 and officially took to market in October. The rest, I suppose, is history.

When I think of my business mentors, history is a very telling and important tutor. In those early days, the civil servants who were trying to pull together the industrial economy, like J J McElligott, Sean Leydon and Sean Lemass, produced that extraordinary Ministry for Supply which kept us supplied during the war. The day of the mandarin, the civil service, as the manager and catalyst to an industrial economy gave way to the new phenomenon which in essence they spawned, which was the semi-state manager. And so you had Aer Lingus, Bord Na Móna and Córas Iompair Éireann. Figures like Todd Andrews, T J O'Driscoll, General Mickey Joe Costelloe of the sugar company, a predecessor of mine, and Jerome Dempsey of Aer Lingus became the great glamour figures of our society and the semi-state companies were the colossi within our industrial society. We then moved from the semi-state company to what I might describe as the new Elizabethans, the people who felt that there were companies in Ireland that were big enough to stand up and plant the flag of Ireland and of excellence in other countries – people like Tony Ryan, Michael Smurfit and Raymond McLoughlin, who played rugby with me – producing a whole new industrial dynamic in this society. I watched that development, participated in it, was a semi-state manager myself both in Bord Bainne and in the sugar company, but then saw that, in terms of reward for effort, private enterprise and international enterprise and the multinational opportunity was something that was attractive to me. I wanted to see if I could play on that bigger stage, in the same way that I had been given a chance as an eighteen-year-old in South Africa in 1955. And so I accepted a job with Heinz and, after two years, went to America and became president of the company.

One of the reasons I am reasonably successful in business is that I work well with a team of people. I don't perceive business as a lone voyage but as a very inter-dependent function. I think anybody who works with me in Heinz would say that Heinz is intensely collegial, both in terms of the flow of information, the allocation of resources and particularly the allocation of compensation and reward. What we have done in Heinz is to make virtually all our management and our workers shareholders in the company, so everyone has a common currency – a share in the company – and they want to optimise that.

I was dining last night with my cousin, Father John Geary, a wonderfully talented and highly educated Holy Ghost Father – I never thought a Jesuit boy would say that about a Holy Ghost Father but there are exceptions, as I told him last night! He made an observation which I thought was a very worthy one. He said that 'really we should all work ceaselessly to enjoy the bliss of solitude'. I think that, after the feverish life I have led in business and in sport, this notion has a great attraction . . .

Maureen Potter

Maureen Potter was born in Dublin in 1925. For fifty years she has been the first lady of Irish comedy, working her way from fit-ups to stage, radio, film and television.

For many years she worked with the great Jimmy O'Dea and then succeeded him in the Gaiety Theatre, Dublin, with the long-running variety show, Gaels of Laughter *and the Christmas pantomimes. She married army captain Jack O'Leary, who became her scriptwriter. Maureen loves cricket and horses and has starred in cabaret in recent years. As she says in the interview, 'I'll keep going until I hear glass . . .'*

I'm a Dub, born in Ballybough, but I lived in Fairview all my early life. I went to St Mary's National School in Fairview, which we lived beside, and this was in some ways handy and in some ways not. Mitching was a bit difficult, although I succeeded twice and was caught twice.

My father died in 1932 when I was seven. He had a car accident and went into hospital to have a leg removed, but in those days there were no antibiotics and he died of pneumonia.

He was a marvellous, marvellous man; very musical. He was a commercial traveller for the Vacuum Oil Company. We saw him only at weekends, but Sunday nights were always musical nights. The local church organist would come in and play the piano and Daddy would sing and Mother would play the piano and sing. Mother had some gold medals for singing, because she was once taught by a marvellous teacher called Desposito. She once appeared on the same platform as John McCormack. It was her proudest moment. We used to hang over the banisters on a Sunday evening and listen to the songs, my mother singing 'One Alone' from *The Desert Song* and things like that. Friday was poker night and we were banished. If I did manage to get into the kitchen where they were playing poker, my father would put me up on the table and have me dance for all his mates in the poker school.

We had a car when Daddy was alive, but, when he died, everything went. A marvellous woman, Dr Barnes, bought the big house opposite the little house we were living in and put us into it. I think we may have been caretakers, but it was a magnificent old house – in bits, but magnificent – with nooks and crannies and a huge garden that we used to look into before we went to live there. There was a conservatory with real grapes, which was most astonishing to us. We used to look over the wall at the apples and the pears and everything. We were very poor but very happy, because it was an adventuresome house. We had a mulberry tree in the garden which was a magnet for every child in the neighbourhood and the bane of their parents' lives because mulberries, as you know, stain like nothing on earth! The kids used to come home with purple stains all over their clothes and their mothers would blame my mother.

I hated every second of school. I didn't stay very long. It was a small school with about three classrooms and there would be three lessons going on at the same time. At home, the boys and I had a rat called Dinah, a black thing which eventually died. I put it in the school harmonium and, after a few weeks, the smell was something else. I got great credit for removing Dinah from the harmonium and putting her in the bin. I was the heroine and nobody knew that I had originally stuck her in there!

I started dancing school the same day as I actually went to school, so I was kind of working. I was a 'pro' at that age. I used to slip out of school when the teacher wasn't looking and run to the Queen's or the Royal, where I might be playing at the time.

On the day of my Confirmation in Marino church, when I was ten, I remember getting as far as the altar and the archbishop slapping my face. I then took off down this huge church to get to the Queen's Theatre by 2.30 in the afternoon to sing 'Sweet Peggy O'Grady'.

The time I enjoyed school best was when we went to Belfast. We were too young in the North to go on stage without going to school, so we went to St Malachy's convent there. I had never been with nuns before. Being visitors, we used to be put at the back of the class and given poetry to learn, which was delightful. I learned a lot of Wordsworth and Chesterton at that time.

At the age of twelve, I took off for England. I did an audition in the Royal in Dublin for Jack Hylton's band and then I forgot all about it. I went on my holidays and, about two months later, a telegram arrived to say would I come over to London and do two broadcasts with Jack Hylton's band. He was very big at the time. I went over for two days and I stayed two years, which was something else.

Connie Ryan, my dancing teacher, or her sister or brother, would accompany us as a chaperon. Occasionally, we would get a sort of governess who would try and teach me the basics, which would be how many penny pencils could you get for sixpence. She didn't teach us a thing, so my schooling really ended when I left Fairview.

My mother was very proud of me, very proud. Not that she got very much money out of it. She was never a stage mother. She was a very reticent and quiet lady.

I was a singer and dancer. I used to do impressions of Shirley Temple, which nearly drove me round the bend, wearing white boots and torturing the straight hair into curls – that was agony. I also did some nice numbers that Jack Hylton picked, lovely dancing numbers. We toured around England and Scotland and Wales with Jack Hylton and then went to Holland and Germany.

We were in Germany in 1938 when Hitler was marching into Austria. I remember those extraordinary broadcasts of Hitler. There were loudspeakers in every street and the streets would be cleared and everyone would have to go home and listen to your man from the Sports Palast making his speeches. He came to see the show with Goering and Goebbels and their wives. He didn't come down to see us afterwards but they did, and they looked exactly like the cartoons, with fat chests and medals and the wives with fat chests and jewellery. We were given a memento of that night, a silver and blue wreath with the date on it. I brought it home and my mother said, 'That filthy man Hitler' and put it in the bin. Their chauffeur got a great crush on my dancing teacher, Connie Ryan, and afterwards he used to call around every night in Hitler's car and take all the lovely singing girls we had in the show out to night clubs. Of course, I had to go to bed, to the pension opposite the theatre, but it was very exciting.

We went back to England in 1938 and carried on at the London Palladium until 1939. On Friday 1 September, all the theatres in London went dark. Jack Hylton sent myself and my friend down to Blackpool to his mother and father's place, just to be out of the way of trouble for the time being. The following Sunday morning, 3 September, Chamberlain made his announcement, and it was very odd to see Blackpool empty. An empty strand with those rolls of barbed wire that they thought would keep Hitler from invading. My mother got the wind up completely and sent for me to come home immediately, so I came home and joined Jimmy O'Dea. He was doing a pantomime that year called *Jimmy and the Leprechaun* and I was the leprechaun, which was very exciting. I had worked with him before I went to Jack Hylton, including in pantomime in 1935 and 1936. I graduated into being his regular feed. I remember my first review was 'Maureen Potter, surprisingly good in a sketch'. From then on we became a sort of double act, Jimmy and I: Dolores and Rosie, the Totties and so on. I stayed with him until he died.

Jimmy was very meticulous and very neat. He had all his clothes hand-made. He wasn't a comic offstage – he could be very cross – but he taught me my business and I'll always be grateful to him for that. He was the best in the business at timing a gag and it was from him I learned my own sense of timing, even though I worked with Arthur Askey and all the great comics in England. Tommy Trinder was another beautiful, kind man, who I played with at the Palladium. He used to play hide and seek with me. And then I loved Frankie Howerd. Not long before he died, he came here one night to see me and we had the time of our lives chatting. Bud Flanagan, too, was a lovely man. They loved the Irish over there. Jimmy and I used to laugh. We were so small that, when we went over there during the war, we could beat our way to the bar quicker than anyone else. They used to think we were Canadians; they couldn't believe that Irish people were articulate and could be understood. There were wonderful comics in England, but Jimmy was the one from whom I learned the most. I always felt that Jimmy O'Dea should have been made a freeman of the city of Dublin. If anyone in this country were to be chosen, it should have been him.

The first time I did a sketch with him, he said, 'A little less characterisation and a little more clarity.' I was acting my guts out but nobody could hear me. He taught me that it is important to be audible on stage if you want to be funny.

I was very lucky when I met Jack O'Leary, my husband. He used to write for me, which was great. The material was completely different from anything that Harry O'Donovan was writing for me and he created the character of Christy that has been with me since 1959. You should hear the audience here at night, when I only have to say 'Come on, Christy!' and they start to laugh before I even go into the sketch. The great thing about Christy is that you can bring him anywhere, because people have to imagine him. He started on radio. I didn't think he would ever work on stage, but he was even better there than on the radio.

On the home front, I had great admiration for Harry O'Donovan. He was the first man in Ireland ever to make his living as a scriptwriter. In those days, nobody was just a scriptwriter; they always had to have another job. But Harry took up with Jimmy O'Dea and wrote all his stuff for him for years and years, so in that way he was a real original – a wonderful man.

Micheál Mac Liammóir and Hilton Edwards were something special. Micheál and I were always the first into the theatre at night. I remember we were doing some sort of a charity concert and all the big guns were on – Peter Ustinov and Siobhán and Milo. The dressing room for everybody was the big number one in the Theatre Royal. I, of course, arrived early and who was there before me, on a big throne-shaped chair at the far end of the room, but Micheál Mac Liammóir, with Mickser Reid standing at his knee. I opened the door and Micheál said, 'Come in darling, come in to this palace of masculinity.' He had a lovely sense of humour and could laugh at himself. I did *The Informer* and *The Man Who Came to Dinner* with Micheál and Hilton, which was marvellous. Hilton would say, 'Potter is infallible, absolutely infallible. Follow Potter,' and then he would change everything. But he tried to make you feel good. I also enjoyed *Androcles and the Lion* with Cyril Cusack. I played the lion and had the time of my life.

In the '40s and '50s, we toured Ireland a fair bit. Jimmy O'Dea loved touring. The train would break down and Jimmy would take the station master and the train driver over to the local pub while everybody else looked for wood to fuel the engine. Jimmy loved meeting the local doctor, the local bank manager and all the local sergeants, while we were doing the work in the theatre.

We always used to bring a rope with a hook to hang our clothes on, because there were no dressing rooms – and the bucket, of course, for the loo, with a curtain between the men and the women. We were an actual 'fit up'. We fitted up our own stage and made our own footlights out of little cooking dishes and put our boards up on the baskets that we brought our clothes in. It could be pretty ropy sometimes getting on and off the stage.

We did sketches and song and dance. Jimmy had sketches like 'Mine's a Pint' and 'Marrying Mary' and I would sing and dance and then we would have acts with accordions and fiddles and maybe jugglers too. We often used to bump into Anew McMaster, who was a joy. I remember meeting him when he was touring with Harold Pinter. Mac used to leave little notes for us if he was in the hotel in town before us, like 'Whatever you do, dear, don't touch the beef' and 'Jimmy, dear, whatever you do, test the beds'. He was a great man and it was an education for me.

I also went into the world of film. I did *The Rising of the Moon* in Kilkee, which was marvellous fun. John Ford took a great liking to me and christened me by the name I had in the film, Pidgie. He asked me over to do a film with Jack Hawkins afterwards. He always kept the people he liked around him. He said to me, 'Pidgie, get in there and make something up. You're the wife of a thief, now make something up.' Luckily, I had worked with Jimmy O'Dea, so I was used to having to ad lib. Then I did *Ulysses*, which I didn't think much of, and *Portrait of an Artist*, which I liked, because I liked the part of Dante.

When Jimmy died, we started *Gaels of Laughter* and the pantomimes. They were very well done – very well dressed and directed and the design was absolutely wonderful. It was my first time to step into number one dressing after Jimmy had gone, which was quite a special kind of feeling.

Pantomime is tough, but it is also great because of the children's participation. It was lovely to frighten them and make them laugh, make them roar at you; it was a marvellous feeling. It's wonderful to see the parents looking, not at the stage, but at their own children to see how they are reacting. Some of the kids can be very tough – the things they yell at you, like 'Pull out his teeth and make a necklace out of them'. It is miraculous after the spate of science fiction movies with fantastic special effects that children still enjoy pantomime. I think that is because they can talk to you and you talk back to them.

We are great cricket and football fans. We used to go to the football finals in Croke Park and Tolka Park and we used to go to Trinity and Malahide and watch the cricket, and we are also great fans of racing on television. Arkle was my absolute passion and a few years ago, in the '70s, Gay Byrne did a television tribute to me. Pat Taaffe was there and he gave me one of Arkle's plates, which I absolutely treasure. I have it hanging inside the door but hanging the right way up, not upside down. We are superstitious about whistling in the dressing room and dropping a comb; we have to step on the comb if we drop it before we pick it up. Also, knitting beside the stage is absolutely horrendous and so is having fresh flowers on the stage.

My husband, Jack, has been a great influence on me. I can't remember not being married to him. I never thought he would have put up with me, but we have two great kids and we still have plenty of laughs together. And to get a good script is the hardest thing in the world, so I am a very lucky woman. It took us years to get married; we kept putting it off and putting it off, but we were good friends, which is a great basis for marriage.

I am sitting here in my dressing room and looking into the mirror, taking a cold hard look at myself. Oh God, I wish I had nice hair! Thelma was sitting next to me and she has beautiful, beautiful hair and I have hair like a dead mouse. As my mother used to say, I have a mouth like a burst slipper and a face like a suet pudding, but, behind this face, there is a very frightened, timid person. I am frightened to death now when I go on the stage. Every time I go on I die. I am in two hours before the show every night, pacing up and down. I remember Jack said once, 'We'll have to get a traffic warden to watch you. And some traffic lights.' I am sometimes physically sick before I go on; the fright is horrendous.

Alexander King, who was a drug addict, wrote *May Your House Be Safe from Tigers* and *Is there Life after Birth?* One of the characters went to his dying grandfather and asked him what he was leaving him when he died. The grandfather just looked up and said, 'Be delighted'! For me, that is a magical thing; to be delighted. I try to be delighted about everything: the first primroses, the nape of a baby's neck. Another writer, Salinger, had a character called Seymour Glass whose family said he was the sort of man you would send to look at horses. Well, that is the sort of person I would like to be – I love horses and I would want to be sent to look at them. I like to think that, just around the corner, something wonderful is going to happen. And that's what keeps me going, keeps me thinking that the next step will be even better.

I have had my ups and downs – mostly ups – but I have been very lucky. I still go onto the stage up to the gills with nerves, but God pulls me through and for that I give thanks. I just 'keep going until I hear glass', as they say.

Feargal Quinn

Feargal Quinn was born in Dublin. He was educated at Newbridge College (on its playing-fields and in its classrooms) and at University College, Dublin. The retail grocery trade was 'in his blood' and he opened his first supermarket in Dundalk, County Louth, in 1960. A dynamic businessman, who introduced many innovative concepts to retailing, Feargal Quinn has built up a chain of sixteen Superquinn stores in the greater Dublin area. He places great importance on listening to his customers and meeting their needs. His concern for the customer is well-documented in his book, Crowning the Customer.

A man of great energy, Feargal Quinn has found time to devote himself to areas of public service, including chairmanship of An Post and membership of Seanad Éireann.

I went to school at Monkstown National School in Blackrock, County Dublin. At an early age, I was given a wooden jigsaw of the United States, in which each state was a jigsaw piece in itself. I am the only person I know who knows every one of the American states! I very often surprise Americans by being able to recognise them on a map and name them. So I suppose my earliest experience of education was the national school in Monkstown and geography.

When we moved from Blackrock over to Clontarf, I went to Kostka College in Seafield Avenue, run by a man called Louis Roden. Even at nine or ten years of age, I was learning French and Latin. I found Latin useful and I encouraged all my children to learn it, if only to help them in things like crosswords and gardening. I have enough French to be able to get by and I enjoy it. We holiday in France quite a lot and can mix with the French, whereas very often our international colleagues at conferences are limited by the language barrier.

I moved on then to second level at Newbridge College, where rugby was very important. I worked very hard at rugby to try and get on the second team, because then you got a chance to get up to Dublin, or wherever the match was being played. I wanted it so badly that I actually ended up on the first team and enjoyed my rugby no end. So part of my education was discovering that, if you are really determined, if you want something badly enough, you can probably get it.

Out of that came a number of other things, one being the power of prayer, because we wanted things so badly that we would make novenas to get them. For instance, in one of our last rugby matches, I was marking Tony O'Reilly. He was the star of the Belvedere team and I was very much the weak link on the Newbridge team. Our only chance would be if we got bad weather, so we prayed for bad weather for 4 March and it turned out to be the worst day ever. It snowed, it stormed, it rained, and we were only beaten by two tries to nil. In other words, the ball only went twice to Tony O'Reilly, so he only scored twice! I think I was educated by the power of prayer as well . . .

On one of the few times I ever scored, the trainer, Father Hegarty said, 'Did you see what Quinn did yesterday? He did everything wrong, but it worked because he did it fast.' In other words, you can make mistakes but, if you move very fast, even a blunder can work. We learned a lot from Father Hegarty. When he was talking about the attacking team and the defending team, I asked him, 'What do you mean by the attacking team? Does it depend on where the ball is on the field?' He said 'No, no. The attacking team is the team in possession of the ball. Even if it's on your own line.' That taught me that even the small boy, the underdog, the fellow who really doesn't stand a chance against the big fellow, if he's in possession, can do a lot with it. So I think you can learn a huge amount from rugby, or from any sport – because we also played a lot of hurling.

Somebody said to me last week that they were surprised at how much influence my teenage years had had on me. I think most young people don't know how important those teenage years are. Almost every day, they are learning things that will be important later in life. It isn't necessarily just the academic end of things, but also the experiences that we have, the things that happen, that can play a very large part in our lives.

By far the greatest influence in my life was my father. I grew up in a holiday camp. That was his business. Since guests who came to Red Island in the Skerries paid for everything on the day they arrived, there was nothing we could do to take money off them; we couldn't sell them anything extra. So my father's one objective was to get them to come back again. That's what I call in my book, *Crowning the Customer,* the 'boomerang principle' – 'Can we get the customer to come back again?' When I went into business in my first shop in Dundalk, I was strongly influenced by this objective that I had obviously inherited from the years spent working side by side with my father, but I discovered that my competitors weren't driven by the same objective. Theirs was to see how much profit they could make from the customer on that visit. Our view was that that was only secondary to getting the customer to come back again.

The holiday camp on Red Island was a great way to grow up. It was a business which covered so many different areas. I worked in the kitchen, I worked as a lounge boy, I worked in the office, I worked almost everywhere. One of the better years I had was working as a photographer. I discovered very early on that the photographs that sold best were those of people smiling. Therefore, one of the photographer's jobs was to get people to laugh. I discovered that I actually enjoyed getting people to laugh, even if I had to use the same routine over and over again, because, like a comedian, it was a different audience each time.

There's an old story about a company, I think it was IBM, which, when they were taking on a salesman, only interviewed people who had a white handkerchief in their breast pocket, because if you didn't wear a white handkerchief in your breast pocket you were unlikely to fit in as an IBM man. Our white pocket test is the ability to smile. So, when we hold interviews at Superquinn, somebody may be very good at giving change and very good at knowing the prices and at filling shelves, but, if they are not able to smile, they probably aren't suitable to be a Superquinn employee. That may seem very tough, but it's better to find out from the beginning rather than be a square peg in a round hole.

I was fortunate enough to get to university in the '50s. We had some very good professors at the time. The famous George O'Brien is the professor that I remember most of all, but he was almost like holy God. I didn't really get to know him at college, but I did later – by accident almost – and I realised then that I hadn't really used college very well. I got my degree in the end, but only by scraping through.

When I went into business, I went to the bank to borrow money for our first supermarket in 1960, and I was cautious enough to borrow more than I needed. When we opened in Finglas, again I went in cautiously and looked for more money than I actually required and, at the end of the year, I had actually made a profit where I thought I would only break even. So one of the great lessons of my university education was one of caution. I had learned there from Michael McCormick and others that, in doing your sums, you don't err on the wrong side. That has been a benefit to me over the years. There was a good mixture of academic and social life at UCD, but I didn't really use the social life as much as I could have. I took a job in a shop in Dun Laoghaire when I was at UCD, which meant that I missed a great deal of the activities I should have become involved in. I've certainly advised my children to use their university time better than I did.

I was an only son and it was assumed that I would go into the hotel or holiday camp business. In my last year in university, I went away to France because I thought France was the centre of the catering world and I would learn about the hotel business. However, I came back enthusiastic about self-service. Not self-service food, funnily enough, but self-service books and magazines, self-service sweets, self-service shoes and so on. In Ireland, when you went to buy a magazine, you asked for the third one from the left. In France, you picked up the magazine and looked through it and then, if you were interested in it, you bought it. I came back to my father and said 'I think there's a great future for self-service retailing.' I was talking about books, magazines, shoes and things, but he was the one who said, 'Well people may not always want to read books, but they will always want to eat food. If you're going to go into business, why not get into the food business?' So that was an education for me. There was also the education involved in going abroad and learning to live on my own. I think it is important to get away from home and to have to live on your own and earn your keep.

There is a danger that too many youngsters nowadays will not be given that chance but will be cosseted right through primary school, secondary school and university.

My father and his father before him had been in the grocery business, so I would have been the third generation except that my father had left the grocery business in the mid-'40s and opened Red Island holiday camp. In 1960, I opened the first shop in Dundalk. There was the excitement of opening a new business in a town which I didn't know, but also of a new way of doing business. Self-service was not very well known then. One of the principal rules I learned very early on was, if you listen to your colleagues, if you listen to your staff, if you listen to your own people, you learn a great deal. I think most of my education has come about from just listening to my own colleagues and people who may even be much junior to me in the company.

Being able to get close to the customer, to listen to the customer, is actually another form of education, because you learn so much from them – the customer who says, 'I'll tell you what I hate . . .' or 'If only you could . . .' or 'I'd come here more often if . . .' That is more education than you get from any book or school, or any headmaster. Of course, market research is important, but not nearly as important as one-to-one contact with the customer who says, 'I'm not coming here again because . . .' Even when they are things you don't want to hear – 'Your prices are too high', 'Your quality's not good enough', 'Your shop's not clean enough', 'Your service isn't friendly enough' – it is very important that you do hear them. There's nothing as bad as a customer *not* telling you why it is they have decided to shop elsewhere. So an important objective is to encourage your customer to complain and I don't think we're very good in Ireland at doing that. We're much happier if we don't get complaints and we sometimes judge success by thinking that the fewer complaints there are the better things are. We've learned a huge amount from customer panels, whereby customers sit down and tell us what they like, what they dislike, what they'd like to see improved. I certainly think I have been far more educated by listening to customers than I have been by reading books.

My wife says I am bad company if I get stuck into a book at home, but the book has to move very fast for me. I'm not very good at academic tomes that are difficult to get through. The reason why my book, *Crowning the Customer*, is written in fairly large print is because I like the experience of getting through something quickly. I also have a rule about sentences and paragraphs not being too long. You then get the sense of moving through the book very quickly.

I got a copy of Tom Peters' *In Search of Excellence* from America the month it was published, got very excited about it and ordered a few more copies and then a few more and then a few more. His book said that those old traditional rules about the boss being a long way away from where the action is do not apply any more. Around that time, a friend called Michael O'Connor from America invited me to join a few other supermarket people to see a great supermarket in Nuremberg which was run by a man called Werner Schmidt. I had never seen such a busy supermarket. It was built alongside a sausage factory, with nothing between except a glass wall. So you could see the sausages being produced. You had to queue up and fight your way through to get those fresh sausages that had just been made across the glass wall. I got very excited.

We had bakeries in our stores at the time and I realised that making our own sausages in full view of the public, just as we make our bread, would be a huge advantage. Nobody could have fresher sausages than those that are made there in front of your eyes. That evening, as we sat around with the four American supermarket people – one of them had twelve hundred stores, one had a thousand, one a hundred and one of them eighty – I was very excited, but I discovered that the Americans felt that the journey had been of no immediate interest to them. One of

them said, 'Feargal, we're too big to do that. We'd have to do it
two hundred times.' That, to me, was an education. It taught
me that being small – we only had eight or nine shops at the
time – meant we could do things that those big fellows with two
or three hundred stores couldn't do. That was a turning-point in
my business life, because I was able to say that not only is small
beautiful but that it could actually be flexible enough to get
things done and know your customer. So, one of the great
benefits of listening to people has been the sort of thing that
Tom Peters has taught – by being close to where the action is
you can actually do things that the big fellows can't.

I don't think we ever finish learning. I've been involved with
the Irish Management Institute for some years now and
regularly attend courses there and I hope there will never be a
time when I don't get benefit from them. When I was asked to
become chairman of An Post ten years ago, I went along to do
a course on how to chair meetings. I learn a lot from being able
to sit and listen to others describe how they run their businesses.
One of the things I always tell our people when they go to
something like an IMI course is not to be shy to ask questions.
We are sometimes a bit nervous of letting ourselves down in
front of our peers. I'm not too shy nowadays to ask quite silly
questions very early on, because it helps me to bring the level
down to the sort of language that I can understand. I don't
think we ever stop educating ourselves.

John Seymour

John Seymour was born in Essex in 1914 to wealthy parents whose lifestyle he ultimately rejected. His formal schooling in England and Switzerland contributed very little to his education. A spell in an agricultural college in Kent enhanced his attachment to the soil, leading to his ultimate conviction that 'we are all soil organisms'.

The African continent was in many ways John Seymour's 'university'. He led a varied life there as farm manager, traveller and soldier. He read widely and learned Swahili. In the Second World War, he saw action with the King's African Rifles in Ethiopia and Burma. After the war, he settled in England and pioneered self-sufficiency on his smallholding. To supplement his income, he began writing – on travel, self-sufficiency and environmental issues. To date, he has published over thirty books, including the bestselling Complete Book of Self-Sufficiency.

John Seymour came to Ireland in 1980 and settled happily in County Wexford, where he set up the John Seymour School for Self-Sufficiency, which is still going strong. He wrote about his adopted country in Blessed Isle: One Man's Ireland.

I would say that, as far as I am educated – which isn't very far – I am completely self-educated. I certainly didn't learn much at school. I learned to speak French and forgot that, I learned a bit of Latin and forgot that. I learned no mathematics; I just couldn't take it in. I was always interested in geography, but I learned that by travelling around the world. I have travelled in about forty or fifty countries now and that is how I learned geography. So, I don't think I got much from either the kindergarten or subsequent prep school in England. I then went to a school in Switzerland on Lake Geneva where I learned quite a few not quite academic things. I learned to row and to climb down the drainpipes and to look at pretty girls!

If anything, my parents influenced me negatively. My mother was American, of a Welsh-American family that went out to Baltimore just after the Pilgrim Fathers got there. My father was Canadian, but my mother made a second marriage to an American businessman. He was a millionaire and I was brought up in a very plush and wealthy household. I didn't like the situation at all. We lived in a large house in Essex with a lot of servants. My friends were all the gardeners and the farm workers around us and I rather reacted against the whole big business world. I found it intensely boring and I contracted out of it as far as I could. I used to spend my holidays sailing fishing smacks off the Essex coast. They still fished under sail in those days and the fishermen and wildfowlers were my friends. So, I learned from my parents insofar as I discovered that I didn't want to live like them.

I didn't really start educating myself until I went to Africa. Before that, though, I was to spend three years in an agricultural college, Wye College in Kent, and I learned quite a bit there about the soil and crops. I also learned to distrust everything I was taught by my professors. Before going to agricultural college, I had worked for a couple of years on farms. On one particular farm in Essex, a small arable farm, there was an old-fashioned farmer who didn't use chemicals on his land at all, not because he had anything against them but because he didn't need them. He grew well above the average yield of wheat, barley, mangolds and other crops. He fattened a lot of cattle on his land and it was the manure from the cattle that kept up the fertility of the land. Then I went to agricultural college, where I was taught that you couldn't farm like that! I knew quite well one could because I had been working for two years on two farms where they farmed like that very successfully. It was then the beginning of the chemical revolution in farming and I mistrusted that because I knew it was possible to farm well and grow good crops without chemicals. There was one old lecturer at Wye College who agreed with me. He was a farmer himself and, in his lectures, used to say the same thing – there is nothing to beat good muck, meaning cattle manure, on the land. I didn't believe the other professors who told us that horses are out, manure is out – and that cattle should be kept on slats not in straw yards because all the fertility you want can be had from a bag. They also told us not to worry about monoculture, growing the same crop year after year on the same land, because the chemists will always come up with something to destroy whatever pest or disease this gives rise to. I didn't agree with it then and I don't agree with it now.

I then went to Africa and that is where my education started – in south-west Africa, in a place called Namibia. I got a job managing a farm. It was very remote, as far into the desert as you could possibly get. It took four days to get there in an ox-wagon from the railway line. There I came across an old box of books with which my boss's father, who was of Scottish descent, had tried to educate himself. There was an enormous amount of English literature in this box, but the white ants had eaten bits out of nearly all the books. White ants like books, but they don't read them; they eat them. So, I would be reading *Henry IV* and I would come to a gap and have to work out for myself what Shakespeare would have said there. I recommend that as an educational device. I had to use my imagination because of the white ants! I read all of the Shakespeare, all of Shaw and Fielding. It was the first time I really knew there was such a thing as English literature and I really got a lot of enjoyment out if it.

I stayed in Namibia for about two and a half years. I was managing a carical sheep farm, a breed of sheep which come from central Asia. Their wool makes fur coats for rich ladies. That was the chief industry of the place. I had to look after about 4,000 sheep and 200 head of beef cattle. I was stuck away in the bush with nothing but African people – I couldn't speak a word of their language and they couldn't speak a word of mine. I learned to speak Afrikaans, which was the *lingua franca*, but I never learned any African language because there were four different language groups on the farm and if I learned one language then I wouldn't be able to speak to the other three-quarters. I loved Africa. I moved from the farm and spent a year deep-sea fishing in the south Atlantic and line-fishing off Capetown. I spent six months copper mining – every young man in those days had to have his term down the mine, otherwise he couldn't hold his head up. Then I got a job inoculating native cattle in Northern Rhodesia, which is now called Zambia. I travelled over a huge area of central Africa. There were no roads and no cars – you walked and you had porters to carry your gear. You lived by your rifle, on what you could kill. I learned a great deal there – how to look after myself and be more or less self-sufficient.

I would call Africa my university. Later on I learned to speak Swahili fluently. I speak it better than I do English, but that was because I joined the army in the Second World War. I was in the King's African Rifles, which was an East African regiment, for six years and we spoke Swahili. There are so many languages in Africa that to learn one is pretty pointless, because if you travel twenty miles you are in another language area, whereas Swahili does take you over the whole of East Africa. I spent six years living in the bush, first in Ethiopia chasing the Italians and then in Burma chasing the Japanese. It was like being in Africa, even though it was Asia, because I was surrounded by Africans. I had a platoon of forty men who were all African. I got to know my men and they got to know me, and there was mutual respect between us. To be with forty men in conditions like that taught me a great deal. The Japanese were a very tough enemy and the jungle was not a friendly place, but we learned to rely on each other and that did me a lot of good.

Having been brought up in an agricultural tradition, I was always interested in the soil, because right from the beginning I realised that we human beings are soil organisms. Everything we eat comes from the soil. I saw the soil being destroyed on the big white-owned farms in Northern Rhodesia. They ploughed land which should never have been ploughed and they grew nothing but maize. I could see the soil was being destroyed and that gave me what has been an abiding obsession for looking after the soil. We can't treat it as something to make money out of – pouring chemicals into it, getting inferior food out of it and selling it for as much profit as we can get. That is not the way we are meant to live. We have to remember that we are soil organisms, we are creatures of the soil, and therefore we must look after it.

After the war I came back to Suffolk and eventually got a little smallholding of five acres. I had a family, a wife and four kids. I set out to become as self-sufficient as I could and we ended up producing all our food – flour, bread, cheese, butter, meat. It was great fun and it kept us fit. I realised that it was a good way to live, but difficult. I earned a living in those days doing a bit of writing and broadcasting.

We spent years without a car. We had a horse and cart then, which was great fun. However, I started doing little jobs for the BBC and had to travel maybe fifteen miles, so I was forced to buy a car – you find yourself being sucked in. Now I have a car and I also have an outboard engine and a couple of boats. When we first came here, we used to row up to New Ross and then, when we got decadent, we got the outboard and used that to get there to do the shopping. It is difficult nowadays to live without a car and if you have one it costs you a lot of money and you have to earn the money somehow. You can't live the Robinson Crusoe existence, you have to compromise.

I have written thirty books now that have been published and I enjoy that, but only if the subject interests me. I started writing travel books, including one about the hard way to travel around India – I travelled overland to India just after the war. I spent a year travelling around India and six or seven years in Africa and then I wrote a book called *One Man's Africa*. Then I started sailing and wrote sailing books and then I got into self-sufficiency and wrote *Self-Sufficiency* and *The Fat of the Land* as well as *The Complete Book of Self-Sufficiency*. I went on grinding out these books – and they were quite successful – until I got sick of it. I then started writing what you might call green books, books about the environment and how we have to look after it.

I love the eighteenth-century novels and essays. If you asked me if I would be more at home in the nineteenth century, I would have to answer that in some ways I would but in others I would have hated it. I would have hated the stuffed shirt part of it, having to wear a collar and tie and so on, but I would have loved the fact that you could have run away to sea if you wanted to and become a sailor or something like that. Nowadays, life is rather more cut and dried than before, although it isn't for me because I haven't allowed it to be. I have always done what I thought would be fun or adventurous, because I wanted to learn. I got a job in a mine because I couldn't imagine what it was like working underground, but now I know. It didn't take me long to find out and then I chucked it, because that was all I had wanted to know. I can't imagine just getting a job and saying, 'I'll hang on here until I get my pension and then I will retire and sit watching television for the rest of my life.'

I live here in the heart of the country. I hardly ever go to Dublin. New Ross is as far as I generally get and that is quite seldom. I only mix with the country people here, the farmers and the fishermen. A lot of my friends are the fishermen down the river. I like their attitude to life. They are hardworking people. The farmers around here are very good farmers by any standards, but apart from that they have a philosophical attitude to life. They always enjoy today and if you meet them in the pub they are always willing to talk. We get singing and music and *craic* in the pubs – you don't that get in England anymore. You can go into a pub here and someone will bring out a violin and someone else will bring out a flute and, before you know it, people will be dancing or singing. I love that. It is the folk culture that I like and I feel at home here. Some of my neighbours have said, 'You are one of God's Irishmen. You were born in the wrong country!' I like it here and would find it very difficult to leave now.

I can't imagine one's education being complete until you topple into the grave, which is an event I am quite looking forward to because I want to see what it is like. However, I want to do an awful lot of things before that happens and I don't intend for it to happen for a long, long time. One thing I want to do is get a Galway hooker and sail around Ireland. I think my education will be considerably advanced by that if we ever get round to it. I am not really an indoor man. I don't spend as much time reading as I should. As a writer, I ought to spend my time in my study and I don't – I spend it out of doors or in a boat or in the pub dancing on a table! There are many books I want to read, so much history I want to learn, it would take me a lifetime to touch even the fringe of the subject. I would like to know the history of China – I know very little about it. I dare not look at an atlas or a globe, because I think, 'Oh, my God, I'd love to go there. What's the centre of Siberia like? I must go there.' Maybe I would rather just stay here, though, which is all I think I will do – except for a bit of sailing.

Patricia Sheehan

1928–1994

Patricia Sheehan was born in Southampton, where her father was a marine engineer with the White Star shipping line. At the outbreak of war in 1939, her mother decided that Patricia and her sister would be safer in Ireland and both girls were sent as boarders to Loreto Convent School in Balbriggan, County Dublin. Patricia then studied medicine at UCD and later married her college sweetheart.

She became involved and quite expert in communication and speech disorders and one of her early pupils was Christy Brown of My Left Foot *fame*. Her husband's sudden death at an early age led Patricia to a study of bereavement and to work as a bereavement counsellor. She later worked with handicapped refugees in Nigeria during that country's civil war in 1966.

Patricia's love of deductive reasoning, à la Agatha Christie's Miss Marple, led her to a serious investigation of the possible connection between a concentration of Down's Syndrome children in County Louth and the fallout from a fire in the Windscale nuclear plant in 1957. She went back to college for a second time in 1985 to upgrade her scientific knowledge in pursuit of her investigation.

Patricia Sheehan died suddenly in July 1994.

I was born and brought up in Southampton. My father was a marine engineer and he went off on long voyages on cruise liners. There was a pattern to family life – when father was at home and when father wasn't at home. Mother didn't drive, so, when father was away, the car was left in the garage in a dust sheet and then, when father came home, there were often battery problems.

Father had very long legs and one of his comments was that, if he walked us to school, he had to walk twice as fast to try and fit in with our little dolly steps because he had a huge stride. That is one of the things I remember most about him. I was Father's pet and had a great bond with him and, whereas my older sister might be baking or sewing with Mother, I would be out with Father. I learned quite a lot that was of use to me later on in life – he decarbonised the car and connected up batteries, he converted American gadgets that were 110 volts d.c. into 220 a.c. When, later on, I came to do physics, it was very useful to have had that experience.

In the early days, Father used to be away for ten weeks at a time on cruises. There was a traumatic time when there was a shipping slump. The Cunard and the White Star lines were rivals, but Father was White Star and they went broke, so there was a period of time when the family was financially strained. Then things brightened up a bit when Father went off to Glasgow as 'platform second' for the launching of the *Queen Mary*. He was there for the installation of all her engines.

Mother was very different. She was a rather aloof sort of person and when I was very small I hurt her deeply without realising it. Shortly after I was born, Grandmama was taken ill and Mother went to be with her. When she died, Mother collapsed and didn't come back for nine months. I had very little mother input for the first nine months of my life, but I had a nanny who adored me. When Mother came back, my sister went running to her, saying, 'Mammy, Mammy, Mammy', but I bawled because I was confronted with a stranger who was taking me from my bonded mother figure. There was always a little something between me and my mother, but I didn't understand it until I pieced that story together much later in life.

Initially, I went to La Sainte Union School in Southampton. It was about a mile away and we walked there and back twice a day. The emphasis there was on training young ladies – it was just pre-war and there was a gentility around the school. We were trained to be diplomats' wives or ladies of leisure who were not going to be making munitions or fighting for emancipation. I remember with great affection the old nun who taught us embroidery. To this day, I still can't start embroidery, even on a cushion cover, without using a knot. When I came to school in Ireland, when war broke out, it was a much more practical approach – we were taught hemming and seaming and buttonholing and darning, but, in Southampton, the emphasis was on embroidery, elocution and music and there was a Montessori approach, which is very good in that it allows you to evolve within a structured setting.

We were on holiday in Ireland when the war broke out and the *Queen Mary* was stopped in mid-Atlantic and sent back to New York. Mother made a rapid decision that Southampton wouldn't be a good place to be and we would probably be evacuated anyway. She was Irish and had been to school in Loreto in Balbriggan, so she arranged, within four days of war breaking out, that my sister and I would be boarders there. It was a bit of a shock, because at first we were on holiday and then we ended up in boarding school, where I spent six years.

We both cried solidly for the first three months, before we settled down. We were a bit of an enigma. We were the only refugees in the school and we had had a different curriculum before we came – the others were only just starting French but we had done French already, and so on. However, I eventually settled in so well that I bawled for the last three months! It was so much a part of my life then that the thought of leaving was traumatic.

There was one old nun who taught us botany and geography and we were all terrified of her – I didn't know at the time that she had had a mastectomy and that she couldn't raise her right arm. She used to call me up to draw flowers on the blackboard and she relied on me to bring in specimens that she could use for the next class. Indirectly, she was responsible for me meeting my husband. When I was at college, I brought in specimens of moss that I had collected to the Botany Department and the professor nearly had a fit! Most pre-meds throw specimens at each other and here was I bringing in beautiful specimens, because old Mother Regis had trained me to be an observant collector. Years later, it was this professor who introduced me to my husband, so I have Mother Regis to thank for that. When I was back in college doing a master's in 1985 to '86, the question arose as to what I would do for a thesis. I set out to measure radiation in seaweed and I went back to the same haunts gathering seaweed and thinking of Mother Regis, right back to square one.

We didn't see Father for four years and he suddenly turned up again in 1944. I was coming up to doing my Leaving Cert in 1945 and, when asked what I would like to do afterwards, I said I would like to do science. I can hear my mother, who herself had taught, saying, 'She should teach, she should teach.' Father looked at me and said, 'Would you not like to go the whole hog and do medicine?' Thinking of him coming up to retirement and six years of fees to be paid, I thought it would be a bit much, but Father said, 'You know very well if you would like to do medicine we will fix it so that you do.' I am very happy now that I did medicine.

I qualified in January 1952 and went back to Southampton to work in Southampton General. When you get your degree you think you know everything, but it is only then that you discover how little you know. I learned more in the first six months of internship from the ward sister, a woman called Clare Leyland, who was a marvellous character. I went back twenty-five years afterwards to the consultant I had worked with and we reminisced about the old days. 'What was the worst thing I ever made you do?' he asked and I said, 'Sit in sister's office during visiting hours.' I had had to sit in sister's office and explain in simple terms to any relative that cáme to visit a patient what was wrong, what had been done, what the prognosis was. I learned an awful lot then that is useful to me now in explaining medical terms in simple language. I also came to understand the psychology of somebody who comes in saying, 'Don't tell me, I don't want to know' when they really do want to know or they want to be reassured. I now do cancer counselling and I often find myself being asked the same questions I was asked forty years ago.

I completed my internship, married in Southampton and came back and set up house in Clonskeagh. For the first month after I was married I would start getting dinner ready at half past three for Robbie coming home at seven! I soon realised I needed something to do. In Southampton, they had been setting up the speech department and I used to assess the children to make sure they didn't have a medical complaint as well as a stammer or whatever. I went to what was then the Dublin Health Authority and spent a day with Dr Brid Lyons Thornton. We had a stimulating conversation, but then she told me that the corporation did not employ married women. She suggested that I go round to the spastic clinic that had just opened in Bull Alley Street, and that is where I met Christy Brown. It was a pivotal day in my life, because, when I found somebody so intelligent, so humorous, so witty and with such difficulty in expressing himself, I made it my *raison d'être* to help spastics to talk. I stayed on working with them for over twelve years.

Children were brought in by voluntary drivers and St John ambulances to have physiotherapy. I started going in three mornings a week and taking the children for speech therapy. The only constant things I had to refer to were the children themselves, their anatomy, the clothes they were wearing and what was in my handbag. I became renowned for my 'bag of junk'. The children would name what I took out and they would categorise what things went together. We also did rhymes and blowing – trying to teach them to suck and blow was quite a problem. Once they had some breath control, they could start to control the sounds they were making.

When Christy Brown began to learn to write, he would flick off his shoe, pick up a pencil and write with the pencil held between his toes. Then he would go home and dictate to his brothers and sisters and they would write down in copy books what he had dictated. When you think of the battles he had to fight to get himself accepted, he really was a tremendous character.

I learned a lot from the kids I was teaching and what I learned from one I could apply to another. I had some wonderful characters there, some who just communicated with yes and no. I got quite good at asking twenty questions until I hit the right question, when there would be joy and relief! Twenty-five years later, I came across another Christy who gained repute, Christy Nolan. I used to encourage his mum when they came up from Mullingar to the Central Remedial Clinic by regaling her with tales of Christy Brown and telling her that I knew her Christy was going to make it too. There was always something about the look in a child's eyes – you didn't have to do psychological tests to know they were sparking. I realised that somebody who has one channel blocked can be very much more alert in others. We don't always realise how important all the channels of learning are.

My marriage ended rather tragically. My husband was a solicitor and he went down to the Four Courts one day, defended his client, then came up to the corner of York Street, turned into Stephen's Green and collapsed over the wheel of his car outside the office. That was one of the greatest shocks that ever befell me, particularly as I had been the one who had been ill. I had had cancer and I was supposed to be the 'creaking door' and the thought of being a widow had never come into my calculations.

Coping with grief led me to become a bereavement counsellor. At the time of the bombings in North Earl Street in 1974, there was a social worker in Jervis Street Hospital who realised that mass grief was something the casualty department was not geared to cope with, so she decided she would run a seminar on grief and bereavement. She arranged with Dr Colin Murray-Parkes to come over from St Christopher's in London and then she told me that he liked to interview somebody during his lecture, somebody who had had a sudden bereavement, or somebody who had nursed a loved one dying of a terminal disease or who had faced up to their own death, preferably somebody who was medical or para-medical. I said, 'Which of my hats do you want me to wear?' Out of that seminar came a course in bereavement counselling and sharing. Until people have come to grips with themselves, they can't really be of any help to anyone else, but there is no better way to learn how to live than to have faced up to death. The mere fact of thinking that you are about to die makes you appreciate life very much more.

Professor Bob Collis was the person who had founded the cerebral palsy clinic and who had discovered Christy Brown. He went off to Nigeria in the early '50s and, while he was there, he begat a handicapped child who didn't talk. He got in touch with me in 1966, just a year after my husband had died, asking how he could stimulate his son to talk. They invited me out to spend Christmas 1966 with them in Lagos. There was very little I could do. The little fellow was very handicapped – he had a multiplicity of problems. I became aware of the rumblings of the civil war that was starting up there and they were looking for medical personnel to help with handicapped refugees, so I volunteered. I ended up running a hospital in the bush in a place called Indubia, which is in East Central state, and that was a tremendous learning experience. It is actually an example of the maturity of a state when they begin to take an interest in their handicapped children. The situation in Nigeria is similar to Ireland thirty years ago and so I have been able to give advice on what we had learned then.

With high technology, you forget that you have hands and eyes and a nose, but when you have no x-rays and no laboratory back-up you see more, you hear more, you smell more and you observe more. It was a matter of making do with things and improvising, the sort of improvisation one learns with the St John Ambulance. I remember some English chaps coming over when I was doing midwifery in the Rotunda and asking where the drip-stand was – this would be in a tenement someplace. I said nothing but just went and got a broom, put the broom handle up and hung the drip out of the sweeping brush! I pity young nurses of the future who won't know how to boil up a scissors or forceps because everything comes pre-packed nowadays.

I am an Agatha Christie fan. I went to a conference in Amsterdam and they nicknamed me Miss Marple. I like deductive reasoning and putting clues together and experiencing the joy of discovery. There are two ways of approaching a problem. The pure Newtonian physicists would go step by step, proving everything as they go with a sort of laser beam approach. Then there is somebody like me who bungles into something – it is like a tangled ball of wool, where you can see cause, you can see effect and you have intuition, and you say, 'Well now, there must be a line that joins this end to that.'

Seventeen years ago, I was working for St Michael's House and a little Down's Syndrome child came in one day with her mother, who was a social worker and had done some research herself. She said she had often wondered about the fact that two or three of the girls she had been at school with had had Down's babies as well. My ears went up like antennae and began to waggle around. She first came up with the fact that there had been an epidemic of 'flu at the school. We contacted as many of the girls as we could and took blood samples to see if we could find a common virus, but, eight years later, all we had discovered was that the epidemic of 'flu had been the common Asian 'flu of 1957. If that virus had caused Down's, then half the countryside would have been affected. Then, by sheer chance, I made the connection that the time they were in bed with the 'flu in the school in Dundalk was the first two weeks of October in 1957, which was when the big fire had happened at Windscale Nuclear Plant at number one pile. I began to investigate the meteorological office reports and eventually got a copy of a White Paper which had been prepared for parliament six weeks after the fire, explaining what the pile physicists had done to try and stop the fire. Things began to fit into place and a picture began to appear. People didn't want to believe me, but I think they are a little less sceptical now since Chernobyl. Measurements were not made directly and it was speculation as to how much radiation the girls had received. Statisticians like large numbers and there were only one hundred and seventy-five girls in the school during that period, so, of course, that is a very small sample. I have since been gathering information about other girls that were day pupils in another school in the same locality and I am working on those statistics at the moment.

This investigation led me back to college to pursue the career in science that I had originally turned down. I had registered as a medical student in 1945 and I registered as a postgraduate forty years on, when a whole new language of radiation had come in. So I went back to college and took to being a student again quite happily, but it was a lot harder to come from being a student back to earth again.

Education goes on day by day. We learn by our mistakes – if everything slotted easily into place we wouldn't learn very much. The other day, I was watching a child with one of those pillar-box toys – they fiddle and fiddle and try to get the round peg into the square hole and eventually they get it and there is a sense of achievement. If they get it first time round, they lose all interest. It is trial and error that helps us to learn.

Those qualities of persistence and observation, *à la* Miss Marple, can be traced back to my formal schooling. I was trained in observation and to stick with a task from a very early age – finishing a jigsaw puzzle, finishing a piece of embroidery. My mother was one of the early time-and-motion people. She was very good on *aides-mémoire*. There was an old monks' bench in the front hall and anything that was downstairs that had to go up was put on the bench and the first one to go upstairs brought it up. On the landing there was a collection of trunks with a cover on them and anything that was upstairs that had to go down was put on the trunks. To this day, I do the same thing at home. If I am going somewhere in the morning and want to bring certain papers or books with me, I put them on the mat in the hall, so I will trip over them if I don't bring them with me. The early training remains all through one's life.

George Otto Simms

1910–1991

George Otto Simms was born in Dublin in 1910 and grew up in Lifford, County Donegal. He was educated in Cheltenham, England, and at Trinity College, Dublin, where he took degrees in arts and divinity before being ordained a priest of the Church of Ireland in 1936. He later spent thirteen years as chaplain at Trinity College. He was Archbishop of Dublin from 1956 to 1969 and Archbishop of Armagh and Primate of Ireland from 1969 to 1980. A scholarly man who had a deep interest in Celtic monasticism, he made a particular study of the Book of Kells. *In later life he wrote a bestselling introduction to that book for young people* – Exploring the Book of Kells – *and he followed that with* Brendan the Navigator *and* St Patrick. *George Otto Simms died in 1991.*

I went to school in 1915. The First World War had broken out in 1914 and this had an effect upon the little town where I lived, the town of Lifford, a dignified town, the county town of Donegal. A refugee family from Belgium came to what was known as the Barrack Yard at that period and one of these was appointed to be governess to me and my younger sister. She taught me my first lessons and some of them were in French. Her English was broken and she got teased when she tried to express herself. I remember one of my first lessons was in the French language, with a Belgian accent – a little rhyme which has stuck in my memory all through the years. Sometimes I bring it out for my grandchildren to make them smile.

> *Mademoiselle, voulez-vous danser*
> *Un Polka?*
> *Non, Monsieur, je ne danse pas,*
> *J'ai trop mal à l'estomac.*

I was the third son of a solicitor. My father was at first a junior partner in the solicitors firm, Wilson and Simms. He wasn't just interested in law, he was also tremendously interested in his country and we were surrounded by history books in the house. Much of his conversation would be concerned with the past. He was probably a unionist in outlook; those were the days just before the First World War when naturally enough the Ulster Volunteers were rallying and dreading Home Rule. My father, interestingly enough, was interested in the Irish language; he had studied O'Growney's Grammar and he had occasion to use Irish in some court cases. He was qualified to practise both in Tyrone and in Donegal, with no special qualification needed for the two-county situation in which he found himself; there were no political boundaries. My mother was from Australia. Her father had gone to Australia from north Germany and had put up a brass plaque there, in Adelaide, saying he was a professor of music.

Then the gold rush came and his interests were diverted. He did rather well at that particular time, so much so that he came back to London, to the stock exchange. So my mother was in touch with Germany, went to school in England, spent a little time in Paris doing an art course and then, when she was aged 22, she married and came to live in Lifford, County Donegal, having been all over the world and in touch with many different places and cultures.

As a family we were four children – we made a four at tennis, which we enjoyed. We all got bitten with the idea of climbing the mountains of Donegal and, as young people do, we collected things and our collection was to be the tops of all the hills in Donegal, and it is amazing how many peaks there are. It was a healthy life, giving us a great love of the countryside, and there was little sense of competition among us. It was a very happy childhood.

Next door to us there was a school called the Prior Endowed School. I went there in 1915 and I spent over four years there before I was sent far away to Surrey, to preparatory school, because they thought that this would give me the opportunity to study classics. Curiously enough, my father, who was a historian and a lawyer, wanted all of us to learn Latin and Greek, but I don't think we felt forced into it. In the Prior School, at that time, the headmaster offered Latin, Greek and Hebrew. It cost two pounds a year to attend the Prior School; fees were moderate but the teaching was of a high standard. The headmaster tried to teach Latin by the direct method: enter, *intra; ne time*, don't be afraid. We used a book called *Ante Limen (Before the Threshold)*. The 'threshold' would be the beginning of learning the language, but 'before the threshold' is where you get the feel of the language from hearing it used: *sta in angulo*, stand in the corner.

Although he was so fond of his own country, my father was rather tempted to make use of what was considered to be the good educational foundation in these independent schools. In a way, when you are far away from home, you get prouder of the country from which you come and you speak more about it; you feel more its distinctiveness. I was fond of school. It was a big wrench to have to go a long way away and never be visited by my parents. My brother took me the first time and then I went on my own. In those days it would have been out of the question for parents to travel just to see you for an afternoon or a weekend and you certainly never came home at half-term. At the same time, I had the full life that such a school provided and I didn't find it a hard life at all. I am still in touch with friends from my preparatory school, as well as from my later time at Cheltenham.

I thought about ordination from about the age of nine, but it wasn't by any means a constant thought; it came and it went. The chaplain at my prep school was a great friend of an eminent Anglican called Bishop Charles Gore. Even at that early stage I was aware of Anglicanism in relation to other church traditions. Charles Gore was very anxious that there should be a coming together and an end to disunity and a little bit of that rubbed off on us, even when we were ten. That white-bearded man, who was so kindly when he came to talk to us in the school chapel, was quite an influence and remains a constant image in the back of my mind.

At one stage I wanted to be a librarian. I suppose my father had given me a love of books and, even at St Edmund's, I was secretary of the literary society. This society was founded by Wystan Auden, who was the head boy when I first went to St Edmund's. He said we ought to be discussing literature, we ought to be reading Chaucer, so we played the Canterbury pilgrims. I was the Clerk of Oxenford and I developed a feeling for literature. I had two or three very good masters at Cheltenham who were so keen on their subjects that it was infectious. One was a minor poet, Hugh Lyon, who was a great friend of Walter de la Mare. He brought in John Drinkwater to read his own poetry to us. In that way we met a real live poet, we were able to ask him how he had become a poet and we also tried to write poetry ourselves.

I was always interested in people – I wanted to know the name of everybody in the school, for instance. My weakness is that I didn't specialise enough. I was so fond of the different subjects that my knowledge of chemistry and physics was a bit shallow at times. We even had a taste of geology and archaeology, as well as Latin and Greek, compositions and writing, verse and translation – all very intensive. I didn't find things like college chapel tedious – I didn't switch off. We worked pretty hard, but I remember how boys came regularly to the voluntary service in Lent, which was a good forty minutes out of their evening which they had to make up somehow. That gave me the kind of support that reassured me that there must be something in this religion, that it is not merely an inherited formal convention.

I came to Trinity College, Dublin, because I realised that I wanted to spend my life in Ireland. Trinity made a lasting impression on me and I feel I am still there. (They very kindly made me an honorary fellow and it is lovely to be there, in the library or occasionally supervising this and that, filling gaps and doing a little talking and instruction.) I took my first degree in classics and in political science and history, then I went on to do the Bachelor of Divinity. So, from 1928 to 1935 I was at Trinity College, living in rooms and meeting very interesting people who have often given me more than some of the lecturers. I think it often happens that you learn from those actually sitting beside you in the class. I said to myself, 'I am going to be a librarian. I am not going to drift into the ministry. It seems to be very easy to get into the Church of Ireland, not too demanding.'

I actually tried to do the Bachelor of Divinity before committing myself to ordination, just because that was a demanding examination. I wrote my thesis on monasticism. It was fascinating to learn about Cassian of Marseilles who had visited the Middle East, the home of monasticism and the Senobitic life, and when you actually read from original sources, you do get steeped in the atmosphere. That thrilled me very much and I thought I would like to work at the British Museum. I wasn't quite sure if this would be for life or just for a while, but I went for an interview. Sir George Hill was the director in those days and he was a very interesting person and we got on quite agreeably at the interview. He said, 'If you want to come we will have you, but go away and think about it,' and of course that brought me to my decision. When I decided to go on with theology, he wrote back and said, 'We would have welcomed you.' At least I knew that there was a choice and that helped me to decide.

There were many people who gave me very good advice. They suggested that, as I was interested in people, it might be that I could give most through the ordained life. If you are ordained, you have an entrée into people's lives, which is very privileged and rather frightening and, of course, full of responsibilities. You are not there as a nosy parker, you are there because you want to share life's possibilities, and ministry really is ultimately that. I still visit the sick – I am privileged to visit old people's homes and celebrate the sacrament with them. I also travel the world to visit leprosy hospitals; these are real people and they have a tremendous amount to teach us.

My first appointment was St Bartholomew's Church in Clyde Road, where they were trying to get an assistant for a vicar who had been there quite a long time. This particular church had been in trouble and it wasn't very popular with many of the people of the Church of Ireland. For instance, it was a church that had a daily Communion service and it was open every day so that people could go in and out as they pleased. It was also a church that tried to reach out to people of other churches and to the world in a special way. I thought that, if I went there, I would learn a lot in a fairly demanding ministry and that greatly appealed to me. When, after three years, I left St Bartholomew's, tears filled my eyes to be leaving after being so involved in people's lives. However, I left there to teach in a theological college for two years and this laid the foundations for the rest of my ministry. I learned about reading and about discussions. I learned about people who had different ways and to tolerate and understand them and, of course, to benefit from the very differences. Then I was brought back to be a chaplain in Trinity and that seemed to be bliss. I wanted to stay there all my life. People come and go and, if you fail with one lot of students, you know they'll move on and a new lot will come. I was thirteen years there as chaplain, until I was asked to go down to the diocese of Cork to look after the cathedral. I was then asked to be bishop and, eventually, asked back to Dublin to be an archbishop.

Trinity was a tremendous learning experience. However, I can never forget the number of suicides there. It was war time and a very difficult time for people on the threshold of any career. I was certainly involved in ten suicides, spread over thirteen years, that is almost one suicide a year. This is shattering of course, it makes you go cold. Every occurrence had some distinctive features. Of course, it is normal to think of the last conversation you had with that person and to ask yourself why you didn't stay longer. There was one boy who told his parents he was going to do it and who also told me. It was a most poignant case. The parents came up and stayed near the college in order to give him all the support possible, but he still did it. Suicide does not happen in isolation – there are relations, friends and companions. On the other hand, it can bring out hidden qualities in friends and families.

We also had a very interesting time in Trinity College, because, at the end of the war, people came from America and England and you would find older people who had already been in jobs seeking holy orders. I had decided to be ordained when I was twenty-three and very young and raw, having led a sheltered life, but here were people who had seen the world and, of all the other ministries, here was something they felt would fulfil them. That taught us an awful lot. I remember teaching Greek to a person who had been a commando and being very particular about getting everything right. The poor man tried to say that his memory was not as good as it had been, but, shocked and upset and physically damaged as he was, I was expecting him to have the fresh, springy memory of a young, undamaged person. However, we learned a lot by talking and trying to understand. 'A shorter course for older men,' he used to say, 'there should be a shorter course for older men . . .'

Books have always been an important part of my life. At home we were very fond of Dickens. I suppose Dickens taught us about people, introduced us to every sort of life – low life and high life. I liked spiritual writing, which I was introduced to by various people I met. I became interested in Celtic Christianity and in the monastic life and then I was asked to help the provost of the college, my Latin professor, whose eyes were growing dim. He had a job on hand, to study the Latin text of the *Book of Kells* in preparation for a Swiss facsimile edition, and that started my interest in the *Book of Kells*. I actually read the text word by word and compared it with standard texts, noting their mistakes and distinctive features. Then the vice-provost suggested that I should present a thesis on the subject for a doctorate, which I did, and that focused me on this particular kind of textual study. Looking at the *Book of Kells* is like looking into a great civilisation, because there is art there and architecture and ancientness, and not just Latin words but a living presentation of a faith – and that has occupied me even to this day.

No one actually teaches you to be a bishop. You don't go into training for episcopal skills; you make mistakes. You are, of course, one of a college of bishops, which is a great help. I have attended many church conferences and I learned a great deal from those. It had never occurred to me that I would be learning from people from different traditions in the Church and finding it enriching, but in fact this is the whole meaning of ecumenism. I was in Dublin in the '60s and they were very interesting and exciting times, mostly because of the changes brought by the second Vatican Council. Everything became more open and, although some people say that nothing is happening today, I think it is but it doesn't get into the headlines.

My father, although he was in the law and saw the seamy side of life, was very gentle and a man of peace. He wanted to appreciate all that was Gaelic as well as all that was 'plantation' in our history. He left this lesson with me: hear the other side, *audi alteram partem.* I often remember that.

Peter Ustinov

Peter Ustinov was born in London in 1921 ('but was conceived in Leningrad and travelled across Europe in embryonic form before making my entrance . . .'). He was educated at Westminster School in London, but dropped out and enrolled at drama school, at his mother's suggestion. From there he has never looked back and has become familiar to a worldwide public as a versatile actor on stage and screen, playwright, set and costume designer, film director, opera producer, author of novels and short stories and all-round brilliant raconteur and entertainer.

A philosophical citizen of the world ('I am life president of my own imaginary country . . .'), Peter Ustinov has been a tireless worker for UNICEF for the past thirty years. For this work and for his services to the arts, he has received numerous decorations, culminating in a knighthood in 1990. His autobiography, Dear Me *('to ensure sanity, there must be at least the elements of an internal disagreement ever present in a personality . . .'), was published in 1977.*

I was an only child. That in itself is not the general experience and it is a trap in a way, because only children are not necessarily spoiled, as the legend goes, but they have a greater contact with adults and they're allowed to sit up at the table because there is no one to play with and so on. They imitate adults and have a superficial sophistication which is really not to be taken seriously. I know that, when I myself fathered more than one child, I was absolutely amazed by the spectacle of sibling rivalry. I would say that only children are very rarely jealous. They are certainly not jealous in the home, unless their parents don't pay sufficient attention to them. I don't think it prepares one very well to be a good partner in life, because you don't acquire the habit of sharing.

I was born as a cosmopolitan, really. I didn't know where I belonged. I was born in London very shortly after the end of the First World War, when British tempers were still frayed and there was talk of 'hang the Kaiser' and all that sort of thing. My father was the first representative in London, after the war, of a German news agency. They thought that he would be less of a target of unpleasantness than somebody with a German name, but what complicated the issue more was that there was a 'von' in front of the name. So at school I was blamed for having personally lost the First World War and when they wanted to be nice to me they said their fathers had told them that the French trenches were deplorable as far as sanitary conditions were concerned. This didn't give me any pleasure, because my mother was of French origin. I had learned to fend for myself, being rather rotund right from the beginning of my life – I became the kind of the boy that couldn't do up his bootlaces but that everybody forgave because he was fat and chubby and pleasant. My schooldays were not particularly happy, but I became rather cunning at avoiding punishment and things like that by playing the part of what I appeared to be.

My grandfather, my mother's father, was the court architect of the Tsar and became overnight the president of the Soviet

Academy of Fine Arts. He was a fairly flexible fellow. He was very, very well thought of by his pupils. I went to visit him in Estonia when I was six. He protected my interests very much because, at that age, I had become a motor car. I was in love with motor cars and I had to play with something, since I didn't have brothers or sisters. I became a motor car, with all the gear changes and the crashed gear boxes and the hooting and all the rest of it. One day my mother had a toothache and I was being a motor car at its most vociferous, changing gear – which was quite unnecessary because Estonia is a flat country – and my mother suddenly flared up at me and told me to stop it. Her father said, 'Don't shout at him. Think of that sound not as that of a motor car but as that of his imagination developing and you will see it will be tolerable.' Of course, it wasn't tolerable, but I was very appreciative of the fact that he came in on my side.

My father didn't really understand children. He was not good with children and I think that is because he was the eldest child, born when his father was fifty-seven, and there were four more to come. So they never really had a father, they only had a grandfather. I think everything was slightly stultified, or petrified, by that relationship. His father was a particularly terrifying old gentleman, who used to wander around naked picking wild asparagus in Palestine. His copious hair and beard weren't enough to cover him properly, but he never realised that he was not wearing clothes. His genes have not come down to me at all.

My first school was Mr Gibbs' Preparatory School. The headmaster was a dear old man who usually cut himself shaving, so every day there were little eruptions of cotton wool over his face, and he used to sing a great deal. He took great pride in his voice, so he used to sing his instructions to me – 'Go upstairs now and fetch the book from which I intend to read.' He was all mock Handel. He liked to broaden our minds with general knowledge quizzes. I hadn't been there long when one of the questions was 'Who was the greatest composer that ever lived?' I said 'Mozart, probably,' but the correct answer was

Beethoven. I was heard to mumble that I thought the whole process was very unfair to Bach and I was made to write out a hundred times 'Beethoven is the greatest composer who ever lived'. It's a miracle I can still stand his music to this day and I've even written a play about him, curiously enough. But then the questions became broader. 'Name one Russian composer.' I put down 'Nikolai Rimsky-Korsakov', but the correct answer, unfortunately, was Tchaikovsky. When the school authorities had looked up 'Rimsky-Korsakov' in the dictionary and found that he existed, I was upbraided in front of the whole school by a woman teacher who said, 'You are showing off.' That was my first premature brush with Thatcherism!

Education has to be entertaining, it has to engage the attention of the young and it should never be dry. When the British government talks about introducing more exams at various stages of life, I know that, first of all, I would never have passed them and, secondly, I would have suffered by being forced to try and pass the damned things. I think it is the wrong way of going about it. There is now, in Bath in England, a small theatre named after me. I'm very honoured and flattered by it and it is used practically the whole time by young people who make their own plays, who criticise their own plays, who perform them and watch them. There is a very, very brilliant young man looking after all this and the young people are fully engaged in it and their minds are broadening all the time. As a result, it has had a palpable effect on delinquency in the town. I'm sure that is the best way of going about education. Things have to be made more attractive. A great enemy of every country at this time – this also goes for Northern Ireland, I would venture to say – is boredom. Quite apart from being unpleasant, it's the real greyness of everything which is so undesirable. In one of my school reports, Mr Gibbs said of me 'He has great originality, which must be curbed at all costs', and there it is in a nutshell.

I don't have particularly happy memories of my second school, Westminster, of the furled umbrellas, top hats and tailed coats. Now, of course, they're dressed sensibly and they're co-educational, which makes an enormous difference. I always thought, even when I was at school, that confining boys of that age to a kind of monastic sense that the world consisted of men and 'the others' was really very, very bad. In our day, we were just overblown schoolchildren being kept in our place by the attitude of 'it must be curbed at all costs'.

Academically, I didn't finish the course. I opted out and went to drama school. That was my mother's decision, really, because I was hopeless. I was a hopeless case because I was top in about three subjects: geography, French and history, and I was bottom in all the others because I had no interest in them at the time. I have acquired enormous interest in practically all of them since. In those days, you had to achieve a certain level in all the subjects; it was the school certificate in those days, not 'O' levels and 'A' levels and all that. My mother knew that I would be humiliated by them and she suggested drama school because I was good at imitation, although critics say it isn't the same thing. It is, of course, because playacting is merely an imitation of the imaginary. I didn't want to go, simply because I didn't understand how actors remembered all those lines. I still don't understand it. I've now played King Lear twice in Stratford in Canada and I got through it all right, but, how I did it, God only knows!

Drama school was very interesting. Again I quarrelled with the methods, because I think they talked too much and did too little. Drama is a curious thing. I think you're wrong to prepare for it too much. There are all the American intellectual methods, which I'm sure are, on the whole, stultifying. They hinder fast reaction and the theatre is a place of extremely fast reaction. If there is too much talk, I think you intellectualise it and turn an art which is based on quick reaction and spontaneity into an art of contemplation. You can't lock yourself in a room to practise acting. And, probably, if you rehearse too much, you lose something. There are many good actors who give you what they've rehearsed. That in itself is a form of laziness, because there are better actors who not only give you what they've rehearsed but who also give you the illusion that what is going on on the stage or on the screen is actually happening at that moment for the first time. And that is an element which I think too many people forget and which gives the theatre or the screen its excitement. It's a manufactured unpredictability which is terribly important.

Alec Guinness told me that, even to this day, before starting rehearsals he always goes to the zoo and watches animals, because you can learn a lot from their reactions. Monkeys are especially fascinating to watch, because humans are often so simian that you can draw a lot of parallels and get a lot of inspiration from doing so. Well, I think that's what they were trying to do at drama school – to broaden our vision. One girl there suffered from all the blights of her age. She was eighteen or so and she had acne, enlarged pores, oily skin and alopecia and she was, poor thing, anaemic too. She came from South Africa at a difficult period and was nostalgic for the open veldt. For patriotic and nostalgic reasons, she offered to become a springbok for the term. It was a very energetic idea. She put an enormous amount of effort into it and she jumped silently on and off furniture the whole term long. She arched her back and sprang about and climbed staircases – *outside* the banister – and she gave us one heart attack after another watching her. And at the end of the term, of course, she had lost a lot of weight, which she could ill afford to lose as an anaemic person, and she was in such a state of mental and moral distress that she went home and we never saw her again. Now I took a lesson from all that and I became a salamander. I just sat on a rock looking for flies, of which there were very few. I had a very restful term!

My dramatic career was interrupted somewhat by Mr Hitler and the war. That was the longest run I've ever been in – the worst parts and very underpaid. I hated every moment of it. However, I knew that it would be wonderful material when it was all over and that I'd be laughing about it. I had every intention of surviving, but I must say, as a worm's eye view of human nature, there's nothing like the army to awaken your absolute aversion and hatred of certain things. I never got into the 'real' action, but anybody who lived in London got into the action enough without wanting to. I saw much more action in London fire-watching on the roof of Wyndham's Theatre with a stirrup pump and a tin hat than I ever did in the army.

I was later attached to the Directorate of Army Psychiatry, not as a client, but as a consultant on the techniques of morale building. Britain needed that very badly at that time – the armies were going backwards everywhere. The Far East was lost and it was a pretty grim show all round. The psychiatrists were given opened letters by the censors and had to try to find out what men wanted from their letters to home, which was probably the most intimate exposition of their feelings about all sorts of matters. It was a fascinating time, but vaguely absurd as all those things are. I couldn't take it terribly seriously.

I wrote a play, which was highly praised – over-praised, I should imagine – by James Agate, and this was actually performed while I was a private in the army. Naturally, the papers gave that wide diffusion. The *Daily Mail* had a photograph of me in uniform, looking pathetic, with the caption 'The Play of the Year'. So that, although I was A1 physically, I was not sent anywhere else but was given willingly to the psychiatrists or to write film scripts, or to do anything, even at my tender age!

When we first went into the army, we had to report to Canterbury and I sat there miserably with my kit bag, in my civilian clothes, in front of a fire. Nobody had yet decided what to do with us and there was an old soldier – an old sweat, a regular – sitting in front of the fire, too, casting his mind back to his own first day. He said, 'I see you're going into the army. I find it difficult to remember the time when I first went in. I'm a volunteer you see, a peace-time soldier, and I never moved up from private. I like it like that. But there was a story I heard when I first went in which might help explain the army to you. There were two soldiers, you see, on latrine duty. It was autumn and I was sweeping up and a sudden gust of wind caught up a piece of used toilet paper. Like an autumn leaf it floated in the air. They couldn't reach it and, before they could prevent it, it floated in through the colonel's window. Now what where they to do? One of them said, "Look, you go on working here. If anybody asks where I am, I've been taken short, right? And meanwhile I'll go up and see if the old man's in and try and recuperate that piece of paper." So the man went off and came back five minutes later and the first one, who was still sweeping, said, "Did you get it?" and the other one said, "No, I was too late, he'd already signed it."'

There was another wonderful day when there was a kit inspection – something I hated, because you had to roll your socks up together to give them a kind of square shape. The army loves symmetry and order of that sort, but, although I made mine square, since they were my socks, when I left them alone, they breathed themselves into rotundity. The sergeant-major came in just before the officer came round, saw my socks and said, 'Wot is that? That's a f . . .' – you can imagine the expletives he used. 'You're gonna get in trouble when the old man comes round, is that clear?' The 'old man' turned out to be an actor who I vaguely knew and he came up to me, didn't look at my kit at all, and said, 'There's a rather good picture of you in *Sphere* this week'. This, of course, mystified the sergeant-major. He came up to me afterwards and said, 'Wot did he say to you?' and I said, 'He said there's a picture of me in *Sphere* this week.' 'In *wot?*' he said. 'Never mind, ask him,' I replied. He turned on his heel and said, 'Ahh, you wait till I get hold of you.' That was the kind of endless paradox in the army. For instance, when I was sent against my wishes to a training place to see whether I was 'officer material', we were told that we would be anonymous. I sat next to an officer at dinner who said how much he had enjoyed my performance at Wyndham's

Theatre. It was very difficult to know whether that was a trap – whether you would get bad marks for having abandoned your anonymity. So I said, 'I don't know what you're talking about, sir.' His brow was furrowed in exasperation and he said, 'Don't pretend that I don't know who you are. I'm going mad in this job, do you hear me?! I'm going to give it up! I can't bear pretending, pretending, pretending!'

I am life president of my own country. All my decisions are made with reference to an imaginary country of which I won't give any details but I know its history, the size of its population, its geographical situation. It is not part of any of the actual treaties – it has a veto in the United Nations because it is tremendously important to me that it should. I use it as a yardstick about what I think about very many things. I don't think this is because I have no 'roots', as the Americans call it. I don't think roots are terribly important, because I have a great affection for Ireland, which must be obvious, but I also have a great affection for Italy – I know what to expect when I arrive there and I'm rarely disappointed. Naturally, I do have prejudices. We all do and we can't avoid it. When my daughter started bringing black students home, she thought it would frighten me because she might marry one. Of course, it didn't at all, but I did tell her, 'Don't think I'm absolutely free from prejudice, because if you came home with a son of a South African apartheid member, I think I might object to that in the family.'

I don't find nationality important, because my father was German by passport and became British. One of his brothers was killed in the First World War as a German officer, another was Canadian and his younger brother is Argentinian and the sister of all those boys is Lebanese. So, how on earth can I take passports seriously. It doesn't make any sense at all. I don't mind what passport I have and in fact I very often travel on a United Nations passport, to which I'm entitled. What is important is the cultural values of each country, which, as an outsider, I can appreciate as much as anybody. I can't stand patriotism, if it is of the variety which is exercised at the expense of other people. This seems to me absolutely barbarous and old-fashioned. Love of a country and its traditions is absolutely natural and a wonderful thing, but I think one can have one's roots in civilised behaviour and I find that even more satisfactory. Without wishing to lose my fascination for my own ethnically filthy roots, of which I'm very proud!

I think that parliamentary democracy is all very well, but it is in disrepute now, because, on the whole, politicians are no longer trusted as they once were, and they are in a difficult situation because they have to try to make themselves attractive. You can see that, in every election in every country, the turnout has to be stimulated, because otherwise relatively few will to turn up to vote. On the other hand, non-government organisations are becoming more important, because they express real human concerns. The first non-government organisation was the Red Cross, which started from one individual's horror on the battlefield at the beginning of the last century. Gradually, the Swiss Red Cross and then the international Red Cross took shape and did something. This is now acknowledged by all nations, but no single government would have been capable of putting such a thing into orbit. It had to be a non-government organisation. We now have Greenpeace, Amnesty International, hundreds of organisations, which came into existence because they correspond to a human, as opposed to a national, need. Curiously, they are getting richer, although they started from very humble roots, just like the Swiss Red Cross. Now, if you have an international congress, the contribution of non-government organisations is far more alive and vital than that of any delegation working under instructions from a capital. I am president of the World Federalist movement, which is a completely unsubversive movement. This is an organisation which has an office in the United Nations and which is at the forefront of those who want an international criminal court, among other things.

In my travels with UNICEF, I see frightful things and I see things which are disturbing. Nowadays, everybody's attention is attracted to Burma, quite rightly, because of the extraordinary character of a single woman, who is handling herself with great cleverness, confronted by a military government of generals. Nobody's going to starve in Burma; you can eat what you want off the trees. But Cambodia's situation is really most distressing and the human race should feel a twinge of conscience. More bombs were dropped on it than on Vietnam, and now the most hideous statistic of all is that over fifty per cent of the population are under 15 years of age, because between two and three million of the older generation were killed, out of a population which was then eight and half million. Flying over it now is like flying over a plucked chicken, because there has been such devastation. The real tragedy of a country like that is that it is practically impossible for it to attract any foreign investment, because of the uncertainty and because of the ruin everywhere. I was sent there on a mission by UNICEF and I was very struck with the contribution UNICEF is making, but external help is not forthcoming on the scale which is needed.

I am learning something now which you really can't learn when you're young – that the human soul doesn't age. I'm sure within myself that I am exactly the same person as I was when I was one year old, or ten or fifteen. I am listened to because I look different and I have more experience. But, as time passes, the body begins to depart from the soul – I can understand why people in the Bible wrote about giving up the ghost. The body becomes more and more strange to you, because it doesn't behave as well as it used to. I feel that, when you are born, you go to a counter which is a kind of Hertz rent-a-body counter and you say to the girl: 'Listen, haven't you got something with a slightly sportier engine?' or 'Oh! a sliding roof, I'd like that very much.' And she says, 'No, wait, they're all out. Take that one or leave it.' And you take it and you're stuck with it all your life, and it becomes much more of a stranger at the end because you begin listening for creaks in the bodywork and there is a noise coming from the back axle which you don't like and so you drive it more slowly than you did before. And you hope that you'll keep your dignity and be able to bring it back to the counter to hand it in and won't be stuck out in the countryside with a red triangle behind you, waiting to be collected. I regard the whole thing with some amusement and am not really frightened of death, simply because I don't remember being frightened of birth. And, after all, the entry and the exit must have something in common! I'm not going to hurry the process. They gave me a new passport, which expires – charming, the word they use for a passport – on 10 April 2000. I really want to make it a point of honour to live as long as my passport, because it is such a waste, otherwise.

I have regrets, but they are not important, because you have to choose a way and if you start regretting you didn't go the other way you are wasting time. Life is much too short, which is a terrible thing, of course, but it would be even worse if it was much too long. Without death, you couldn't assess anything. It's like a map without a scale. If you start to think about what you could have done, you lose the initiative, and life is nothing but a mass of initiatives which you simply have to take. You can't get out of yourself. You're stuck with yourself for better or worse and there is no use in having enormous regrets that you are not this way or that way. You can be a Walter Mitty secretly. I am a Walter Mitty, because I'm my own country, where I have no great difficulty in suppressing the opposition. Although it's a democratic country, you understand. Of course, it is a country in which there is a modicum of freedom, but certain things are in the hands of a government, with a whole ministry devoted to consultation. I think consultation is very important, otherwise I wouldn't have called my autobiography *Dear Me* and divided myself into two. I don't give a concrete answer to any question, instead the two sides of my nature argue it out, which I think is not only more democratic but also more revealing.

Jean Vanier

Jean Vanier was born in 1928, the son of the man who would later become Governor-General of Canada. After an early career in the navy, he studied philosophy in Paris. At the age of twenty-one he met a man who would change the direction of his life completely – Père Thomas Philippe, who later became chaplain to an asylum. Both men were unhappy at the exclusion of people with mental disabilities from normal everyday life in the community. Thus was born the concept of L'Arche (The Ark) – a simple residence in which Jean initially lived with two mentally disabled men. L'Arche offered a haven of peace to those who were disturbed, of sharing to those who were excluded, of hope to those who lived in despair.

From that tiny beginning, the L'Arche movement has spread all over the world. There are now 105 L'Arche communities, which welcome people of all faiths. As Jean Vanier says, 'the only passport required to enter L'Arche is pain...'

I was born in Switzerland. My father was military adviser to the Canadian delegation at the League of Nations and he then went as a diplomat to Canada House in London. I was in England from 1931 to 1939 and I went to a Jesuit school there, the prep school of Beaumont College, and then in Canada I went again to a Jesuit Loyola College in Montreal. Two years later, in 1942, I left for England to join the navy.

Dad and Mum were both people of prayer and deeply committed to honesty, to integrity, to serving the country, to serving people, but even more deeply to love of the Church and being present to the poor. They were obviously a very strong influence on my life.

Probably the most important thing that happened in the formation of my *being* was asking my Dad if I could join the navy. He asked me why and, although I don't know what I answered, I remember his answer: 'I trust you'. I often say that the trust of my father whom I loved was my second birth, because it permitted me to trust myself; he was saying I trust your intuition and I trust you. I was thirteen years old.

I think what remains from my naval training is the discipline. Though the discipline was hard, it gave me a dynamism and a capacity to adapt and to live difficult situations.

I was twenty-one when I left the navy and went to a small community near Paris which was founded by a French Dominican called Thomas Philippe and that was a very deep experience. I came there both mature and immature. Mature, because I had assumed a lot of responsibility and done a lot of things in the navy – probably a lot maturer than many young people of the same age – but quite immature in my capacity to relate and from the point of view of my intellectual and cultural development. I was seeking to grow intellectually and spiritually.

I spent a number of years in that community. I received a good intellectual foundation and, particularly through Père Thomas, a deep spiritual formation; he led me into a life of quiet prayer. His talks touched me deeply, intellectually and spiritually, so there was a sort of communication between himself and myself which was of the order of spiritual rebirth.

I think Père Thomas brought together three elements – a mystical element, a real union with Jesus leading into silence; a whole vision of metaphysics and theology; and also a vision of the needs of young people, particularly in the period after World War Two. He was a man who was very interested in people. In this community there were people from many different countries, particularly the Middle East. Through these three elements, I was nourished and formed intellectually, metaphysically and theologically and I was led into a life of prayer. I finished my studies at the Catholic Institute in Paris and started teaching at St Michael's College in Toronto.

In 1963, I went to visit Père Thomas, who had become chaplain of a small institute for thirty men with mental disabilities. He had suggested that I come and meet his 'new friends'. I went to visit them with much fear and some misgivings, because I didn't know how to communicate with people who had a mental handicap. How do you speak with people who can't speak? And even if they did speak, what would we talk about? I was very touched by these men with all that was broken in them, their handicaps, their incapacities. Each one was thirsting for a relationship. Each was asking, 'Do you love me? Will you be my friend?' My students in philosophy wanted my head but not my heart. They were interested in the courses I could give them so that they could pass their exams and move on. They were not saying, 'Do you love me?', they were saying, 'What can you give me to pass my exam?'

I loved teaching, but it was not really my purpose in life. I was seeking my life's work, not just a job. In the navy, and then in the world of studies, I had been in the world of the strong, the 'winners'. Here, I was opened up to the whole world of the poor, the broken, the 'losers' of humanity. I was touched by their cry and by their terrible situations. Many had been living for a long time in institutions or psychiatric hospitals, where you would find a hundred men roaming around in one room, with no work, nothing to do.

Père Thomas encouraged me to take two men from an asylum and live with them. Raphael had had meningitis when he was young and would fall over easily. Philippe had had encephalitis when he was young and had one paralysed leg and one paralysed arm; he also had a mental handicap, though he could speak well. We started living together – and so began the adventure of *L'Arche*.

I think *L'Arche* is a discovery that people with handicaps are beautiful people. They may be slow and more fragile, but, if they are loved and appreciated, they are incredibly beautiful. They have great wisdom, but most of the time they are pushed aside; people don't listen to them, so they are unable to give out their beauty, their wisdom and their kindness.

Our civilisation has been influenced by rational philosophies: man is a rational animal; we are only human if we can develop our intelligence. In the Catholic Church, for example, people with mental disabilities were not allowed to receive Communion, because they could not understand. In our society, people are frightened of death and of anything that is a sign of death. A child who is born with a profound handicap is a sign of death, a sign of brokenness, and so is often put aside. How can parents who want their children to be beautiful and to have a good life easily accept a child who is a sign of death? Frequently, having a child with a handicap is regarded as a punishment from God! Or sometimes society makes parents feel that in some way they are the cause of their child's difficulties. Children sense that they are a source of pain instead of joy for their parents. They can act as a nuisance, with strange and difficult behaviour, because they know that others only see them as a nuisance. It is true that they are different, but can we not see the difference as a treasure, rather than a threat?

'*L'Arche*' is the French word for 'the ark' of Noah in the Bible. It carries with it a beautiful image, because Noah's ark saved people from the deluge. Many people today, particularly those with mental disabilities, are caught up in the deluge of our civilisation of technology, efficiency, rapidity, faxes, unemployment and so on. *L'Arche* is a community where they can find refuge. Our communities welcome people from different Christian traditions; in India, we welcome Hindus and Muslims as well. The 'passport' to enter *L'Arche* is not baptism but pain, suffering, rejection. We are trying to create communities where we appreciate each other, where we belong to each other. In the Gospel of Luke (14: 12–14), Jesus tells us that, when we give a meal, we should not invite members of our family (even though Jesus is 'pro-family'), nor our rich neighbours, nor our friends, but when we give a really good meal we should invite 'the poor, the lame, the disabled and the blind' and then we will be blessed. In *L'Arche*, we are discovering the blessing of eating at the same table as the poor, the lame, the disabled and the blind! To eat together in biblical language means to become friends. The ultimate meaning of *L'Arche* is to become friends, to belong to each other.

Our main difficulty is to find young men and women 'assistants', who want to come and share their lives, to serve in the spirit of the Gospel, which means putting down roots in a community which is simple and poor, living together a life of pain, work, celebration and prayer, day after day. Some people come for short periods of a year or two; others stay on for the rest of their lives, because they discover that *L'Arche* is a vocation, a real calling. Almost all are transformed in one way or another by their contact with the people at the heart of our communities.

As I lived with Raphael and Philippe and others, I discovered that I had to change. I had to listen more to them. They were not calling me just to be generous, to *do* good things *for* people, but to enter into a vulnerable, permanent relationship with people who have disabilities. I discovered the communion of hearts, which is different to generosity. It was difficult, a total reversal for me, as I used to be quite serious and austere. Our meals together would take a long time; we would relax, play games, have times of quiet prayer and few words. Little by little, I was learning what it was to be human. I soon learned that Raphael and Phillipe weren't terribly keen to live with an ex-naval officer who thought he could tell everybody what to do. So I have had to change and learn to work with other people.

Gandhi is one of the people who influenced me a lot. I admired his vision of non-violence, his vision of the *harijans* – the untouchables – whom he called the children of God, and his desire to live with them and be part of their lives (in the ashram his job was always to wash the toilets) and also his desire for unity between Hindus and Muslims. He had a sense of what humanity was called to be and he was also a man of deep prayer. His vision formed my mind and my heart and helped me to discover more fully the Gospel message, just as Père Thomas and Mother Teresa had.

Then, in 1980, I took a sabbatical. I left the responsibility of the community and lived for a year in one of our homes which welcome ten men and women with profound disabilities. I lived with Eric, who was blind, deaf, could not walk and could not eat by himself, and Loic, who was about twenty-five but looked like a young boy of six – he could not speak, but was able to walk a little. Living with them, spending time with them – giving them their baths, helping them to eat, trying to understand their bodily gestures – was quite a revelation for me. It is an incredible thing to enter into a deep relationship of love and communion with people who are so weak and fragile. They teach us how to be at peace and to be quiet inside. Moments of silence can be even more important and 'expressive' than talking.

In our *L'Arche* communities, we are frequently confronted with crisis, but we are learning from these crises. They help us see the importance of evaluation and of giving better support and formation; they call us to be more open to new things and to evolve. Crises call us to be truthful, to come together and do the best we can; to grow in trust in one another and in providence. Some of our communities that were in great difficulty a few years ago are very beautiful and blossoming today. There is crisis, but then something happens, help arrives, and the community begins to flower again. Some of our communities are in difficulty because they are lacking good medical and psychiatric help; others have difficulty finding support and understanding from the churches. Some crises have come from lack of assistants. There have been many different crises.

In our society there is still a lot of prejudice against people with mental disabilities or against places like *L'Arche*. Parents of people with disabilities may be happy that *L'Arche* exists, but often parents of assistants who come to live in *L'Arche* are much less happy! They often get upset when their son or daughter comes to *L'Arche*, especially when he or she feels called to *L'Arche* as a lifelong vocation. It is not very honourable to spend your life with broken people. Our societies often reject the values and vision of the gospels.

Our communities are constantly swimming against the tide of culture, as our societies today value efficiency, power, money and success more than littleness, service and compassion. Little by little, however, *L'Arche* is gaining recognition. I know that, here in Ireland, through our three communities in Cork, Kilkenny and Dublin, people are seeing *L'Arche* as a sign of hope and as a sign of what is possible for people with disabilities. Perhaps the fullness of the message of *L'Arche* is not yet recognised; we are not seen as a new form of Christian community for the Church today.

In *L'Arche*, the good news is being announced to and by the poor. Who, except the poor, can tell us this good news? It is not the wise men nor even the theologians who can say, 'I have discovered what it means to be loved.'

Not too long ago, a young lad of eleven with a mental handicap made his First Communion. Afterwards, there was a family celebration and the uncle said to the mother: 'Wasn't it a beautiful liturgy? The only sad thing is that he understood nothing.' The boy heard that and he looked at his mother with tears in his eyes and said, 'Don't worry, Mummy, Jesus loves me as I am.' The weak and the fragile seek the *presence* of God, whereas people who are more clever intellectually seek *knowledge about* God. People with disabilities don't want knowledge but the presence of God. Isn't that what the whole of the mystery of the incarnation is about? Certainly, we have something to teach the poor, but even more fundamentally they have something to teach us. *L'Arche* is founded on the beatitudes. People with disabilities in many ways live close to the beatitudes – they *are* the poor in spirit, they *are* the persecuted, they *are* those who weep, they *are* gentle, they *are* the pure of heart, they *are* in some way peacemakers. So, in order to discover what the beatitudes are about, we are called to live with the poor and the broken.

The poor evangelise us, they change us, if we let them touch our hearts. I believe that you can learn more about humanity in prisons and psychiatric hospitals than in universities. There you find what I would call 'naked humanity', people on their knees, people who are angry, who are depressed, who have known oppression and pain, who have hurt people because they have been hurt. They teach us about humanity and that the immense cry of humanity is a cry of loneliness: 'Who will be my friend?' The weak and the broken teach us something about this cry for love. In that sense, they are the prophets of today. The poor are always the prophets and when I talk of the poor, I do not just mean the poor of Ireland or France, but also the poor of Rwanda or India, people in slums, refugees. They teach us about humanity. That is why Jesus says that, if we eat at the same table with the poor, the lame, the disabled and the blind, we will be blessed, because we will discover something about humanity and something about God.

The seeds of *L'Arche* were sown by Père Thomas, a man who had suffered, a man who revealed to me what I call the secret of people with handicaps, their closeness to God. I could easily have gone into the world of philosophy and the world of the powerful, but he led me into the world of the poor. The seeds of *L'Arche* were sown in the union between Père Thomas and myself. The mystery of the Church is in the unity of lay people and priests together. Père Thomas had a hidden role as a spiritual adviser and often I was the one who made the decisions. Père Thomas carried the seed in his heart, he gave it to me and together we looked after it.

The first years of *L'Arche* were years of joy. We would laugh, we would sing and dance; they were fun. If I had not been with *L'Arche*, I would have been studying philosophy. People with disabilities brought me to the place of fun – not fun with a lot of drinking, not fun that is vulgarity, not fun which is just looking at television, but a coming together and celebrating life together, celebrating our common humanity and our sense of belonging to each other. *L'Arche* is a place of celebration.

Ken Whitaker

Ken Whitaker was born in County Down in 1916 and moved to Drogheda, County Louth, in 1922. He had a distinguished career in the Irish civil service, rising to secretary of the Department of Finance, from 1956 to 1969. He inspired the writing of Economic Development *(1958), which marked the opening up of the Irish economy to the outside world. He was governor of the Central Bank of Ireland from 1969 to 1976. A former senator in the Irish parliament, he was also president of the Royal Irish Academy. He has had a lifelong commitment to the Irish language and served as chairman of Bord na Gaeilge. He was elected chancellor of the National University of Ireland in 1976.*

I was born in Rostrevor, County Down, in 1916. My parents were very upright people, very pious people, and they were also very economical people. My father had a Victorian sense of values. He would never spend money if it depended on borrowing. Hire purchase was anathema to him. I remember when my sister and I were learning to play the piano and we needed a new one, but we had to wait until he had saved up the money for it. No question of hire purchase. I often wonder if that affected my thinking on economics in later life! Certainly, I'm very much against our going so heavily into debt, particularly internationally, and I had a particular objection to our borrowing money abroad for purely current domestic purposes.

My sister and I were the product of a second marriage, so our father was rather older than a father would normally be. We revered him rather than loved him. He was very good to us all, but he was distanced from us by time and authority, and one of my regrets was that I never really got to know him properly. Just when I had grown up and got married he died, so we never had an adult relationship. I was closer to my mother who lived to be 100, so we saw a lot of her. She lived to see her great-grandchildren and that was a good influence for all the children, particularly the grandchildren, growing up.

We moved from Rostrevor in County Down to Drogheda in about 1922, just as the Civil War was going on. One of my earliest memories was of looking out the window and seeing a dishevelled man with a gun running down the street. I spent virtually all my school years until Leaving Certificate with the Christian Brothers in Drogheda. In the secondary school, particularly in the last three or four years, I was extremely fortunate to have excellent teachers. One, Brother Burke, who taught us English and maths, and the other, a lay teacher, a little man who came from Newry, Peadar McCann, who taught us Irish and history, and between them I got an absolutely superb education. Brother Burke was, at the time, compiling his anthology of English poetry, *Flowers from Many Gardens*, and we were allowed to help correct the proofs. Peadar McCann really encouraged an interest in Irish which has endured for me to this day. I'm extremely grateful to him for enriching my life in that way. He also took such an interest in his pupils that he took a handful of us for French classes before school every morning for a couple of years without any recompense whatsoever. French wasn't on the Christian Brothers' curriculum.

I managed to get an intermediate scholarship, which enabled me to buy a bicycle, and I was in fact working for a university scholarship after the Leaving Certificate when the news that I had done well in the civil service examination came. We had a council of war at home. My father had just retired, and we decided that there wasn't much prospect of our being able to afford university, even if I got a scholarship for medicine – a long course – as I was planning at the time. So we took the bird in the hand and I made as good use of that as I could and climbed the civil service ladder.

Growing up in Drogheda was in itself an education; a wonderful historic town with St Laurence Gate only a stone's throw away from where I lived and all the great Boyne Valley with its megaliths behind us. As I grew up, I got friendly with a Dominican lay brother, Brother Andrew Ryan, who had had a marvellous life. He had been employed by the order to raise money all around the country and he had a great personality. He had a very sophisticated knowledge of lots of things, like breeding cocker spaniels and tending roses. We used to go for swims with him and he introduced us to shooting rabbits up near Dowth and Newgrange and swimming in the Boyne there and so on.

At that time I could identify with Wordsworth's *Intimations of Immortality*. I remember cycling out to Newgrange, before Newgrange was restored, and there was a tangled mass of thorn trees on top of it and rabbits scampering around. You could feel, as you peered through the gate, a cold air wafting out, some kind of mystic experience – being in association with the past.

In my teenage years, I spent many summers in Rann na
Feirste in County Donegal, where I improved my fluency in the
Irish language. It has completely enriched my life because it
introduced me to so many people in the Gaeltacht with whom
I established great friendships and it introduced me to literature
written in the Irish language – modern Irish in particular. In the
case of literature since the sixteenth century, I was happy when
I was chairman of Bord na Gaeilge to induce two excellent
people, Sean Ó Tuama and Thomas Kinsella, the poet, who was
my private secretary for a while, to join together in producing
An Duanaire, the collection of *Poems of the Dispossessed*, as they
called it. I had always thought that many of the people who
referred to the great age of poetry and literature in the Irish
language were just paying it lip service, that they knew damn all
about it, and I thought it was very important to produce the
poetry, or a good sample of the poetry, with a competent poetic
translation into English facing it, and that's what we did in *An
Duanaire*.

For boys who had a Christian Brothers education at the time
there were very few outlets. The civil service and local
authorities and a few other jobs of that kind were the only
things on offer. In the very early days when I was in the civil
service commission, I sat with a man who was the father of
Eithne Fitzgerald. Our job was somewhat like that of Laocoön,
who was wrestling with all the serpents in that famous
sculpture. We were wrestling with great big sheets of sticky
paper on which we had to put the marks for various
examinations. We then had to put them into numerical order,
which meant getting all these narrow perforated sheets and
putting them back on a new background – a very sticky and
unexciting job! However, we were rescued from that because,
once you're in the civil service commission and want to do
another competitive examination, you are hounded out to
somewhere else for fear you might see the papers in advance. I
was sent to the Department of Education at a very early stage

and actually became private secretary to Tomás Ó Deirg, who was the minister at the time.

I wasn't too impressed with Education as a department. My impression of it was that people did not co-operate well. There were a lot of people whose main interest was not to help you but to 'walk you up the garden'. There was a great deal of unnecessary competitiveness. They didn't have enough input from outside; the kind of graduate intake that Finance and some other departments had was not available to them and that continued for quite some time.

I spent a little while in Revenue as an assistant inspector of taxes, which was another rung of the ladder. For that examination, economics, or commerce, was on the syllabus. I had never heard of economics until then, so I decided I had to do something about it. I started doing first of all a London University arts degree in mathematics and Celtic studies, Latin and law. I got some credit for the mathematics to do an economic/science degree at London by correspondence, as an external student. Later on I completed it by doing a master of science/economics, as they put it.

I went to Finance in 1938. I have always likened it to entering an officer corps. No matter how junior you were, you had access to the officers' mess, you could ask the general something and you wouldn't be frozen out. It was a completely new experience, an exhilarating one, to be in a place where that kind of *esprit de corps* existed. It was very much like an academic institution. There was a good deal of talking amongst ourselves about economic problems. There were people there in my time like Paddy Lynch and Jack Nagle, with whom one could talk over problems one had with one's own study.

In my thirty-one years in Finance, one of my great mentors was Arthur Codling, an Englishman who stayed after the Treaty to help in the new department and who became assistant secretary there. He was quite a disciplinarian; you made sure that you got your file numbers correct on your documents and so on. He was also someone who, by his own example, taught you how to mix intuition and logic to good advantage.

Professor George O'Brien of UCD was also extremely helpful to me. I was somebody outside his own immediate sphere, somebody who had never gone to university, but I was always included by him amongst those he called his 'swans', the people he invited to dinner and pleasant debates in congenial company.

Anyone who grew up in my generation couldn't help but be influenced by the socialists, who got a great innings from the first Penguin and Pelican books – Harold Lasky and G D H Cole and so on. In 1936, Keynes' great book, *General Theory of Interest, Employment and Money*, came out and Keynes was the focus of discussion for years after that.

As for Ministers for Finance, I was there in Sean T O'Kelly's time, and then Frank Aiken would have been there from about 1946 to 1948, before the first inter-party government came in. At that time Aiken was extremely interested in cheap money – Mr Dalton, the British Chancellor of the Exchequer, was a great proponent of cheap money. I was just a junior officer, so he kept asking the senior people all sorts of awkward questions and they turned to me. I had to endure long sessions of discussion and query and then do my own research, trying to keep at least one step ahead of him. The result was that I was able to put together – with his encouragement – a book on financing by credit creation during the last war in Britain and the United States. I cured him slightly of his preoccupation with cheap money, but we did manage to use all our expertise and persuasion against the banks of the time to induce them to provide money at a much more reasonable rate for the exchequer on exchequer bills.

In the post-war period, Sean Lemass was one of my great political heroes. I admired him a lot for being a man of decisiveness. He was a pragmatic patriot, a man who was in the right place at the right time, though perhaps not timely enough.

I would agree with those who think that de Valera probably stayed on too long.

It was clear to everyone, and became clear to Lemass in particular, that protectionist policies, the self-sufficiency policies, were outmoded, so, after the war, Lemass began the process of dismantling it all. First of all, he introduced a bill to restrict protection, to force the infant industries to become adult. However, that was never passed, because in 1948 there was a change of government. Once he came back into power and we reassessed policies in the mid-1950s, I think everyone agreed that there was no future for either employment or improved standards in Ireland if we were relying on an impoverished home market. We had to break out, we had to sell in the export markets competitively.

We also learned a lot from civil servants like John Leydon and J J McElligott. We observed them when we went on trade talks or negotiations of an economic kind to London or Paris. We were the young people briefing them, doing the groundwork, but also watching how they dealt with cross-table discussion and argument. Leydon in particular was quite a fierce terrier in those situations.

In the late 1950s, we prepared the programme for economic development. It made the change from a self-sufficiency policy to an open export-oriented policy. The significant thing about it was that it was a product of the most unlikely place in the world – the hard-bitten, negative Department of Finance. People were impressed and said there must be something in it, there must really be some potential for development in the country if those people in Finance say there is. I think that helped to create confidence, that psychological factor which I would regard as one of the most important factors of production.

De Valera, who was just in his last months as Prime Minister, had the magnanimity to say we should publish the book and let it be known that the authorship was a group of civil servants. That was a big step for him, because other people, like Sean

McEntee, opposed it. De Valera, Lemass and Dr Jim Ryan said publish and be damned, as it were. Of course, they were very astute politically in doing so, because it would have been much harder for them to embrace a complete reversal of traditional policy on their own account, much easier when it was apparently the advice of objective non-political civil servants.

It was a time of great satisfaction, because most of us who were engaged in that felt that we were the first privileged generation of the new Ireland. We'd had good jobs, a good education, and here was a chance to apply what we had learned for the benefit of the country, as we saw it. That was a source of great satisfaction. Indeed, I remember thinking, going back to Wordsworth, how apt it was when he said 'bliss it was in that dawn to be alive, but to be young was very heaven'.

The worldwide phase of buoyancy in the '60s was an enormous help to us, because it is extremely difficult for any small country to pull itself up by its own bootstraps. That has been the problem in recent years – the external environment has been unfavourable. But now that it is beginning to improve, we can start to hope for better things.

I was the only public servant ever to have been nominated to the Senate, particularly by two different Taoisigh, Jack Lynch and Garret FitzGerald. Although it was a great honour when Jack Lynch asked me to accept the nomination, I initially refused, because I felt that a former civil servant couldn't become identified with any political party. He assured me that I would be free to express myself in whatever way I wished, so on the basis of being independent I accepted. Very soon after the nomination, I found myself being very critical of a proposal by Jack Lynch himself to establish an economic ministry as distinct from the Department of Finance. I asked him how he liked this dog biting the hand that fed him and he said forget about it; that was what he had wanted me to do. I relished the opportunity to say what I thought, having spent so many years in the background slipping furtive notes to ministers and hoping that they would deal well with the gist of what I had said. I thought the Senate did good work, in being a forum for very serious and enlightened debate without interruptions. The first time I came home after being there, my wife asked me how I had found it. 'It's a wonderful place,' I said, 'the only place I know where a man can speak for a quarter of an hour without being interrupted!'

It is a place where you can have a very high-level debate on important issues like Northern Ireland or extradition or things of that kind, where the political animus doesn't enter into the debate to the same extent as in the Dáil. And I also thought it very good as a reviewing chamber, where people with such legal expertise as the late Alexis Fitzgerald could get to grips with complicated bills like Landlord and Tenant, or Sale of Goods, and really help the whole process of perfecting the bill. It contributed to my own education.

Becoming chancellor of the National University of Ireland was a great honour for me – and a great education. I am also the government's appointee as chairman of the council of the Dublin Institute for Advanced Studies. I relish this position – being in charge of something I only barely understand. There are three schools there: Celtic studies, of which I know a little, cosmic physics and theoretical physics, of which I know nothing whatsoever. I discovered, after being a civil servant, that the principles of management are very much the same no matter where you apply them, whether in the public service or in businesses like a bank or Guinness or institutions of learning.

I think it is extremely important to refresh and update one's learning continually. I have always said, to the annoyance and dismay of people, that, although you may think you are wonderful now that you have a BA honours in economics, unless you keep up the subject over the years it will melt away and be of no use to you. It was important for those of us who were working on economic planning to feel that we had the same competence as a university lecturer in the subject.

Coming to more recent times, I found when I left the Central Bank that it was a refreshing experience to get into private concerns, like the Bank of Ireland and Guinness, and then into the educational sphere and even into salmon research. Then I was asked to chair the penal system inquiry and, more recently still, to review the common fisheries policy for the benefit of the Minister for the Marine. All this was a great enlargement of my sphere of interest and it was refreshing and invigorating.

To go back finally to my schooldays, I remember Peadar McCann, when teaching us history – particularly the French Revolution – always used the phrase 'whether for good or ill'. We regarded it, as boys, as a cliché and used to make little notes of how many times it was said in the course of a class. It was afterwards that it got embedded in my mind as one of the best cautions that anyone could give you in school – not to take something for granted, not to take history, as written, as the last word. You ought to apply your own intelligence, make your own assessment of events and make up your own mind about historical developments.

Gordon Wilson

1927–1995

The self-proclaimed 'ordinary wee draper' from Enniskillen was born in Manorhamilton, County Leitrim, in 1927. He was educated at Wesley College, Dublin, before joining the family drapery business in Enniskillen, County Fermanagh, in 1945.

For forty-two years, Gordon lived an ordinary, uneventful life as businessman and family man – until Remembrance Sunday, November 1987, when the IRA bomb at the Enniskillen Cenotaph killed his daughter, Marie, and ten others and injured many more, including Gordon. When he forgave the bombers in a BBC television interview, he was immediately cast into world prominence. Gordon Wilson said those words simply because he believed them, and he went on to repeat them and tell his 'wee story from Enniskillen' in an untiring crusade to end the violence. His message was simple and basic – 'The bottom line is love'.

Further tragedy befell his family when his son, Peter, was killed in a road accident.

Gordon Wilson died suddenly in 1995.

I'll always be proud to say that I was born in Manorhamilton in County Leitrim – not that far from Enniskillen, but the other side of the border, of course. A wee town by any standards. My folk came from about a mile out the road. They were small farmers, and I mean small farmers; the land in County Leitrim is not great. I am sometimes reminded by my wife that I am from the bogs of Leitrim and, if I get very uppity, she'll mention the particular bog.

My father went as an apprentice into a local draper's shop. I'm talking of a town of a thousand souls – seventeen pubs, but one thousand people; if indeed as many as that. Manorhamilton's chief claim to fame was that it was on the railway line between Enniskillen and Sligo and the railway workshops were there. Indeed, when they closed in the '40s, Manorhamilton, in a way, died a death and, in my opinion, it has never since picked up in terms of life, activity, industry, or whatever. Eventually, in 1925, my father bought the shop. He was a very strong influence on my life. In 1938, he bought his first new car for one hundred pounds. That was a big deal for us, and the night he got it he, my mother, my three sisters and I piled in and went to Bundoran, twenty-eight miles down the road. What was on in Bundoran but Duffy's circus and my father went up to the desk and asked for tickets for two adults and four kids and she said, 'That's six shillings' – a shilling each. He said 'Four of them are kids, they should be half price,' and she said, 'No, at the evening performance there's no half price for kids.' My father refused to pay it and I remember thinking he was a miserable old so-and-so. But it shows how hard times were.

In 1926 he married and in 1927 I was born. My mother's surname was Conn and she was of farming stock up in the county of Derry in a place called Ballykelly. She was a nurse – in the same hospital, indeed, as Marie went to later – and she became what would now be called a community nurse. So my background was one of living with a father and mother who came, not quite from different traditions, but certainly from different parts of the country. Mother's family were strong, solid Presbyterians and my father was a Methodist, a 'southerner'. A balance had to be struck all the time and that would certainly have had a bearing on my thinking. We, as Protestants, would have been perhaps five per cent of the local community and, as far as I was concerned as a boy growing up in Manorhamilton, I certainly never had nor was I ever aware of a community relations problem there.

We were regular church attenders and we were brought up strictly – very strictly by modern standards. For example, I remember during the war how, on a Sunday, my father would listen to the one o'clock news and, when it was over, no matter what came on, he would say, 'Turn that off.' On a Sunday you could listen to the news, but you couldn't listen to music or discussion or whatever.

I went to the Masterson School, a Protestant primary school. Mrs Boyd was an Irish language fanatic and she taught us the language colloquially. She used the cane and she put manners on us and I, like the others, sometimes got my backside warmed. When I left that school to go to Wesley College in Dublin as a boarder, my knowledge of the Irish language was such that I could talk freely in Irish and I could understand the news in Irish. When I hit the grammar school in Dublin, Irish was another subject, like French or English, and they threw a grammar book at us and that had to be a mistake. By the time I came to sit my Leaving Cert, where one had to pass Irish to get the Certificate, I finished up with forty and two-thirds per cent, just a pass, because I had lost the use and meaning of the words, whereas, at the age of eleven, I had been all but thinking in Irish.

Wesley was hard going at the time. Growing cubs need a lot of food, but we were on bread and butter for tea most evenings. For me, it was a shock to come from the country to the middle of Dublin city, but I warmed to it. On my first Christmas holiday, my father, who in the meantime had leased the business which I later ran in Enniskillen, said to me, 'Would you think of leaving? You could live over the shop in Enniskillen and go to Portora Royal School as a day boy.' I said, 'No, I like it there. I'm settled and I'd like to go back.' So I did.

I wasn't one of the brightest pupils, but I did a good Inter Cert, good enough in maths to put me in a class with Dr John Conway, who wanted me to do a sizarship in maths for Trinity. I wasn't too long at that when I realised that I wasn't really that good and opted to go back into the general course. We had a Dr Sammy Powell who taught us history and that was really the first time in my life when I appreciated the influence of history on people. He was a good man and a good teacher. This man was a Catholic, whereas all the pupils in Wesley, with the exception of a ten per cent Jewish element, would have been Protestant of one denomination or another. Dr Powell said that the next lesson would be about Cromwell and he added, 'I don't take that lesson. I couldn't give a lesson on Cromwell without showing bias, so I have the permission of the headmaster to skip it – you're going to have to learn that one for yourselves.' I am in no doubt that the first time the impact of history touched me was through Dr Sammy Powell.

No member of staff in the six years I was in Wesley ever asked me, or any other pupil as far as I was aware, the question 'What are you going to do when you leave school?' The headmaster, the late Dr Irwin, wrote to me with my Leaving Cert results saying, 'I presume you mean to go into the family business, but, if not, would you think about medicine?' Fool that I was, I didn't relish the thought of sitting down to more books.

Business was frustrating to a certain extent. You had to get the customer what he wanted and then you had another, very often longer, wrangle over the price, particularly on fair days. However, I decided I would be able to handle that and I think the old man thought so too. So, in September 1945, I went to Enniskillen.

[3;3]ort=3ort

I immediately became aware that there were two communities in the North. I had to learn a little about that, because it was new to me. Until I went to live there, I hadn't realised just how strong opinions were and how many hard things were being said and being reported in the local paper. Yet one would read in the local paper that Sir Basil Brooke and Cahir Healy, the nationalist MP in Enniskillen, were blood and gut enemies but later one read that they travelled up from Enniskillen together and home together in the one car. So that's where you begin to ask the question, is it just talk, because they feel it has to be said for their tribe, as it were.

I was in the front line at the counter, meeting people. To me, frankly, it didn't make a lot of difference whether a man was Protestant or Catholic. If he was a decent fellow, I could trust him and, hopefully, he could have a little trust in me too. I tell a story which in a way is symptomatic of the sort of ongoing difference there is in our community. We used to sell underwear that was made in Yorkshire, heavy lambswool underwear. The label in the underwear carried the Union Jack and I had decent Catholic farmers who wouldn't buy it – they thought it was waving the flag. I found a firm in County Dublin which made the same sort of lambswool underwear and I bought it. It had a label which said 'Made in the Republic of Ireland' and then I had decent Protestant farmers who wouldn't buy it! In one way it's funny, but in another it's sad. Sad maybe, but even so we were dealing with both sides of the community.

My wife, Joan, came from farming stock, seven miles out of town. Her dad had gone, probably under-aged, to fight in France in the Great War and lost a leg, after which he was nursed by the nuns in a Dublin hospital. His war experiences were the reason for me attending the Remembrance Day service, right up to Remembrance Sunday 1987, which is the day that changed my life in more ways than one.

I wouldn't be honest if I didn't say that our life at home, and in three thousand other homes in Northern Ireland, has become a before and after. I had the trauma of physical injuries and shock myself and, like a lot of others, had to cope with that as best one could. I blush when people say I'm famous. I'm not famous – I'm an ordinary guy. Nevertheless, the fact remains that my face and the words I used made page one on every newspaper in the world and item one on every radio and television broadcast. The penny didn't drop on that one for me until the night after the bomb. Things were happening over which I had no control and what I had said, which to me was perfectly natural, was becoming perceived as newsworthy, for want of a better word. The BBC producer, who came from Enniskillen, rang me that evening and said, 'Gordon, it's only fair to warn you that your story is big. I've seen guys cry that don't cry too often.'

Of course, looking at it clinically and coldly, my story of Marie's death and her words to me was big news. Her words of love to me at the end were wonderful words. They were glorious words for a twenty-year-old who knew that she was on the edge of death. She would know enough to know that she was fatally injured and yet she didn't complain, she didn't talk about herself. She said, 'Daddy, I love you very much.' That helped me and allowed me to accept a little of the grace of God. So that, when Mike Gaston, the interviewer, without warning asked, 'How do you feel about the guys who planted the bomb?', I said what I said – which, although I didn't use the word 'forgiveness', had to be forgiveness. That seemed to catch people's attention. Here was a guy in the midst of grief, who that day had lost his daughter, forgiving the people who had killed her. I didn't say those words because they were the words people would expect me to say, or because it was a nice thing to say, I said them because I believed them. I went on to say that I would pray for those guys that night and every night, and I still do. I haven't changed my views on that since then. People say, the man's potty – how could he, now that he has lost his daughter, how could he? I don't claim any personal credit. I thank God that he gave me the grace to say those words. I believe there is a God and that God loves me. I try to love him and I accept his word when he said, 'A new commandment I give unto you, that you love one another.' I accept his word when he taught us the Lord's Prayer with the words, 'Forgive us our trespasses as we forgive those who trespass against us.' You either believe that or you don't. And I do.

The response was enormous by any standards – letters and flowers and the media. I even had to go ex-directory. Six weeks later, I lost my memory. Something had to give.

I never forget that ten other people were killed in Enniskillen, never mind the three thousand who have been killed altogether. I was perceived as a spokesman for Enniskillen – the face of Enniskillen, the voice of Enniskillen. I couldn't and didn't ever assume that mantle. I spoke for Gordon Wilson and my family, and I still do. When Mrs Carmencita Hederman, the Lord Mayor of Dublin, came to Enniskillen two weeks after the bomb to bring the Book of Condolences from Dublin, I was asked to receive it on behalf of the relatives and the town, but I refused. Why should it always be Gordon Wilson? When Princess Di and Prince Charles came to Enniskillen and we were to meet them in private, the guy in charge came to me and said, 'We want you to be the first to meet them.' I was back in the spotlight where I didn't want to be and it was getting worse rather than better. I was even getting phonecalls from America in the middle of the night. I wasn't aware of the pressure I was under until I lost my memory.

There is no formula, there is no list of rules that you can throw to people who are grieving and say follow these rules and you'll be alright. Everybody has to make their own reconciliation, find their own way forward. I know this for sure, because my wife, Joan, and Peter and Julianne and myself, got through it in different ways. Of course, we ask ourselves 'Why?' and of course the loss is there. I wouldn't be honest if I didn't say that we have times when we miss Marie very much. Of course, we will never forget. People say time is a healer. Time helps one to cope a little better. Life goes on, life goes on. There is no point in sitting at home feeling sorry for oneself, one has to get on with it, and this is no disrespect to the dead.

I have the assurance that it is the will of God I will meet Marie again. I will again hold her hand. That is one of the things that keeps me going. I am now retired from business; to be frank, after the bomb I didn't really want to know about business. Retirement is something that doesn't just happen. One has to apply oneself. Thankfully, I have had the wit to get out, meet friends, play some golf, stay involved. There are lots of days when I could be alone in the house and that to me would be a death trap.

I have the highest regard for the New England poet, John Greenleaf Whittier. Very often I try, unsuccessfully, to find words to talk about forgiveness and reconciliation and, above all, to talk about love, because to me the bottom line is loving my neighbour. So I ask myself the question, 'Who is my neighbour?' and the answer I get is that my neighbour is not just my Protestant neighbour nor is it just my Catholic neighbour. I must include my terrorist neighbour, if I believe what I am trying to say. It is true to say that Christ died for them, too, and they are the children of God, just as I am, and they must repent if they are going to get God's forgiveness, just as I must. That is why I like these words of Whittier.

Follow with reverent steps the great example
Of him whose holy work was doing good.
So shall the wide earth seem our Father's temple,
Each loving life a psalm of gratitude.

Then shall all shackles fall,
The stormy clangour of wild war music o'er the earth shall cease,
Love shall tread out the baleful fire of anger
And in its ashes plant the tree of peace.